Trade, Industrial Activity and the Environment in China

Wu Shanshan

Paths International Ltd

中国财经出版传媒集团
中国财政经济出版社

Preface

This book explores four topics within the broad area of trade, industrial activity and the environment in China. The research is immediately motivated by a concern regarding possible changes of industrial specialization patterns in China due to the pollution haven hypothesis—a theoretical viewpoint in the existing literature on trade and environment. According to this argument, since the stringency of environmental regulations in China is relatively lax, China tends to specialize more likely in pollution – intensive industries. Chapter 2 of this book thus examines whether the specialization of the pollution – intensive industries is higher or increasing more rapidly than other industries, given possible determinants of industrial specialization. Chapter 3 thereafter aims to examine the factors that determine industrial air pollution within a framework of the demand for, and supply of, environmental services. Given the concern that industrial specialization patterns change in China, Chapter 4 examines the effects of industrial specialization on environmental specialization across regions and based on the study of chapter 4, chapter 5 further investigates the spatial distribution of pollution across regions in China.

Results reveal that different from the prediction of the pollution haven hypothesis, the specialization of pollution - intensive industries is neither higher nor increasing more rapidly in China, and the reason is that traditional factor endowments such as physical capital still remains significant in determining the industrial specialization patterns. It is found in China that an industry's physical capital is negatively related to its degree of specialization, meanwhile, pollution intensive industries are also physical capital intensive, therefore, physical capital may compete with the relatively lax stringency of regulations in determining the specialization of pollution intensive industries. This research also finds that energy use, human capital intensity, productivity and investment in innovation, are the most significant determinants of industrial air pollution. The industrial specialization is increasing overtime in China but generally does not impact the environmental specialization of China. However, a significant impact of industrial specialization on environmental specialization is obvious. When focusing on regions of China, Lastly, the inequality of pollution distribution in China is not as serious as that in developed economies, however, in certain regions of China the issue of pollution inequality has become more and more serious.

Acknowledgements

This book emanates from my Ph. D research undertaken at the University of Birmingham, UK. My special appreciation goes to my Ph. D supervisors, Professor Robert J. R. Elliott and Professor Matthew A. Cole for their patient guidance and support throughout my PhD research. I am also indebted to my fellow man Dr. Jing Zhang for her help and encouragement during our Ph. D time at Birmingham.

I would like to thank research fundings from the National Natural Science Foundation of China [Grant No. 71803193], the Liberal Arts and Social Sciences Foundation of the Ministry of Education in China [Grant No. 17YJC790166], and Major Program of National Social Science Foundation of China [Grant No. 18ZDA038]

Finally, Chapter 3 reuses material in Cole, M. A., Elliott, R. J. R. and Wu, S., 'Industrial Activity and the Environment in China: An Industry – Level Analysis', 2008, *China Economic Review*, 19, 393 – 408. Chapter 5 reuses material in Wu, S. and Hueng, C. J., 2019, 'Concentration of Industrial Pollution in China', *Applied Economics Letters*, 26 (16), 1339 – 1344.

To my parents.

Contents

Chapter 1

Introduction

The motivation of the research in this book is to investigate the impact of industrial activity on China's natural environment. Particular attention will be paid to industrial and environmental specialization, the spatial distribution of pollution and the role played by environmental regulations.

China's economy has rapidly and continuously developed since the late 1970s, and then China has faced challenges of several environmental problems that developed countries have gone through in their industrialization. The rapid growth of the economy and critical environmental problems simultaneously present, raising a growing conflict between environment and development. In China there are organic pollutants directly discharged into watershed, in some urban areas, atmospheric concentrations of pollutants such as suspended particulates and sulphur dioxide (SO_2) sometimes exceed World

Health Organization safety standards by certain margins. As a result, the number of pollution - related respiratory diseases increases each year (Wheeler, Wang and Dasgupta, 2000).

There is no doubt that the Chinese industry primarily generates several environmental problems. Based on the estimates from the National Environmental Protection Agency (NEPA) in China, industrial activity is responsible for 70% of discharged wastewater, 72% of sulphur dioxide (SO_2) emissions, 75% of flue dust emissions (a major component of suspended particulates) and 87% of solid waste (data updated to 2007). Many polluting industries are located in densely - populated metropolitan areas, where pollution exposure could possibly cause serious damage to human health. ①

The Chinese government and pollution control agencies have been aware of the environmental problems and started to respond though not quickly at that time. Following the Stockholm Conference in 1972, China intended to set up a system of pollution charge. The idea was formally adopted by the central government in 1978. By the end of 1981, 27 of 29 provinces, autonomous regions and municipalities have established certain types of environmental regulations. From early 1980's to 1996, Chinese regulators have collected about 3.75 billion U. S dollars from more than 500000 Chinese polluters, and a large percentage of the levy has been invested in the pollution control.

Investment in pollution control was approximately 0.5% of GDP in 1996, which is low compared to that in most developed countries. However, during China's 9th Five - Year Plan (1996 - 2000), the

① Data source: NEPA.

Chinese government increased the investment in pollution control by a significant amount. Between 1996 and 1999, the investment of pollution control increased up to 31 billion U. S dollars and the share of this investment in GDP also increased, the investment takes 1% of GDP in 1999 and 1.3% in 2000. ①

Wastewater treatment has used up most expenditures on pollution abatements, followed by air, solid waste, and noise treatments. The investment of wastewater treatment reached 0.59 billion U. S dollars in 1996, which is nearly twice the investment amount of air pollution treatment (0.35 billion U. S dollars), and it reached 1.65 billion U. S dollars in 2000, followed by 2.45 billion U. S dollars in 2003. Many industrial enterprises reduce emissions through end - of - pipe equipment, improvement on production process and material recycling. For industrial water pollution, after taking stronger enforcement measures, many Chinese provinces have seen a substantial decline in plants' water pollution intensity even though the industry is still growing rapidly at the same time. However, the situation is different for industrial air pollution. Although the investment of air pollution abatement has been increasing over time, namely 1.17 billion U. S dollars in 2000 to 1.88 billion U. S dollars in 2003 with a growth rate of 18% on average②, it has not seen that industrial air pollution significantly decrease at the same time.

An increase of investment in pollution abatement and more stringent environmental regulations are both obvious in China, but compared to developed economies, China has still remained behind. Chi-

①② Data source: China Statistical Yearbook.

na spent about 1% of GDP on pollution control while other developed countries such as US, UK and Germany, spent over 2% of GDP on pollution control (data updated to 2007). Meantime, since local agencies are generally responsible for taking environmental enforcement measures, under pressure of unemployment and taxation, the efficiency of the enforcement remains questionable.

Given that the environmental regulations in China appear to be less stringent (and less enforced) compared to developed economies, it is reasonable to believe that China may have experienced a comparative advantage in pollution intensive production, as postulated by the pollution haven hypothesis (PHH). If true, we may then expect greater flows of investment and trade, within pollution intensive industries, to China. Since the late 1970s, market – oriented economic reforms have gradually turned China into one of the most attractive destinations for foreign direct investment in the world. In particular, China's accession to the WTO (World Trade Organization) in 2001 has further boosted the flows of investment and trade from the world. As a WTO member, China is likely to significantly increase its exports , leading to a rapid production expansion in certain industrial sectors. We thus begin our research with an examination of industrial specialization patterns in China.

There are only a few theoretical models that distinguish environmental regulations from the traditional factor endowments as a source of comparative advantage (e. g. Antweiler *et al.* , 2001). Following these theories, a number of empirical studies examined the economic effects of environmental regulations and the extent to which they shape a country's comparative advantage (e. g. Toby, 1990; Cole and Elliott, 2003, 2004; Kahn, 2003). However, evidence of the migration or displacement of dirty industries from high regulation developed countries is mixed and a number of arguments have emerged to explain why clearer evidence of pollution haven pressures has not been found.

The research focuses on one argument out of those that have emerged. It argues that environmental regulations and traditional factor endowments are competing with each other when determining specialization patterns in a country. We thus have missing evidence of the PHH because traditional factor endowments such as physical capital play a significant role and may counteract environmental regulations in determining the specialization patterns. One of the first goals of this book is therefore to test such competing effects in our target country – China.

If China is to successfully tackle its industrial pollution, a more comprehensive understanding of the relationship between industrial activity and pollution is required. To date, a large majority of the research in this area has been undertaken for the US (e. g. Kahn, 1999; Gray and Shadbegian, 1995, 2002, 2003 and 2004). The lack of studies outside of the US are largely a consequence of a scarcity of data on pollution emissions at the sub – national level and particularly at the industry and plant level. We have recently produced a dataset for China that provides industry specific pollution emissions for a range of air pollutants. The dataset allows us to investigate the possible linkages between industrial activity and industrial air pollution in China and it may therefore provide an understanding of such a relationship in a developing country context, the second key contribution of this book.

Previous studies have suggested that industrial energy use, physical and human capital intensity, productivity, average firm size, plant vintage, and investment in research and development all matter for the pollution intensity of an industry in a developed country (e. g. Antweiler, 2001; Cole and Elliott, 2003; Cole, Elliott and Shimamoto, 2005; Poter and Van der Linde, 1995). Since China differs from developed countries, industrial activities in China may have determined industrial pollution in quite different ways. Previous research also suggests that regional characteristics such as unemployment rate, population density and level of education, play a role in determining industrial pollution in a region (Bartik, 1998; Gray and Shadbegian, 2002, 2004; Hamilton, 1993; Henderson, 1996; Helland and Whitford, 2003; Kahn, 1999; Levinson, 1996). Regional characteristics also matter because they have impacts on communities' power to 'informally' regulate the polluters and they are most likely to influence the stringency of regulations. In China, these regional characteristics as a determinant of informal regulations appear to be more important due to the weak formal environmental policies in China at present. An attempt to investigate the link between regional characteristics and industrial pollution is thus worthwhile.

Next, the book investigates two issues that can both augment the impact of industrial pollution on human health: environmental specialization and the spatial distribution of pollution.

Firstly, I consider environmental specialization. Aside from a country's level of total emissions, the composition of pollution may be an important determinant of environmental risks. Exposure to a certain amount of pollution of a similar type or category may cause significantly more health risks than exposure to the same (or even a greater) amount of pollution of a large number of types or categories (i. e. exposure to 10 units of a single pollutant may be more damaging than exposure to 10 units of 20 different types of pollution). One reason for this is the existence of threshold effects that refer to the minimum level of toxins to which humans may be exposed before suffering any adverse effects. Such effects have been shown to exist (e. g. Doull, 1996; Chestnut *et al.*, 1991). Thus, the specialization in a similar type of pollution could more easily result in a level of toxins exceeding the minimum limit and thus yield large health risks.

Secondly, I measure the composition of pollution in terms of environmental specialization. Environmental specialization refers to a given locale exposed to a similar type of pollution. Given two regions where environmental quality in terms of pollution levels have gradually improved, the environmental specialization of the region where the composition of the remaining pollution is of similar type, would be greater than that in the other region where the composition of the remaining pollution is of a large number of types. The region with greater environmental specialization is therefore more likely to suffer from detrimental health effects. One study has found that industrial specialization is the most likely contributor to environmental specialization in the US (Millimet and Slottje, 2003). My research provides evidence for a rising industrial specialization in China, whether it may also contribute to environmental specialization as it did in the US is the motivation of our research. This is the third contribution of the book.

Finally, I examine the related issue of the spatial distribution of pollution. While a large number of studies examine the spatial distribution of income, very few studies examine the spatial distribution of pollution (Millimet and Slottje (2002) being one exception). I adopt the principles used in the income inequality literature and apply them to the distribution of pollution. Some studies have found evidence of a strong link between income inequality and pollution inequality (e. g. Heil and Wodon, 2000; List, 1999), and there is evidence of an increasing level of income inequality in China (Wan and Zhou, 2005; Wang, 2006; Benjamin *et al.*, 2005; Kanbur and Zhang, 2005). Thus, whether there is a high level of pollution inequality as a result of a rising income inequality, or whether pollution inequality currently remains at a low level in China and thus may be able to mitigate health risks generated by environmental specialization, is the motivation of our research. This is the fourth and final contribution of the book.

There are four main chapters in this book. Each chapter can be studied in isolation but chapters are internally linked and are arranged in logical order. This book is primarily empirical in nature but all chapters are based on theoretical models that have been verified in the existing literature.

The major data source in my research is the China Statistical Yearbook, which is the government official statistic yearbook. My research mainly employed three kinds of data, including trade data, industry data and pollution data. The economist has provided a guide (developed by Goldman Sachs) to the reliability of official Chinese numbers. It gives a score to different sets of statistics as 5 being the most reliable, and 0 the least. According to this guide, foreign trade data has a score of 5 whilst industry – level data has a score of 4, which demonstrates the reliability of these two kinds of data in China. Referring to the pollution data, I have checked out the data numbers collected from different sources, such as the environment section in the China Statistical Yearbook, China Environment Yearbook, and a series of regional statistical yearbook. I found that the numbers are consistent across sources and thus provide evidence for the reliability of pollution data. Therefore, the data collected are reliable for the research in this book and I undertake our empirical analysis on the basis of such data collection. In this book I don't study the issue of Tibet, Taiwan, Hongkong of China.

Chapter 2 begins with a study of the specialization in manufacturing sectors in China through introducing several measures of specialization. Based on the PHH, environmental regulations now potentially play an increasingly important role in shaping a country's comparative advantage, thus raises the possibility that pollution intensive industries will relocate from high regulation countries to developing regions where environmental regulations may be less stringent. Therefore, the objective of this chapter is to examine whether China's specialization in pollution intensive sectors is higher or rising more rapidly than in other manufacturing sectors due to the less stringent regulations in China. The results are not as the PHH predicts: China's specialization in pollution intensive sectors is neither higher nor rising more rapidly than in other sectors. I offer an explanation for this finding. My analysis suggests that pollution intensive industries are also intensive in the use of physical capital whilst the physical capital intensity of an industry negatively determines that industry's degree of specialization in China, explaining why the specialization in pollution intensive sectors in China is neither higher nor rising more rapidly than in other sectors. It therefore demonstrates the competing effects of factor intensities and environmental regulations on industrial specialization.

Chapter 3 examines and quantifies the complex linkages between industrial activity, environmental regulations and air pollution from the manufacturing sectors, in which it further demonstrates the close relationship between an industry's pollution intensity and its physical capital intensity as suggested in chapter two. Couched in terms of the demand for, and the supply of, environmental services, the determinants of industrial air pollution are therefore defined as a variety of industrial characteristics as well as formal and informal environmental regulations. The introduction of informal regulation is a complement to formal regulation particularly if formal regulation is weak in some developing countries including China. Since informal regulation is actually the activity performed by local communities, it is thus determined by various regional characteristics relevant to the power of local communities. Our findings suggest that out of a range of industrial characteristics, energy use, productivity and expenditure on innovation are the most significant determinants of industrial air pollution, whilst the effect of both formal and informal regulations on controlling air pollution is not very strong.

Chapter 4 examines environmental specialization at the provincial level in China. It employs several types of specialization measures. The objective of this chapter is to test the possible linkage between environmental and industrial specialization. If a region specializes in relatively clean industries then it may reduce the possibility of emitting a similar type of pollution. In contrast, if a region specializes in pollution intensive industries then it may increase the possibility of emitting a similar type of pollution. The existing literature suggests that low value – added industries that perform poorly in terms of the environment may be transferred from developed countries in Europe, the US and Japan to China, and then from eastern China to central and western China.[①] Thus industrial specialization patterns would be different throughout regions in China. I separately focus on the area of the entire country, all East coast regions and all interior regions. My findings suggest that over the entire country, industrial specialization appears to have no significant impact on environmental specialization, however, within the area of the East coast and interior regions significant effects are detected.

Chapter 5 extends the work in chapter 4 to investigate the spatial distribution of pollution in China using a number of inequality measures including the Gini coefficient and a family of entropy indices. As discussed previously, if pollution is spatially distributed in a relatively equal way over an area, it can actually reduce detrimental effects caused by a high level of pollution specialization in that area. I again undertake the analysis for the entire country as well as the area of East coast regions and the interior regions separately. My findings suggest that the distribution of pollution varies by pollutant, perhaps reflecting regional industrial production patterns.

The book concludes with a review of results and insights, a dis-

① Source: Environmental and trade implications of China's WTO accession – a preliminary analysis, prepared for the working group on trade and environment, China council for international cooperation on environment and development, September 2000.

cussion of possible improvements in data and methodology, and an outline of the potential for future research.

Chapter 2

The Effects of Environmental Regulations and Factor Intensities on Chinese Industrial Specialization

2.1 Introduction

The Chinese opening has been strengthened by an accession to the World Trade Organization (WTO) after two decades since the "open door" policy in late 1970s. After a series of tough negotiations for 15 years, on November 10th, 2001 at WTO Ministerial Conference in Doha, WTO members formally approved the accession package for China and China thereafter became a full member, the WTO's 143rd, on December 11th, 2001. The accession to WTO is meaningful to the industries in developed world. Taking US as an example, in 2000 China was its 4th trading partner and its 10th international market abroad. We therefore expect more flows of investment, trade, and even more migration of industries from developed countries to China.

On the other hand, the US refused to ratify the Kyoto Protocol climate change treaty since the treaty excludes the developing world from binding emissions reductions. The US thus believed that the Kyoto Protocol would create a powerful incentive for industries to 'export jobs, capital and pollution'①, and increased environmental regulations in the US would lead to the migration of energy – intensive production—such as the chemicals, steel, petroleum refining, mining industries – from the developed countries to the developing countries'②.

Meanwhile, although the environmental protection legislation and system have been well established over years in China, the relatively weak enforcement of regulations implies Chinese environmental regulations may be less demanding relative to those in many developed countries. Thus, it is possible that the production of industries, particularly pollution – intensive industries, may be moving to developing countries such as China where an increasing degree of openness exists. The aim of this chapter is to examine whether China's relatively lax environmental regulations have had an impact on its trade flows.

Theoretical studies on this issue, for instance, Baumol and

① AFL – CIO Executive Council February 20th 1997.

② From a letter by the President of the Business Roundtable to President Clinton, May 12th 1998.

Oates (1988) state that those countries that do not control pollution emissions, whilst others do, will "voluntarily become the repository of the world's dirtiest industries." Chichilnisky (1994) has provided similar conclusions. As a result of this debate there is a growing body of literature that examines the economic effects of environmental regulations and the extent to which they shape a country's comparative advantage. Some studies base on industrialized economies (Toby, 1990; Antweiler*et al.*, 2001; Cole and Elliott, 2003, 2004; Kahn, 2003); others are based on developing economies (Chai, 2002; Dasgupta *et al.*, 1997). However, from those empirical studies the evidence of the migration or displacement of dirty industries from high regulation economies is mixed and many studies offer explanations for such mixed findings. Some argue that environmental regulations may be endogenously determined by trade since they may be used as secondary trade barriers, i. e. a means of protecting domestic industry (Levinson and Taylor, 2008). Other explanations include the fact that environmental compliance costs are likely to form a small proportion of a firm's total costs, the dependence of heavy industries on home markets, the fact that low regulation countries may have certain characteristics that deter inward investment such as corruption, poor infrastructure and uncertain or unreliable legislation, and the possibility that foreign investors may be concerned about their international reputation and do not wish to be perceived to be taking advantage of slack environmental regulations. ①

In my research I employ a range of industrial specialization indices

① See Neumayer (2001) for a review of these issues.

to investigate whether the effect of relatively lax environmental regulations in China has resulted in high and/or increasing specialization in 'dirty' industries as predicted by many scholars. I find that specialization in 'dirty' industries in China is neither higher, nor increasing more rapidly than in other industries. One explanation is that pollution intensive industries are typically more intensive in the use of physical capital than clean industries, and the empirical results of this chapter indeed reveal that physical capital intensity is a negative determinant of an industry's specialization in China. Thus, there is little specialization in dirty industries that require high levels of physical capital intensity even though the enforcement of environmental regulations is relatively low in China. The results show no evidence that an industry's specialization is related to its human capital intensity in China.

The rest of the chapter is organized as follows: Section 2 reviews the relevant literature, Section 3 introduces the specialization measures, Section 4 discusses the data, Section 5 provides background information, Section 6 describes the econometric methodology, and Section 7 provides the main results and sensitivity checks and Section 8 finally concludes.

2.2 Literature Review

There has been a growing body of literature discussing the trade liberalization and environment nexus. On one hand, it is concentrated on the industry dimension, discussing the impact of stringent environmental regulations on dirty industries. On the other hand, more emphases have been put on the relationship between the patterns of trade and environmental regulations. Most empirical studies test the possibility that more dirty industries will move to developing countries to take advantage of lax environmental regulations and more dirty products will be produced in the South, resulting in a new trade pattern between North and South, however, the evidence of this possibility is mixed so far. It requires more investigation in future.

2.2.1 Trade and the Environment

One hypothesis that has emerged from the trade and environment literature is the "pollution haven hypothesis", which suggests that regulatory stringency in developed countries shifts polluting industries to the developing world where less stringent regulations are implemented. In a widely cited review Jaffe *et al.* (1995), notes "there is relatively little evidence to support the hypothesis that environmental regulations have had a serious side effect on competitiveness." One explanation points to the small fraction of costs represented by pollution abatement in the total production cost and therefore implies that more stringent environmental regulations only have a small effect on firm's costs and international competitiveness (e.g. Ederington and Minier, 2003; Levinson and Taylor, 2008). Some other empirical studies witnessed larger and more significant pollution haven effects for less pollution-intensive industries. A few even found evidences that industries with relatively high pollution abatement costs are leading exporters. ① The

① See Levinson and Taylor (2008) for reference.

positive link between regulatory stringency and exports underlies the Porter hypothesis (Porter and van der Linde (1997)) that regulation brings cost – reducing innovation.

Levinson and Taylor (2008) re – examine the link between abatement costs and trade flows using a simple, multi – sector, partial – equilibrium model, they argue that the problems involved in estimation are responsible for the mixed results from tests of the ‘pollution haven hypothesis’ rather than other reasons introduced above. These estimating problems include unobserved heterogeneity, unobserved foreign pollution taxes and aggregation bias. After controlling for these criteria using instrumental variables, they estimate the effect of regulations on trade flows using data providing US imports in 133 three – digit manufacturing industries from Mexico and Canada over year 1977 to 1986, and found a positive, statistically significant, and empirically plausible relationship between industry pollution abatement costs and net imports into the US.

Some other papers consider the pollution haven hypothesis within the context of the composition effect that states that following an episode of trade liberalization, the industrial structure of an economy may change as each country increasingly specializes in those activities that have a comparative advantage (e. g. Cole and Elliott, 2003a). The environmental regulation effect (ERE) states that a country's comparative advantage is determined by the relative stringency of environmental regulations. Since there is a high correlation between a country's per capita income level and the stringency of its environmental regulation (e. g. S. Dasgupta *et al.*, 1995), the pure ERE therefore implies that developing countries or regions (the south) with lax environmental regulations have an advantage in pollution intensive production whilst the developed world (the north) with relatively stringent environmental regulations will specialize in clean production. In contrast, the pure capital – labour effect (KLE) believes that the North is more capital – abundant than the South and thus specializes in capital intensive as well as pollution intensive production, whilst the South specializes in relatively clean, labour – intensive production that generates an opposite effect to that stemming from the ERE.

So far, only Antweiler *et al.* (2001) has provided theoretical model distinguishing the competing effects of environmental regulations and traditional factor endowments. Antweiler *et al.* test their theory in terms of site – specific concentrations of sulphur dioxide (SO_2) and claim to find evidence that both environmental regulations and traditional factor endowments are driving comparative advantage. There is a reduced form of equation that is central to Antweiler's whole theory, namely

$$\hat{z} = \gamma_1 \hat{S} + \gamma_2 \hat{k} - \gamma_3 \hat{I} - \gamma_4 \hat{T} + \gamma_5 \hat{p}^w + \gamma_6 \hat{\beta}$$

where all γ_i are positive, z denotes pollution, k denotes the capital – labour ratio, I represents real per capita income, T represents 'country type', p^w and β denotes the common world price of one good and trade frictions, respectively, and therefore the domestic price of one good is expressed as: $p = \beta p^w$. Trade liberalization can result in $\hat{\beta} > 0$ for a dirty good exporter and $\hat{\beta} < 0$ for a dirty good importer, implying that trade liberalization, will increase emissions in a country having a comparative advantage in pollution intensive output (a dirty good exporter) and reduce pollution in a country having a comparative advantage in clean output (a dirty good importer). According to this model, holding other determinants of emissions constant, trade liberalization does not have a unique relationship with emissions. Rather, the effect of liberalization on the environment is country specific and depends crucially on a country's comparative advantage. The results provide evidence for both the ERE and the KLE, suggesting that, *ceteris paribus*, the level of pollution, will drop in a country with a low K/L ratio after trade liberalization, whilst rise in a low – income country (with a low level of environmental regulations) since dirty production deepens after trade openness and fall in a high – income country. Thus, both relative factor endowments and relative income differences appear to determine a country's comparative advantage.

Based on Antweiler's model, Cole and Elliott (2003) test the trade – induced composition effect using emissions of pollutants rather than concentrations. They find evidence of both the ERE and the KLE for the pollutants SO_2 and carbon dioxide (CO_2), however, the findings for nitrogen oxides (NO_x) and biochemical oxygen demand (BOD) are quite different. The estimates of NO_x and BOD are opposite to SO_2 and CO_2. They thus argue that such difference amongst pollutants may be caused by the different sources of pollution where emissions of NO_x come from the transport sector and BOD come from agricultural sector. Antweiler *et al.* (2001) does not consider the difference.

In an earlier study of trade and the environment, Chichilnisky (1994) examined environment issues using a model of North – South trade and found that other than the factor endowments, environmental policy can be one of the motives that leads to changes of the world trade patterns. The North has better – defined property rights for environmental goods than the South, explaining some puzzling aspects of the trade patterns between the North and the South. The South exports environmentally intensive goods even if it is not well endowed with them because the South with ill – defined property rights overuses the environment as an input to production, and such ill – defined property rights by themselves create a comparative advantage for the South. In addition, tax policies for the environment in the South could also lead to more resource extractions so that the trade patterns change. Thus, Chichilnisky (1994) suggests that environmental policies can be one of the determinants on trade patterns besides the well – known determinants of factor endowments.

An empirical study by Tobey (1990) discusses the impact of environmental control measures on trade patterns using the Heckscher – Ohlin – Vanek (HOV) model. The HOV model is a multi – factor, multi – commodity extension of the Heckscher – Ohlin (H – O) model for international trade. The empirical test conducted using the HOV model found no evidence that the introduction of environmental control measures has caused trade patterns to deviate from the HOV predictions, implying that the world's distribution of 'dirty' industries cannot be simply changed by differing the country – level environmental stringency. Furthermore, Tobey quoted Bowen *et al.* (1987) who questioned the accuracy of the cross – section HOV model and argued that since the HOV model makes no reference to factor input intensities it is only a weak test of the HOV hypothesis. In addition, the nature of the pollution – intensive commodity groups and violations of the assumptions of the HOV model also interfere with the test to pick up the effect of environmental policy.

Cole and Elliott (2003) examine the impacts of environmental regulations on trade patterns within the context of the traditional comparative advantage model and the 'new' trade – theoretic framework. Their work extends Tobey's (1990) analysis in a number of ways. Firstly, they use a larger and more up to date dataset; Secondly, they test two alternative measures of environmental regulations; thirdly, they include industry dummies to control for unobserved industry characteristics that may affect the relationship between regulations and net exports, and finally they control for the potential endogeneity of environmental regulations. Their empirical results estimated on a basis of the HOV model suggest that environmental regulation does not significantly determine net exports of dirty goods, trade patterns are still dominated by traditional comparative advantages. However, the estimation within the 'new' trade – theoretic framework provides evidence that environmental regulation differentials are influencing trade patterns. Since the 'new' trade model focuses on bilateral trade and controls for the determinants of intra – industry trade, it may be more appropriate to model issues such as the pollution haven hypothesis.

2.2.2 The Study of Industrialized Countries

Due to the availability of data, the US is the subject of the majority of empirical studies. Cole and Elliott (2004) examine the competing effects of environmental regulations and factor intensities on the specialization in US industry whilst only a few early studies touched on such link between environmental regulations and industry specialization before. They adopt an index of revealed comparative advantage (RCA) (originally proposed in an international trade context by Balassa, 1965, 1979 and 1986) as a measure of industry specialization and a greater value of RCA indicates a high level of specialization. They find dirty industries in the US experiencing an increase in RCA even after more stringent regulations are enforced in the US. The finding therefore indicates that there is no systematic tendency for the US specialization to decline in pollution intensive industries. Moreoaver, they find no evidence suggesting that dirty sectors have lower average values of RCA than clean sectors. One explanation refers to the industry characteristics in the US, particularly the physical and human capital intensity. The RCA of an US industry is heavily determined by its human and physical capital requirements, despite of the stringent enforcement of regulations, the US does not appear to have experienced low or reduced specialization in pollution intensive industries.

The estimation function of Cole and Elliott (2004) is given by:

$$SPEC_{it} = \gamma_i + \tau_i + \beta_1 PAOCva_{it} + \beta_2 PCI_{it} + \beta_3 (PCI_{it})^2 + \beta_4 HCI_{it} + \beta_5 (HCI_{it})^2 + \beta_6 tariff_{it} + \varepsilon_{it}$$

where $SPEC_{it}$ denotes a specialization measures, namely RSCA, the MICHAELY index or net exports per unit value added;① $PAOCva$ is defined as pollution abatement cost per unit value added; PCI is physical capital intensity defined as the non – wage share of value added

① $MICHAELY_{it} = \frac{X_{it}}{\sum_i X_{it}} - \frac{M_{it}}{\sum_i M_{it}}$. X and M are exports and imports of sector i in year t, respectively. It ranges between plus and minus one; a positive (negative) value means a country is specialized (under – specialized) in that sector.

and HCI is human capital intensity defined as the share of value added that is paid to skilled workers. Tariff denotes import duties per unit of imports within each industry, whilst γ and τ are industry and time specific effects, respectively. Their empirical results suggest that in the US the specialization of an industry is negatively determined by its pollution abatement cost (the stringency of environmental regulations) and positively determined by its physical and human capital intensity.

Kahn (2003) uses the following estimation similar to Cole and Elliott (2004):

$$Log(Yjt) = B1 \times Dirty + B2 \times Dirty \times time + B3 \times HighEmissionIndustry + U$$

where the dependent variable Y is defined as the ratio of Imports to Consumption in the US. Evidence that would support the pollution haven hypothesis is that the estimates of B1, B2 and B3 should be positive. The estimate of B3 takes the same consideration as in Cole and Elliott (2004), which implies that a dirty industry, defined as a high emission industry, would import more than a low emission industry.

It is surprising that the results of Kahn (2003) find no increase in the share of import for high air emissions industries between year 1972 and 1994 after the Clean Air Act was enacted in the US in the early 1970s. However, after taking shipment cost into account, Kahn (2003) considers a smaller sample size to concentrate on 'light' or 'footloose' industries, the results show that the light and high emissions industries increasingly imported after the Clean Air Act was enacted. Kahn (2003) therefore draws a conclusion that there is no evidence that dirty trade increases even after the environmental regulations become more stringent in the US, and shipping costs may play a key role in explaining why the evidence of the pollution haven hypothesis is weak.

2.2.3 The Study of China

As the Chinese manufacturing base grows, a concern about its impacts on the environment also grows. Although some literatures have been working on this issue, the studies that examine the impact of the trade liberalization on China's environment are still quite limited.

Chai (2002) examines the relationship between trade and the environment using evidence from the Chinese manufacturing sector. Their research begins with testing both the positive and negative effects of trade liberalization on China's environment. It is believed that trade liberalization promotes specialization in sectors with comparative advantages, where in China such sectors are relatively less pollution intensive. Trade liberalization provides opportunities for China to access and adopt the best practices of international pollution abatement technologies and enables China to transfer environmental costs to other countries through importing intermediate products whose production may cause degradation to the environment. These positive effects of the trade liberalization on environment are however overwhelmed by the largely negative scale effect created by a rapidly growing demand for the Chinese export.

The standard approach in the literature of trade and the environment is to decompose the environmental impact into scale, composition and technique effects. Chai (2002) applies these groupings to the Chinese manufacturing sectors and finds positive composition and technique effects. One explanation is that the composition effect shifts the pattern of the Chinese manufacturing exports from pollution intensive sectors, such as petroleum processing, coal products and chemicals, to the clean sectors, such as garments and machinery. The technique effect leads China to increase levels of environmental standards, close up polluted enterprises and enforce pollution charges. As a consequence of both effects, the pollution intensity of the Chinese manufacturing sectors significantly declines. Nevertheless, such positive impact is overwhelmed by the huge negative scale effect since China has increased its manufacturing exports by a striking percentage of 796% in the observed period (year 1980 – 1996). Therefore, although China has been significantly reducing total emissions of water, air and solid waste due to the composition and technique effects of trade, the reduction does not catch up with the expansion of the Chinese manufacturing exports and the negative scale effect of trade on environment remains dominant.

Additionally, the relationship between trade and environment in China is highlighted in a report from the World Bank Development Group (Dasgupta *et al.*, 1995). One section of the report discusses the trends of the five most heavily – polluting industry sectors: Chemicals, Pulp and Paper, Non – Ferrous Metals, Ferrous Metals, and Non – Metallic Minerals. They firstly find the share of the output from the five 'dirty' sectors in total industrial output has decreased in the observed period from 1977 to 1992, and there is no evidence of shift toward pollution – intensive production in the long run. Secondly, the net imports of products from the five 'dirty' sectors have been rapidly growing since 1987, implying that China lost comparative advantage in pollution – intensive industries. Lastly, the ratio of consumption to production of the five 'dirty' sectors has remained well above one throughout the period, again suggesting that China does not have comparative advantage in 'dirty' production, therefore China remains as a net importer of pollution – intensive goods. Overall, the report concludes that in the era of trade liberalization, China deepens its revealed comparative advantage in non – pollution – intensive goods. Although all industries have experienced rapid growth throughout the period, the cleaner ones have been growing even faster, both domestically and internationally. For China, increasing openness generally has had 'clean' impact on improving the composition of industrial output.

2.3 Specialization Index

In this section I demonstrate various methodologies for measuring specialization. A traditional index of specialization is called "revealed comparative advantage (RCA)", which was originally proposed by Balassa (1965).

Comparative advantage determines the reallocation of resources. The way to find out the comparative advantage of one country is to make cost – comparisons based on census of production using identical methods of investigation in all countries. One case of cost – comparison is between the US and the UK where inter – industry cost – comparisons were made in 1950 in a study prepared for the Organization for European Economic Co - operation (OECD). However, the study at that time excluded material costs and therefore underestimated value of comparisons.

Another study, prepared for the National Industrial Conference Board, provides some information on production costs of domestic and foreign operations of American firms that 147 companies that take business in the US and abroad have provided such information. However, the problem is, without a cross - classification on countries and industries, no information is identified for the comparative advantage of foreign countries. Therefore, since data of the production cost is not easily available across countries and industries, it is more likely to rely on the prevailing theories of international specialization to determine patterns of comparative advantage. Out of these doctrines, the Heckscher - Ohlin theory and the classical theory of comparative advantage deserve our attention.

In the Heckscher - Ohlin framework, for example, relative factor supplies are characterised in terms of 'abundance' or 'scarcity', and countries are supposed to export goods produced intensively using abundant factors as inputs. One difficulty in the Heckscher - Ohlin theory arises if there is zero or unity elasticity of substitution among the factors of production. Arrow *et al.* (1961) firstly claims that elasticities of substitution are generally lower than unity, and also differ among industries, implying that relative factor intensities should not be defined independently of factor prices. While wage rates rise relative to the price of capital, one industry where the elasticity of substitution is high may increase its capital intensity, and other industry where the elasticity is low may have no much change in terms of intensity. Even though the production of the industry is labour intensive, after a rise in wage, because of high elasticity of substitution, the industry will quickly switch its input from labour to capital and become a capital – intensive sector, therefore, relying on identifying relative factor endowments only will not uniquely determine comparative advantage.

Another difficulty is that the Heckscher – Ohlin theory cannot be applied in a case of three factors. The comparative advantage of one country can be determined by ranking industries according to their relative factor intensities, in the case of two factors, there is a unique ranking, but within three factors, more than one ranking in terms of the relative factor intensities can be found, to determine comparative advantage is thus more difficult. Similarly, the difficulty arises when applying the theory on the case of more than two countries. Since all these issues complicate the identification, the Heckscher – Ohlin theory offer limited guide for evaluating comparative advantage. On the other hand, the classical theory of comparative advantage does not account for non – price variables, though quality – differences, goodwill, servicing, the existence of repair facilities and differences in weights and measures all matter for determining the pattern of international trade in industrial countries.

After an overview on the difficulties of evaluating comparative advantage using the Heckshcher – Ohlin theory, Balassa (1965) proposed "revealed comparative advantage (RCA)" to evaluate trade performance on manufacturing products for industrialized countries. RCA has considered relative costs of production as well as differences of non – price factors that overcomes those issues raised in the Heckshcher – Ohlin theory.

For a single country, the RCA index is defined as:

$$RCA_{it} = \left(\frac{X_i / \sum_i X_i}{X_{iw} / \sum_i X_{iw}} \right)$$

the numerator denotes the percentage share of a given sector in total exports in a particular country where X_i are exports from sector i in a given year. The denominator stands for the percentage share of a given sector in world exports (where subscript w denotes world). For a given sector, RCA index with value of one means the percentage share of that sector in a particular country is equal to the world's average. RCA value higher (lower) than one indicates specialization or that a country has a comparative advantage (under – specialized or has a comparative disadvantage) in that sector. Since this measure "revealed comparative advantage (RCA)" was introduced by Balassa in 1965, it has been widely employed in several reports (e.g. UNIDO, 1986; World Bank, 1994) and academic publications to measure the specialization of international trade.

The other measure of specialization is simply net exports, expressed as a share of individual industry's value added:

$$NETXva_{it} = \frac{(X_{it} - M_{it})}{VA_{it}} \tag{1}$$

where VA_{it} is the value added of sector i in year t. Increasing NETXva for a specific industry implies the export is increasing relative to the import and the specialization of this industry is increasing.

The difference between RCA and NETXva is that RCA compares exports of an industry relative to the exports of other industries and other countries, while NETXva compares exports of an industry relative to imports of the same industry. RCA index may be more appropriate to measure the specialization of a sector in one country because it compares a country to other countries or to the world on average, which exactly matches the goal of evaluating a country's comparative advantage. However, imports are not included in the RCA index, a barrier for the intra – trade consideration. In contrast, NETXva has taken into account both sides of exports and imports of a given sector and is better for evaluating intra – trade within one industry, however, NETXva concentrates on one country only and provides no comparison across countries, limiting our study on a country's comparative advantage. Nevertheless, an industry can be identified as highly specialized in one country if it has a large value of net exports. Given that both measures have pros and cons, I use both of them for my empirical research.

2.4 Data Description

I construct RCA index for 19 industries and NETXva for 14 industries based on the 3 – digit International System of Industry Classification (ISIC). In later regressions where I set up an industry – level panel data, pollution variables are available for only 14 industries due to the data limitation. In order to keep consistency, NETXva is estimated for 14 industries so that it can be employed as dependent variable in regressions.

The China Statistical Yearbook revised the section of pollution data in 2001 and the number of industries changed thereafter. Although the Yearbook classifies the industry on a basis of the ISIC three – digit classification, the classification in the Yearbook and the ISIC are not exactly identical. Several three – digit sectors are merged and reported as one sector before 2001. For example, Food products (ISIC311), Beverage (ISIC313) and Tobacco (ISIC314) are reported as one sector ‘Food, beverage and tobacco industry’ prior to 2001. Likewise, Textile (ISIC321) and Wearing apparel except footwear (ISIC322) are reported together as ‘Textile industry’. Machinery except electrical (ISIC382), Machinery electric (ISIC383), Transports equipment (ISIC384) and Professional and scientific equipment (ISIC385) are reported together as ‘Machine building, electric machinery and electronic equipment manufacturing’. However, these sectors integrated before 2001 was again separated after 2001.

On the other hand, I have to merge several small 3 – digit ISIC industries into one industry because of data issue, for instance, ‘Chemicals’ incorporates Industrial chemicals (ISIC351) and Other chemicals (ISIC352), ‘Non – metallic mineral products’ incorporates Pottery china earthenware (ISIC361), Glass and products (ISIC362) and Other non – metallic mineral products (ISIC369). Furthermore, I drop two industries, ‘Wood products except furniture (ISIC331)’ and ‘Furniture except metal (ISIC332)’ because they have no pollution data.

My sample finally identifies 14 industries. The estimate of NETXva is also available for the 14 industries since it is defined as the dependent variable in regressions. The estimate of RCA will not be used in regressions and is only introduced for general analysis because of its short timeline. My sample starts from 1996 to 2003 and data of estimating RCA is available from 1992 to 1999, only four years are covered by both datasets that are not long enough for regressions, therefore, I have an estimate of RCA for 19 industries from 1992 to 1999.

The Chinese pollution data raise several problems as described above. However, the trade data in this study is not straightforward either. In the section of foreign trade of China Statistical Yearbook, commodities imported and exported are classified in terms of the Commodity Classification from the Chinese Customs Statistics, which is based on the Harmonized Commodity Description and Coding System (HS for short) and has made some modifications to meet China's special needs. Since all other variables are reported in terms of the ISIC Classification, I made an attempt on matching HS to ISIC for the Chinese trade data (see Table A2. 1 in the appendix). Other data are collected from the China Statistical Yearbook while the average wage data is obtained from the China Labour Statistical Yearbook (see appendix for data information).

2. 5 Background

2. 5. 1 Revealed comparative advantage (RCA) in China

In recent decades, the Chinese economy has achieved rapid growth followed by diverse economic and social consequences partly because the expansion in foreign trade for industrial products. In 1980, which is the second year after the "open – door" policy was implemented in China, the total value of foreign trade was $31.8 billion for industrial products, and in 1999 it had grown to $344 billion, 9.8 times the value in 1980 with annual growth rate of 13.3% on average. Exports of industrial products increased from $15 billion to $184 billion by a multiple of 11.2 and had an average annual growth rate of 14.1%; imports increased from $16.8 billion to $161 billion, 8.5 times larger and had an average annual growth rate of 12.6%. Although these numbers are impressive, at present China is still a manufacturing centre where low value – added and labour – intensive industrial products are produced. ①

The specialization pattern in one country is determined by that country's comparative advantage. According to the prediction of the HOV model, a country will highly specialize in industries that have comparative advantages, while in contrast the production of industries with comparative disadvantage may shrink and eventually disappear. One indicator that examines the specialization pattern is the RCA index. The RCA index for China is calculated using the Chinese exports data for 19 industries from 1992 to 1999.

Table 2.1 presents the RCA for 19 three – digit ISIC industry sectors in China. RCA values averaged over 1992 – 1999 is greater than one in seven of the nineteen sectors, with the greatest degree of specialization displayed by Wearing apparel except footwear (ISIC322), Leather products (ISIC323), Non – metallic mineral products

① Data source: China Statistical Yearbook.

(ISIC361 +362 +369) and Textiles (ISIC321). China traditionally has a large comparative advantage in the Wearing apparel sector except footwear (ISIC322), Leather products (ISIC323) and Textiles (ISIC321). From 1980 to 2003 Wearing apparel except footwear, is the only sector that has stable and substantial comparative advantage and such advantage appears to deepen through exports with annual growth rate of 13.5% on average while this growth rate of the whole world is 6.1%. The export from the sectors that has great comparative advantage takes 36.1% of total exports in China, in which Wearing apparel except footwear (ISIC322) contributes the most, accounting for 24.6% of total exports. Other sectors with RCA around one include Food products (ISIC311), Plastic products (ISIC356), and Iron and steel (ISIC371). Apparently, these sectors have one thing in common that they are labour intensive and relatively clean but with low value - added and antiquated technologies. ①

In contrast, the industry sectors that have the lowest values of RCA in Table 2.1 are Transport equipment (ISIC384), Paper and products (ISIC341) and Printing and publishing (ISIC342). Not surprisingly, China has a comparative disadvantage in these industries, for instance, the export of the paper industry averaged over 1992 to 1999 accounts for only 0.7% of total exports in China. Compared to the industries with a comparative advantage, these disadvantaged industries in China are more likely to be capital intensive and high - tech industries. It is interesting that the pattern of the Chinese specialization is just a mirror of the US specialization pattern, where the

① Data source: China Industrial Development Report (2005).

industries that have the highest RCA in US are Printing and publishing (ISIC342), Chemicals (ISIC351 +352), Machinery (ISIC382 +383), and Transport equipment (ISIC384), and those industries with the lowest RCA are Leather products (ISIC323) and Wearing apparel (ISIC322).

Table 2.1 The RCA indices of China

ISIC		Ave. 1992 – 1995	Ave. 1996 – 1999	Ave. 1992 – 1999
311	Food products	**1.41**	**1.14**	**1.28**
313	Beverages	0.37	0.31	0.34
314	Tobacco	**1.17**	0.81	0.98
321	Textiles	**2.19**	**1.75**	**1.97**
322	Wearing apparel except footwear	**5.63**	**5.43**	**5.53**
323	Leather products	**4.81**	**4.54**	**4.67**
341	Paper and products	0.22	0.23	0.22
342	Printing and publishing	0.16	0.27	0.22
351 +352	Industrial chemicals and other chemicals	0.46	0.48	0.47
353	Petroleum processing and coking	0.34	0.30	0.32
355	Rubber products	0.43	0.56	0.50
356	Plastic products	**1.18**	**1.47**	**1.32**
361 +362 +369	Non – metallic mineral products	**4.15**	**3.79**	**3.97**
371	Iron and steel	**1.10**	**1.46**	**1.28**
372	Non – ferrous metals	0.56	0.69	0.62
381	Fabricated metal products	0.48	0.52	0.50

Continued

ISIC		Ave. 1992 – 1995	Ave. 1996 – 1999	Ave. 1992 – 1999
382 + 383	Machinery except electrical and machinery electric	0. 53	0. 70	0. 61
384	Transport equipment	0. 14	0. 20	0. 17
385	Professional and scientific equipment	0. 85	0. 94	0. 89

Note: the value of RCA more than one is highlighted in bold.

Figure 2. 1 illustrates the RCA for 19 industries in China. The highest three bars stand for the three highly specialized industries, Wearing apparel expect footwear (ISIC322), Leather products (ISIC323) and Non – metallic mineral products (ISIC361 + 362 + 369), production of these sectors heavily depends on the endowments of labour and natural resources. There are seven bars that have value of RCA more than one and each bar represents a specialized industry in China.

Before examining RCA indices for the pollution intensive industries, it is important to clarify the relative stringency of environmental regulations in China. I have no comparable cross – country data of regulations to help determine the relative stringency of the Chinese environmental regulations, however, several studies suggest that the stringency of a country's environmental regulations is highly correlated with its per capita income (e. g. S. Dasgupta *et al.*, 1995). Per capita income of China is not as high as that of developed economies, it is reasonable to suggest that the stringency of the environmental regulation in China stays at a low level relative to many of its trading partners. The pure environmental regulation effect (ERE) implies that one source of comparative advantage could be a relatively lax stringency of environmental regulation, and a country with such an advantage would specialize in pollution – intensive production. Therefore, as predicted by ERE, the specialization of dirty industries in China may be higher or increasing more rapidly than that of clean industries.

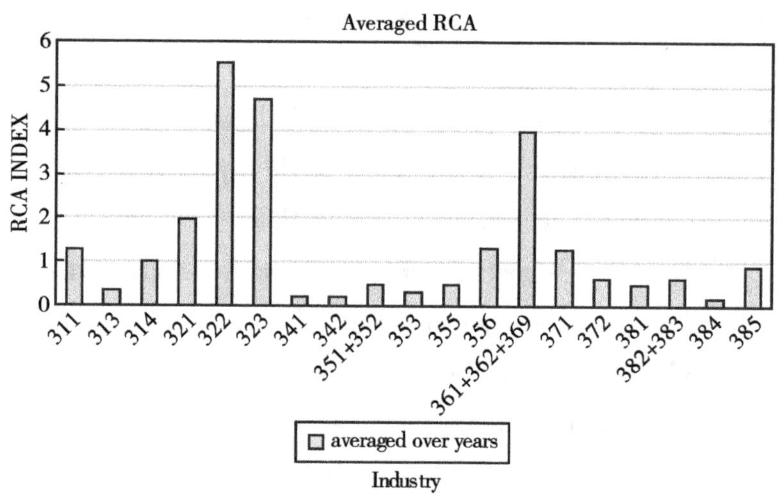

Figure 2.1 RCA indices for 19 industry sectors in China

In Figure 2.2, we plot RCA indices for the five dirtiest industries (as defined by the sectors producing the largest amount of pollution per unit of value added)[①]. The five dirtiest industries are Paper and products (ISIC341), Industrial chemicals and other chemicals (ISIC351 + 352), Non – ferrous metals (ISIC372), Iron and steel (ISIC371) and Non – metallic mineral products (ISIC361 + 362 +

① See Figure A2.1, A2.2, and A2.3 in the appendix.

369), respectively. There are three major findings derivated from Figure 2. 1 and 2. 2. Firstly, of the five dirtiest industries, Non - metallic mineral products (ISIC361 + 3621 + 369) and Iron and steel (ISIC371) show an average RCA greater than one and others show an average RCA much less than one. This may suggest that, of the five dirtiest industries, two sectors at most have a revealed comparative advantage in China. Secondly, it is seen that the RCA of the five dirtiest industries remains fairly stable from 1992 to 1999, and there is no evidence showing a deepening specialization for dirty industries in China. Thirdly, relatively clean industries report an average RCA much greater than that of dirty industries, for instance, the average RCA is 1. 97 for Textiles (ISIC321), 5. 53 for Wearing apparel except footwear (ISIC322), and 4. 67 for Leather products (ISIC323), which implies China maintains its comparative advantage mostly in relatively clean industries.

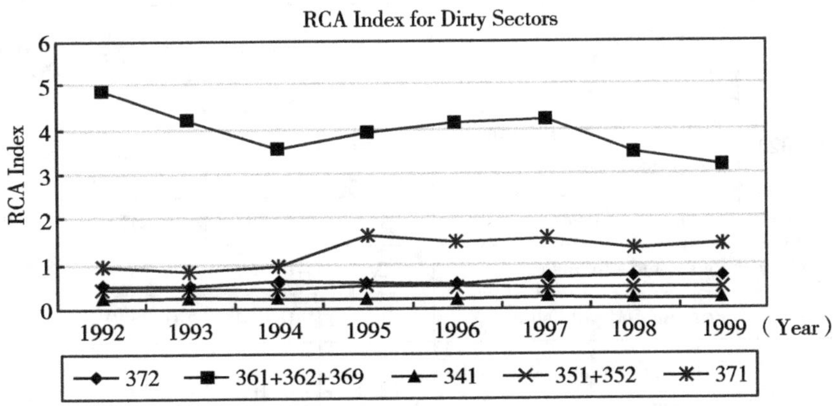

Figure 2. 2 RCA Indices for the five dirtiest Sectors in China

2.5.2 Net exports (NETXva) of the Chinese industry

The second measure of specialization is estimated using an industry's net exports scaled by its value added (NETXva). Table 2.2 provides NETXva for 14 sectors in China, each sector has an estimate of NETXva averaged over the first half period (1992 – 1997), the second half period (1998 – 2003) and the whole period (1992 – 2003), respectively. Table 2.2 also presents the ratio of each sector's value added to the total value added of the manufacturing industry, which indicates the relative size of 14 sectors.

Table 2.2 NETXva and relative size of 14 sectors in China

ISIC		NETXva			
		% VA	Ave. 1992 – 1997	Ave. 1998 – 2003	Ave. 1992 – 2003
311 + 313 + 314	Food products, beverage, tobacco	15.5	0.119	0.0976	0.108
321 + 322	Textiles, wearing apparel except footwear	9.9	1.145	1.446	1.296
323	Leather products	1.9	1.035	1.047	1.041
341	Paper and products	2.2	−0.767	−0.909	−0.838
342	Printing and publishing	1.2	−0.034	0.0520	0.00921
351 + 352	Industrial chemicals and other chemicals	12.1	−0.103	−0.205	−0.154
353	Petroleum processing and coking	4.0	−0.249	−0.176	−0.212
355	Rubber products	1.3	−0.159	−0.139	−0.149

Continued

ISIC		NETXva			
		% VA	Ave. 1992 – 1997	Ave. 1998 – 2003	Ave. 1992 – 2003
356	Plastic products	2. 4	- 1. 319	- 1. 292	- 1. 306
361 + 362 + 369	Non – metallic mineral products	6. 3	0. 0145	-0. 615	-0. 300
371	Iron and steel	7. 2	-0. 251	-0. 224	-0. 238
372	Non – ferrous metals	2. 5	-0. 408	-0. 613	-0. 511
381	Fabricated metal products	3. 3	0. 316	0. 417	0. 367
382 + 383 + 384 + 385	Machinery except electrical and machinery electric, transport equipment, professional and scientific equipment	30. 3	-0. 581	-0. 138	-0. 359

Note: % VA measures each sector's share of total value added.

First, while examining NETXva over the whole sample period (1992 – 2003), out of 14 industries, only five industries are net exporters that demonstrate comparative advantages in China, Specifically Food products, beverage and tobacco (ISIC311 + 313 + 314), Textiles and wearing apparel except footwear (ISIC321 + 322), Leather products (ISIC323), Printing and publishing (ISIC342) and Metal products (ISIC381). The remaining nine industries are net importers that demonstrate comparative disadvantages and the five dirtiest industries are found to be within these nine industries. Along with findings from Figure 2. 3, there are five bars above zero, each of which indicates a net exporter, respectively. There are nine bars below zero, and each of them indicates a net importer and five of them stand for the dirtiest industries.

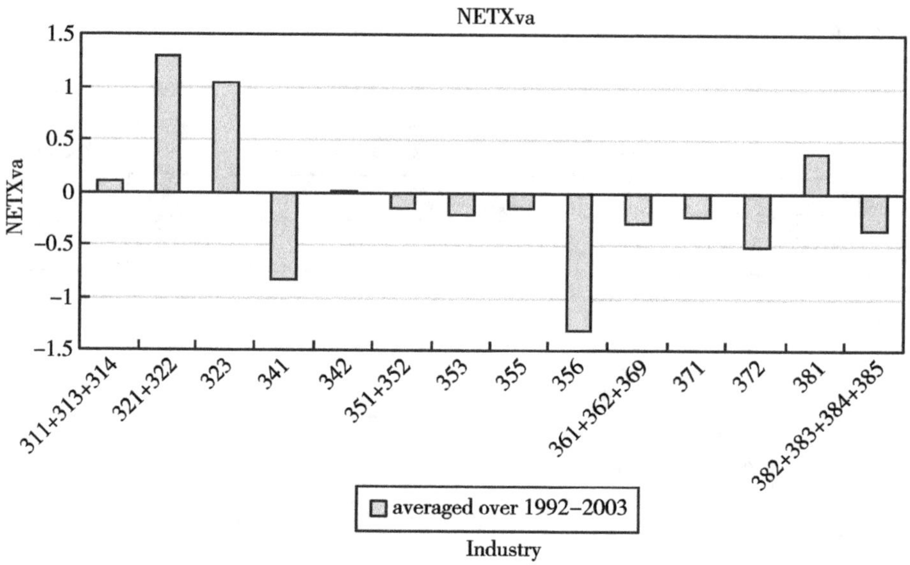

Figure 2. 3 NETXva averaged over years for Chinese industry

Secondly, Table 2. 2 also presents estimates of NETXva averaged over two half periods, respectively. In this way I can examine the time trend of the Chinese industrial specialization. There are nine industries that show an increase in NETXva over time, they are relatively clean industries such as Textiles, wearing apparel except footwear (ISIC321 + 322), Leather products (ISIC323), Printing and publishing (ISIC342) and Metal products (ISIC381). The other five industries report a decreasing NETXva over time, and four of them are defined as dirtiest industries. The data suggests that China has not seen an increasing degree of specialization for dirty industries as predicted by the pure environmental regulation effect (ERE).

Meantime, Figure 2.4 plots NETXva over 1992 – 2003 for the five dirtiest industries and it has been obviously declining since 1996, so that the specialization of dirty industries in China is not increasing though the stringency of environmental regulations is relatively lax compared to developed economies.

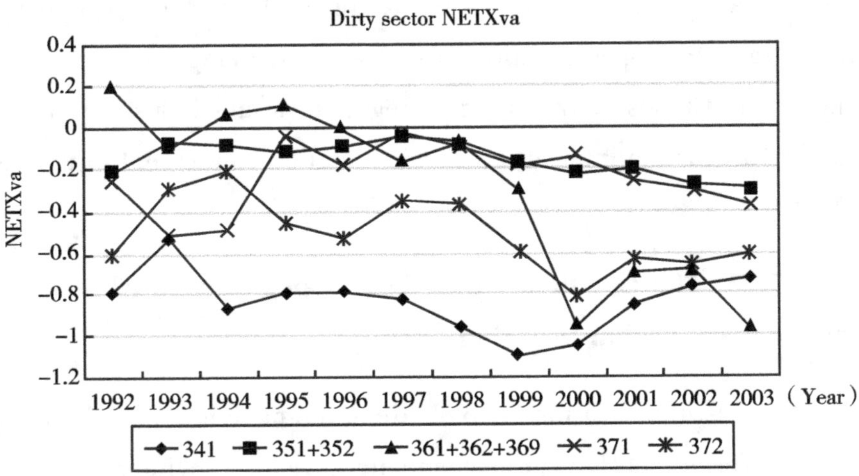

Figure 2.4 NETXva for the five dirtiest sectors in China

It is also necessary to examine the relative size of each sector and Table 2.2 shows that the relative size significantly varies across sectors. The sector Various machinery (ISIC382 + 383 + 384 + 385) presents the largest size and its value added takes about 30.3% of total value added. The sector Printing and publishing (ISIC342) presents the smallest size and its value added takes 1.2% of total value added. There are certain sectors that are also relatively large in size including food products, beverage and tobacco (ISIC311 + 313 + 314), textiles, wearing apparel expect footwear (ISIC321 + 322), and industrial chemicals and other chemicals (ISIC351 + 352).

These sectors may work as outliers in regressions later on, therefore, need more attention while taking analysis on the results.

To conclude, both specialization measures of RCA and NETXva indicate that the specialization of dirty industries is neither higher nor increasing in China even though the stringency of environmental regulations is lax relative to the world's average. To further explain patterns of industrial specialization in China, I will emphasize on understanding the Chinese environmental regulations and industrial characteristics such as the intensity of physical and human capital in the next section.

2.5.3 The Legislation and Governance System of the Environmental Protection in China

The constitution of the People's Republic of China (PRC) stipulates, "The State shall protect and improve the environment where people live and the ecological environment. It shall control pollution and other public hazards." Since 1949, the National People's Congress (NPC) and its Standing Committee have had formulated nine laws on environmental protection and fifteen laws on the protection of natural resources. Since 1996, the State has formulated or revised a number of laws on environmental protection and laws closely related to environmental protection. The State Council has formulated or revised over 50 administrative regulations. Relevant departments of the State Council, People's Congresses at local level as well as local governments have, within the extent of their jurisdiction, formulated and promulgated over 660 rules and regulations either at national or at local level.

China has established national and local levels of environmental protection standards. Standards at national level include environmental quality standards, pollutant discharge (control) standards, and standards of environmental samples, while standards at local levels include environmental quality and pollutant discharge standards. By the end of 2005, the State had promulgated over 800 environmental protection standards.

China has also strengthened enforcement of environmental legislation. The State has inspected the regulation enforcement for the prevention and control of air, water and solid waste pollution. The State has promulgated the Interim Regulations of the Punishment of Violations of Environmental Protection Laws or Disciplines. The State initiated special campaigns of environmental protection to identify enterprises that violate laws through discharging pollution. In three years, the campaigns have processed over 75000 violation cases, closed up 16000 enterprises, and issued more than 10000 warnings to polluters urging them to make improvement. ①

Although the establishment of the environmental protection system appears to be on the right track for China, when compared to developed economies, gaps still remain and barriers still prevail. First, different from many other countries, China's national environmental agency, the State Environmental Protection Administration (SEPA), plays a minor role in the day – to – day enforcement of environmental rules, instead, Environmental Protection Bureau (EPBs), a part of local government, executes a majority of pollution control regulations

① Data sourec: China. org. cn.

as required by the national government. Under circumstances of such a governance system, the execution of EPBs thus is supposed to be supervised by the local government. For example, when a pollution intensive company is at the same time a major source of jobs for local residents as well as a big tax payer, local EPB may have to be cautious when taking enforcement. Moreover, because the courts in China do not often settle environmental disputes, and local EPBs cannot rely on lawsuit to manage environmental violation cases. Meantime, the role of Non – governmental organizations (NGOs) in China is not as prominent as they are in developed economies while resolving the environmental problems.

Secondly, the standard of environmental rules in China sometimes are not defined as clearly as those in developed economies. For example, there are standards of discharge permitted for only four contaminants of wastewater pollution, standards for other contaminants are quite ambiguous, while in US for example, there are discharging standards for more than thirty contaminants. Thirdly, due to the lack of well – defined procedures in response to non – compliance environmental activities in China, local EPBs may have tailored the national environmental rules under circumstances of particular violations during execution, which gives a high degree of flexibility on taking enforcement. All barriers discussed above significantly impact the level of stringency for the Chinese environmental regulation enforcement.

2.5.4 Industrial Air Pollution Abatement in China

The estimations of this research concentrate on industrial air pollution abatement in China. Air pollution is one of the most significant pollutants produced by the Chinese industry. However, investment of air pollution control is much less than that spent on water pollution control, also less efforts have been devoted to the enforcement of regulating air pollution. Fortunately, the Chinese government has noticed the problems and began to take actions.

There are two critical regions where the government put a great deal of efforts on controlling air pollution, namely 'the acid rain – controlled region' and 'the SO_2 controlled region'. Both regions have covered as many as 175 cities over 27 provinces (there are 31 provinces in total in China), where these cities are population intensive and developed with geographic area taking 11.4% of the national geographic area and emissions of SO_2 taking over 60% of the national total (data updated to 2007). In these control regions, a specially designed 'pollution permits' system sets up standards for level of SO_2 emissions allowed. The government encourages dirty firms to replace traditional energy source such as coal with relatively clean energy source, for example natural gas, and at the same time imposes an increasing levy on polluters. As a result, 70.8% of total firms in the two regions have reached the standard of emissions and the quality of air also gradually improves in the region. ①

The research takes pollution abatement cost as a proxy for the stringency of environmental regulations across fourteen industries in China. Figure 2.5 demonstrates pollution abatement cost defined as pollution abatement operating cost per unit of value added for individual industry. There are six of fourteen sectors that have quite large

① Data source: China Environment Yearbook.

cost of pollution abatement as displayed by high bars, including Paper and products (ISIC341), Industrial chemicals and other chemicals (ISIC351 + 352), Petroleum processing and coking (ISIC353), Non – metallic mineral products (ISIC361 + 362 + 369), Iron and steel (ISIC371), Non – ferrous metals (ISIC372), five of which are the dirtiest sectors in China. In contrast, relatively clean industries such as Textile and wearing apparel except footwear (ISIC321 + 322), leather products (ISIC323), printing and publishing (ISIC342), plastic products (ISIC356), and machinery except electrical and machinery electric, transport equipment, professional and scientific equipment (ISIC382 + 383 + 384 + 385), all have much lower levels of pollution abatement cost as displayed by low bars in Figure 2. 5.

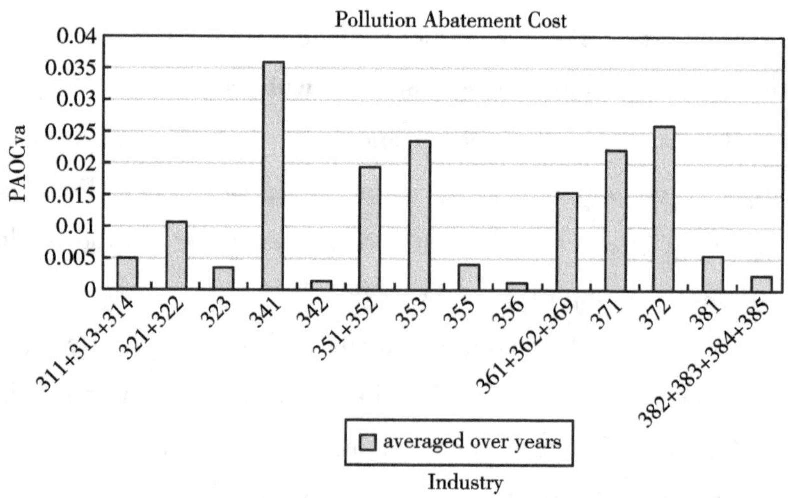

Figure 2. 5 Pollution abatement cost per unit of value added for individual sectors in China

In addition to the pollution abatement cost, an alternative measure of pollution removed per unit of value added is also employed to measure the stringency of environmental regulations. Figure 2.6 demonstrates SO_2 removed across sectors. Apparently, the highest bar of the sector non – ferrous metals (ISIC372) has removed the largest volume of SO_2 emissions. It is hardly to observe bars for the other sectors, however, these bars standing for the five dirtiest sectors, paper and products (ISIC341), industrial chemicals and other chemicals (ISIC351 + 352), petroleum processing and coking (ISIC353), non – metallic mineral products (ISIC361 + 362 + 369) and iron and steel (ISIC371), are relatively higher than other bars, indicating more pollution abatement cost may have been spent in these sectors to remove SO_2 emissions.

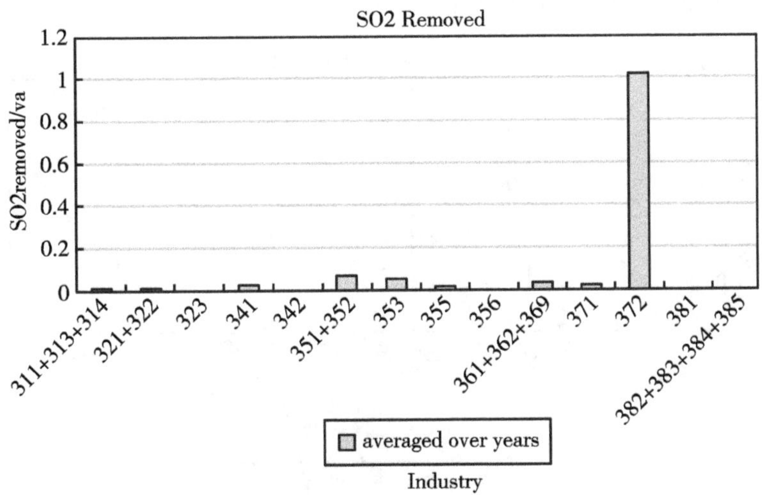

Figure 2.6 SO_2 removed per unit of value added for individual sectors in China

Figure 2. 7 demonstrates SOOT removed per unit of value added across sectors, and again the higher bars stand for the five dirtiest industries. It is the same in Figure 2. 8 that demonstrates DUST removed per unit of value added. Three high bars stand for non – metallic mineral products (ISIC361 + 362 + 369), iron and steel (ISIC371) and non – ferrous metals (ISIC372), respectively. These findings suggest that the abatement cost of removing soot and dust emissions of each dirtiest industry is quite larger than cost of other industries, and it may imply high levels of environmental stringency imposed on dirty sectors.

Along with previous analysis on RCA and NETXva, I can conclude that enforcement of environmental regulations imposed on dirty sectors in China is not as weak as we imagine, and dirty sectors are not found to be specialized in China.

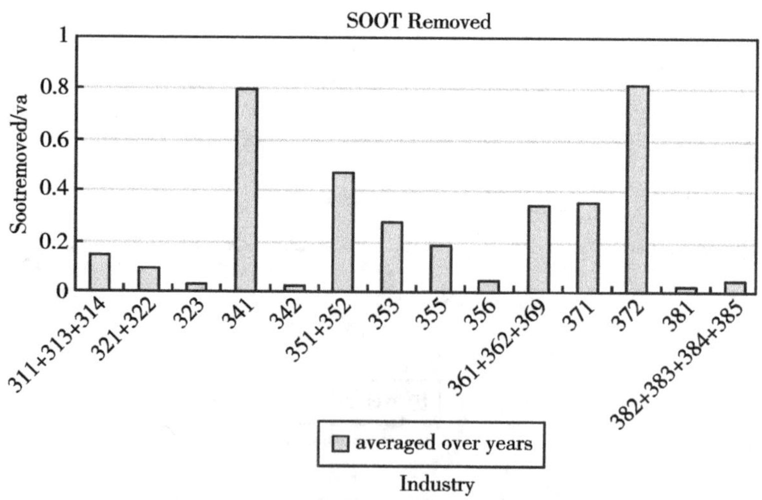

Figure 2. 7 SOOT removed per unit of value added for individual sectors in China

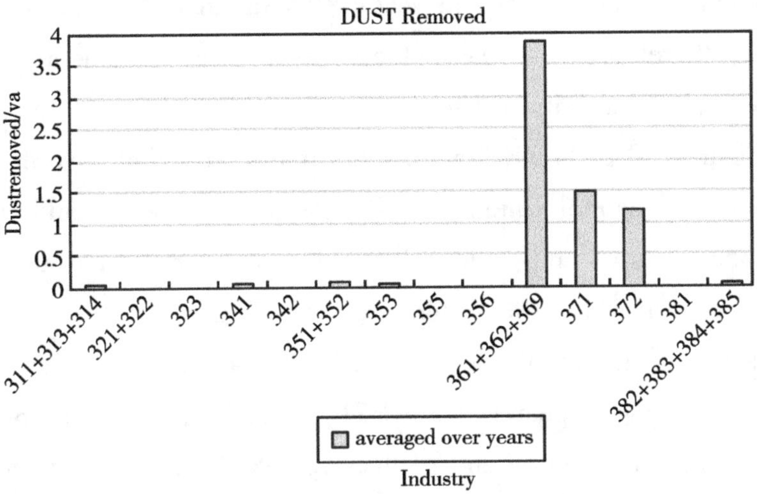

Figure 2. 8 DUST removed per unit of value added for individual sectors in China

2. 5. 5 Physical Capital Intensity (PCI) and Human Capital Intensity (HCI) in China

No evidence suggest that the specialization of pollution intensive industries tends to be relatively high or rapidly increasing in China over time. To find out explanations, a further investigation on characteristics of industry is necessary and more attention should be paid to physical and human capital intensity. In this research, individual industry physical capital intensity (PCI) is defined as total fixed capital divided by the number of workers and human capital intensity (HCI) is defined as average wage paid to skilled worker. Using the average wage as a proxy for human capital may not be ideal because in some small – sized sectors average wage is likely to be high but human capital intensity may not be high at the same time. However, China has generally higher wages in sectors that intensively employ human capital, therefore, it is reasonable to use average wage as a proxy for human capital intensity in China.

Figure 2. 9 plots NETXva for the three sectors that have the highest physical capital intensity, Petroleum processing and coking (ISIC353), Iron and steel (ISIC371) and Non – ferrous metals (ISIC372), in which two sectors are dirty. Figure 2. 9 also shows the three sectors that have the least physical capital intensity, Textiles including wearing apparel (ISIC321 + 322), Leather products (ISIC323), and Printing and publishing (ISIC342), which are relatively clean. ① Notice that all three physical capital intensive sectors have estimates of NETXva lower than that of three least physical capital intensive sectors, suggesting a close and negative relationship between the specialization of an industry and its physical capital intensity. Figure 2. 10 plots NETXva for the three sectors that have the highest average wage, Petroleum processing and coking (ISIC353), Iron and steel (ISIC371) and Non – ferrous metals (ISIC372); and for the three sectors that have the least average wage, namely Textiles including wearing apparel (ISIC321 + 322), Non – metallic mineral products (ISIC361 + 362 + 369) and Paper and products (ISIC341). ② The relationship between NETXva and average wage cannot be clearly observed in Figure 2. 10.

① See Figure A2. 4 in the appendix for the selection of sectors.

② See Figure A2. 5 in the appendix for the selection of sectors.

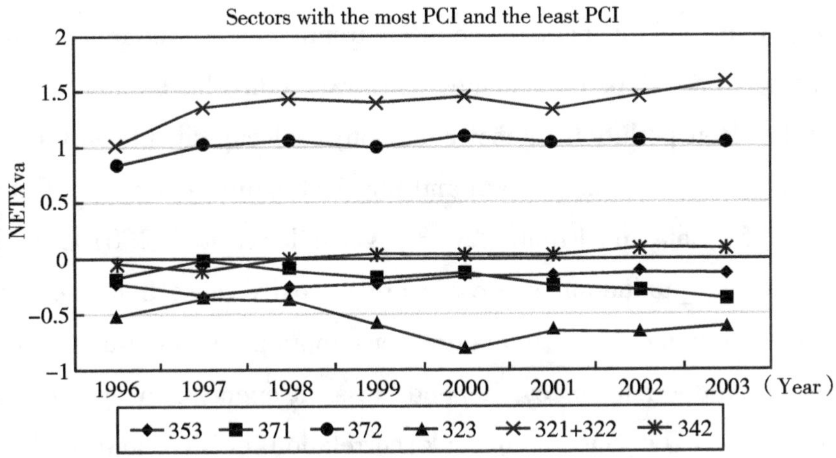

Figure 2. 9 Chinese NETXva for the most and the least physical capital – intensive sectors.

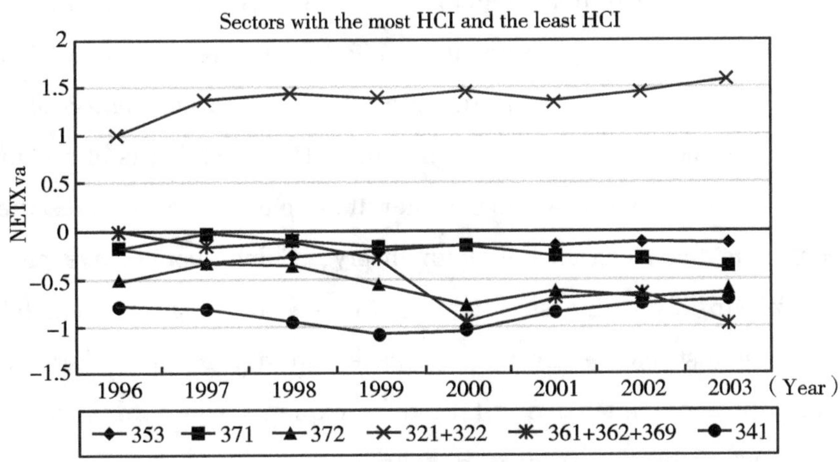

Figure 2. 10 Chinese NETXva for the most and the least human capital – intensive sectors.

The analysis discussed above may explain why the specialization of pollution intensive industries is neither high nor increasing despite relatively low enforcement levels of environmental regulations in China compared to developed economies. Several studies have found a correlation between pollution intensity and physical capital intensity or between pollution abatement costs and physical capital intensity (Cole *et al.*, 2005; Cole and Elliott, 2003; Antweiler *et al.*, 2001). Pollution intensive production processes are typically those that use heavy machinery relying on great energy consumption. In contrast, labour intensive production process depends less on energy and is thus relatively clean. The Spearman rank correlation of PCI and pollution abatement costs per unit value added (PAOCva) in the sample of this research is 0.49 (significant at 1%). When considering alternative measures of pollution abatement costs, a correlation of PCI and SO_2 removed is 0.51 (significant at 1%), a correlation of PCI and SOOT removed is 0.40 (significant at 1%) and a correlation of PCI and DUST removed is 0.49 (significant at 1%). China is abundantly endowed with labour resources rather than physical capital resource. According to the Hechscher – Ohlin theory, China should have greatly specialized in labour intensive industries instead of in physical capital – intensive industries. Meantime, because pollution intensive industries are also physical intensive, it therefor explains why China has low levels of specialization in dirty industries.

The relationship between pollution intensity, physical capital intensity and industrial specialization appears to be well defined in China. Using industrial data from US, Cole and Elliott (2004) also found a significant correlation between an industry's human capital requirements and its pollution intensity. The correlation suggests that clean industries tend to rely on low skilled workers while complicated industrial processes that typically depend on large energy consumption require greater amount of human capital. However, such a significant correlation barely exists in China. In the five dirtiest industries, two of them (Iron and steel, Non – ferrous metals) are in the sectors that have the highest average wage, while the other two (Non – metallic mineral products, Paper and products) are in the sectors that have the least average wage. Moreover, the Spearman rank correlation test also indicates little correlation between an industry's human capital intensity and regulation variables. There is a correlation of 0.21 for HCI and PAOCva, 0.23 for HCI and SO_2 removed, and 0.17 for HCI and DUST removed, and there is even no correlation between HCI and SOOT removed. Unlike the industry in US, the industry in China is not evident by a clear relationship between an industry's pollution intensity (or pollution abatement costs) and its human capital intensity.

2.6 Econometric Analysis

Previous analysis provides some evidence that in China pollution intensive sectors with high cost of pollution abatement either have low levels of specialization or the degree of their specialization is not deepening over time. The pollution abatement cost or pollution removed is thus expected to be one of the determinants of an industry's specialization. It is also expected that an industry's physical capital intensity negatively determines its degree of specialization. Moreover, the regression controls for an industry's human capital intensity.

Using a panel data of 14 three – digit ISIC industrial sectors from 1996 to 2003,[①] the regression estimates determinants of industrial specialization in China, it is given by:

$$SPEC_{it} = \gamma_i + \tau_t + \beta_1 PAOCva_{it} + \beta_2 PCI_{it} + \beta_3 HCI_{it} + \varepsilon \quad (2)$$

where $SPEC_{it}$ denotes net exports per unit of value added. *PAOCva* is categorized into two alternative measures, pollution abatement operating costs per unit of value added (PAOCva), and the removal of air pollutants per unit of value added (SO_2 removed, SOOT removed and DUST removed). *PCI* and *HCI* are previously defined, whilst γ and τ represent industry and time specific effects, respectively.[②] The estimates are expected as $\beta_1 < 0$, $\beta_2 < 0$, and the sign of β_3 is ambiguous.

Equation (1) is a panel data regression, and it requires both cross – sectional and time series dimensions. The methodology includes fixed effects and random effects specifications.[③] The fixed effects estimation assumes that the coefficient of the explanatory variables is not same across sectors, let the constant term vary to account for the sector fixed effect. The error term in the fixed effects estimation is homoskedastic and uncorrelated, both over time and across sectors, which allows for the estimation by pooled OLS. In the random effects estimations, unobserved effects are left in the error term and it has

① Average wage data (HCI) by industry proved unattainable before 1996, thereby restricting our sample.

② See Appendix for definitions and sources of variables.

③ Econometric software STATA 9.0 is applied to run the regression in this research, and the major syntaxes inclue *xtreg* with *fe* and *re robust*.

caused error terms to be correlated with each other as well as correlated with the explanatory variable, therefore, the OLS estimates are no longer efficient. As a result, the random effects estimations use the generalized least squares (GLS) estimation that can transform the error term into homoscedastic and produce efficient GLS estimates. The significant difference between the two approaches is that the fixed effects estimation accounts for the within sector effects only, and the random effects estimation accounts for both within and between sector effects that may provide strong estimates than the fixed effects estimates.

There is one critical issue raised in the estimation. Several studies suggest that an industry's abatement costs may be endogenously determined by its net exports (Levinson and Taylor, 2004), in this case, the explanatory variable and the error term are correlated in the estimation and the OLS estimates are thus inefficient. In this research there are two major sources of endogeneity.

First, imports may impact abatement costs. Levinson and Taylor (2004) suggest that most studies use data at 3 – digit industry level and each of the 3 – digit industry is a heterogenous mix of 4 – digit industries, incurring the issue of endogeneity. Stringent regulations have increased cost of pollution abatement of 4 – digit pollution intensive sectors, as a result, imports from these sectors gradually grow and domestic production of these sectors experience contraction. Then average pollution intensity of production for 3 – digit sectors also decline and pollution abatement cost therefore decreases. Second, environmental regulations may be used as secondary trade barriers. Ederington and Minier (2003) claim that countries may relax environmental regulations in those industries facing the greatest import penetration. Due to these potential sources of endogeneity, the estimates may not be efficient and more tests should be carried out in order to acquire reliable estimates.

2. 7 Results

2. 7. 1 Main Results

Table 2. 3 presents the main results using both fixed and random effects estimations. The dependent variable is the net exports per unit of value added (NETXva) and there are two alternative explanatory variables that measure the stringency of environmental regulations, one is the pollution abatement operating costs per unit of value added (PAOCva), and the other one is the volume of pollution removed per unit of value added, i. e. SO_2 removed, SOOT removed, and DUST removed. When using pollution removed as the explanatory variable in the regression, I drop a sector out of the sample, the sector (Non-ferrous metals ISIC372) is an outlier because Figure 2. 6 finds its SO_2 removed extremely large and data of this sector remains questionable.

I run the Chow test to examine the poolability of sectors (i. e. homogeneity of regression coefficients across sectors). A Chow test is simple and just examines if the estimate is equal across sectors. When the test does not fail, both fixed and random effects estimations can be applied with our panel data. Results of the Chow test are presented in Table A2. 8 of the appendix. The F-statistics from the Chow test

Table 2. 3 **The determinants of NETXva**

NETXva	FIXED EFFECTS				RANDOM EFFECTS			
	(1)	(2)	(3)	(4)	(5)	(6)	(7)	(8)
PAOCva	-2. 866 (-1. 08) [2. 5]				-3. 265 (-1. 07) [2. 3]			
SO_2rem		0. 000298 (2. 79) *** [0. 00]				0. 000296 (2. 69) *** [0. 00]		
Sootrem			-0. 0000904 (-3. 16) *** [0. 00]				-0. 0000941 (-3. 84) *** [0. 00]	
Dustrem				-0. 0000133 (-0. 91) [0. 00]				-0. 000013 (-1. 16) [0. 00]
PCI	-0. 00553 (-0. 67) [0. 01]	-0. 174 (-2. 25) ** [0. 01]	-0. 166 (-2. 10) ** [0. 01]	-0. 00847 (0. 87) [0. 01]	-0. 00678 (-0. 89) [0. 01]	-0. 0189 (-2. 74) *** [0. 01]	-0. 0175 (-2. 46) ** [0. 01]	-0. 00975 (-1. 31) [0. 01]

Continued

NETXva	FIXED EFFECTS				RANDOM EFFECTS			
	(1)	(2)	(3)	(4)	(5)	(6)	(7)	(8)
HCI	0.0000552 (0.92) [0.00]	0.0000818 (1.34) [0.00]	0.000077 (1.35) [0.00]	0.0000595 (0.87) [0.00]	0.0000528 (0.91) [0.00]	0.0000824 (1.43) [0.00]	0.0000758 (1.37) [0.00]	0.0000596 (0.96) [0.00]
Constant	-0.233 (-1.45)	-0.300 (-2.10)**	-0.0437 (-0.28)	-0.171 (-0.78)	-0.217 (-0.80)	-0.295 (-1.10)	-0.0282 (-0.10)	-0.167 (-0.57)
R^2	0.114	0.143	0.194	0.124	0.0532	0.0163	0.204	0.0581
Hausman (*FE. V RE.*)					0.16 (1.0000)	0.35 (1.0000)	0.21 (1.0000)	0.31 (1.0000)
n	112	104	104	104	112	104	104	104

Note: t-statistics in parentheses for fixed effects and z-statistics in parentheses for random effects. Standard errors that are clustered by industry are reported in square parentheses. Time dummies are included.

* significant at 10% level; ** significant at 5% level; *** significant at 1% level.

are insignificant across sectors, indicating that I cannot reject the hypothesis that estimates of all sectors are equal, therefore, data of each sector can be pooled to set up a panel and both fixed and random effects estimations can be applied. I also run a Hausman specification test to examine if the estimates from random effects estimations are consistent and efficient as the true parameters, a rejection of the null hypothesis implies random effects estimates are not reliable. The results of the Hausman tests in Table 2. 3 show consistent and efficient estimates from random effects estimations.

Model (1) and (5) of Table 2. 3 present estimates respectively for the fixed and random effects specifications using pollution abatement operating costs per unit of value added (PAOCva) as the regulation variable. PAOCva and PCI are both negative, HCI is positive, but no estimate is significant in these two models. The value of R – squared is not high either. ① The results therefore indicate that an industry's pollution abatement cost is not significant when determining industrial specialization. The literature suggests that the level of environmental regulation in one country is closely related to its level of income. Compared to developed economies, level of income in China stays relatively low and the stringency of regulations could not be as high as that in developed economies. Therefore, pollution abatement cost may account for only a small fraction of an industry's total cost and it is not surprising that its impact on industry's specialization is not significant. On the other hand, these sectors are relatively in a

① All estimations use heteroscedastic – robust standard errors. R^2 within is reported for fixed effects specifications, and R^2 overall is reported for random effects specifications.

large size including various machinery, food products, beverage and tobacco, and Textiles and wearing apparel except footwear, however, their abatement cost is relatively low, which may have impact on the significance of the estimates. Lastly, the issue of endogeneity may have caused insignificance of PAOCva.

Table 2. 3 also presents estimates using pollution removed as the regulation variable. SOOT removed and DUST removed are found to be negative, however, only estimate of SOOT removed is statistically significant. SO_2 removed turns to be positive and significant in Model (2) and (6), which is not as previously predicted, but the value of R – squared is quite low in both models, so that I do not rely on the estimates of SO_2 removed to explain the story.

However, an inconsistency between the estimate of SO_2 removed and estimates of SOOT removed and DUST removed needs more analysis. Figure 2. 11 draws the marginal abatement cost curve (MAC). The cost is increasing with the level of pollution abated, which means that one additional unit of pollution increases as more and more pollution have been removed. It is not hard to understand because it is extremely easy to abate the first unit of pollution and the marginal cost is thus low, after then, it becomes more difficult to abate an extra unit of pollution and the marginal cost is certainly increasing. Back to Figure 2. 6 and 2. 7, the level of SO_2 removed is quite low across sectors, according to the MAC in Figure 2. 11, the abatement cost of removing SO_2 should be much less than the abatement cost of removing SOOT, therefore, it is not surprising that their estimates are different in terms of sign and significance. Since the abatement cost is little for SO_2 and it is not expected to play a role in determining industrial specialization, I rely on the estimates of SOOT removed to explain the causality of regulation stringency on specialization.

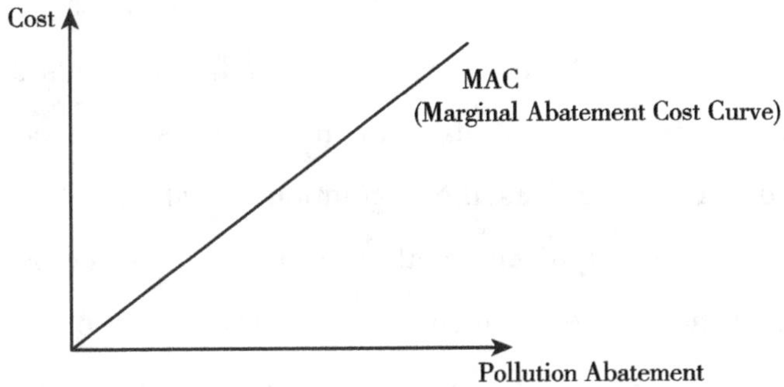

Figure 2.11 Marginal Abatement Cost Curve

The estimates of physical capital intensity are negative in all models and statistically significant in model (2), (3), (6) and (7). These are exactly empirical evidence for that an industry's physical capital intensity negatively determines its degree of specialization in China, other things being equal. The estimates of human capital intensity are positively signed but insignificant throughout all models, which suggests that presently the human capital intensity is not a significant determinant of industrial specialization in China.

2.7.2 Sensitivity Checks

Since the proxy for the stringency of environmental regulations is insignificant when taking pollution abatement operating cost per unit value added as the regulation variable, and the proxy is not consistently signed when taking pollution removed as the regulation variable, it is necessary to perform sensitivity analysis to check the robustness of the main results. I take the sensitivity analysis in this way: drop one sector out of the sample each time and re – estimate equation (1). This methodology may take out any outlier that have caused issues to the main results.

Table 2.4 and 2.5 present estimates of fixed effects and random effects regressions using pollution abatement operating cost per unit value added (PAOCva) as the regulation variable. The estimate of PAOCva has remained negative after dropping one sector out of the sample each time. More interesting, after dropping the sector Textiles and Wearing apparel (ISIC321 + 322), the estimate of PAOCva in the random effects regression turns to be statistically significant. The estimate of PCI has remained negative over time and is statistically significant sometimes. There is no major change for the estimate of HCI. The sensitivity checks in Table 2.4 and 2.5 have proved the robustness of the main results.

Table 2.4 The determinants of NETXva, employing PAOCva and dropping one sector at a time (fixed effects)

NETXva	FIXED EFFECTS					
	PAOCva	PCI	HCI	Constant	R^2	n
311 +313 +314	-2.892 (-1.07)	-0.00536 (-0.64)	0.0000559 (0.92)	-0.252 (-1.54)	0.125	104
321 +322	-3.775 (-1.43)	-0.00255 (-0.31)	0.0000788 (1.27)	-0.401 (-2.34) **	0.163	104
323	-2.736 (-1.03)	-0.00211 (-0.25)	0.000054 (0.85)	-0.320 (-1.81) *	0.0054	104
341	-3.990 (-0.87)	-0.0174 (-1.71) *	0.000109 (1.61)	-0.288 (-1.69) *	0.164	104

Continued

NETXva	FIXED EFFECTS					
	PAOCva	PCI	HCI	Constant	R^2	n
342	-2. 787 (-1. 04)	-0. 00331 (-0. 38)	0. 0000471 (0. 78)	-0. 224 (-1. 36)	0. 127	104
351 +352	-4. 538 (-1. 56)	-0. 00286 (-0. 35)	0. 0000413 (0. 67)	-0. 196 (-1. 20)	0. 118	104
353	-1. 719 (-0. 72)	-0. 0235 (-1. 80) *	0. 0000458 (0. 74)	-0. 138 (-0. 90)	0. 157	104
355	-2. 964 (-0. 98)	-0. 00508 (-0. 60)	0. 0000522 (0. 82)	-0. 212 (-1. 21)	0. 108	104
356	-2. 715 (-1. 01)	-0. 00610 (-0. 71)	0. 0000608 (0. 99)	-0. 155 (-0. 93)	0. 112	104
361 +362 +369	-1. 968 (-0. 78)	0. 00114 (0. 16)	-0. 000039 (-0. 91)	0. 00983 (0. 08)	0. 152	104
371	-1. 098 (-0. 45)	-0. 00788 (-0. 98)	0. 000111 (1. 78) *	-0. 395 (-2. 53) **	0. 140	104
372	-3. 536 (-1. 27)	-0. 00761 (-0. 90)	0. 000069 (1. 10)	-0. 229 (-1. 41)	0. 111	104
381	-2. 958 (-1. 11)	-0. 00459 (-0. 54)	0. 0000529 (0. 88)	-0. 263 (-1. 60)	0. 121	104
382 +383 + 384 +385	-2. 791 (-1. 07)	-0. 00275 (-0. 27)	0. 0000388 (0. 54)	-0. 171 (-0. 92)	0. 103	104

Note: t – statistics in parentheses. Time dummies are included.

* significant at 10% level; ** significant at 5% level; *** significant at 1% level.

Table 2.5 The determinants of NETXva, employing PAOCva and dropping one sector at a time (random effects)

NETXva	RANDOM EFFECTS					
	PAOCva	PCI	HCI	Constant	R^2	n
311 +313 +314	-3.260 (-1.05)	-0.00660 (-0.86)	0.0000538 (0.92)	-0.237 (-0.82)	0.0477	104
321 +322	-4.322 (-1.69) *	-0.00433 (-0.58)	0.0000801 (1.38)	-0.391 (-1.62)	0.0855	104
323	-3.055 (-0.97)	-0.00311 (-0.41)	0.0000512 (0.84)	-0.303 (-1.06)	0.0131	104
341	-4.267 (-0.84)	-0.0183 (-1.86) *	0.000105 (1.56)	-0.270 (-0.95)	0.0205	104
342	-3.173 (-1.03)	-0.00458 (-0.58)	0.0000451 (0.77)	-0.208 (-0.72)	0.0376	104
351 +352	-4.927 (-1.45)	-0.00396 (-0.52)	0.000039 (0.66)	-0.182 (-0.64)	0.0637	104
353	-2.030 (-0.70)	-0.0278 (-2.28) **	0.0000428 (0.73)	-0.110 (-0.43)	0.273	104
355	-3.432 (-1.00)	-0.00630 (-0.81)	0.0000494 (0.80)	-0.194 (-0.66)	0.0586	104
356	-3.776 (-1.15)	-0.00746 (-0.94)	0.0000516 (0.86)	-0.110 (-0.42)	0.128	104
361 +362 +369	-2.141 (-0.79)	0.000648 (0.10)	-0.0000398 (-1.00)	0.0162 (0.07)	0.0903	104
371	-1.591 (-0.54)	-0.00903 (-1.21)	0.00105 (1.74) *	-0.369 (-1.26)	0.0026	104
372	-3.795 (-1.20)	-0.00891 (-1.15)	0.0000681 (1.13)	-0.219 (-0.78)	0.0546	104

Continued

NETXva	RANDOM EFFECTS					
	PAOCva	PCI	HCI	Constant	R^2	n
381	-3.299 (-1.07)	-0.00582 (-0.75)	0.0000512 (0.88)	-0.249 (-0.87)	0.0427	104
382 +383 + 384 +385	-3.212 (-1.05)	-0.00436 (-0.46)	0.0000384 (0.55)	-0.158 (-0.54)	0.0612	104

Note: z - statistics in parentheses. Time dummies are included.
* significant at 10% level; ** significant at 5% level; *** significant at 1% level.

Table 2.6 and 2.7 present fixed effects and random effects estimates using SO_2 removed per unit value added as the regulation variable. The estimate of SO_2 removed remains significantly positive after dropping one sector at a time except for dropping the sector of Petroleum processing and coking (ISIC353). After dropping this sector, the estimate of SO_2 removed turns insignificant in both fixed effects and random effects regressions, therefore, the positive and significant estimate of SO_2 removed from the main results is not robust, and I suggest that SO_2 removed should not be a reliable proxy for the regulation stringency in China.

Table 2.6 The determinants of NETXva, employing SO_2 removed and dropping one sector at a time (fixed effects)

NETXva	FIXED EFFECTS					
	SO_2rem	PCI	HCI	Constant	R^2	n
311 +313 +314	0.000296 (2.71) ***	-0.0172 (-2.20) **	0.0000825 (1.34)	-0.323 (-2.22) **	0.150	96
321 +322	0.000253 (2.43) **	-0.0144 (-1.86) *	0.000106 (1.65)	-0.477 (-2.99) ***	0.175	96

Continued

NETXva	FIXED EFFECTS					
	SO_2rem	PCI	HCI	Constant	R^2	n
323	0.00028 (2.46)**	-0.0147 (-1.77)*	0.0000805 (1.25)	-0.386 (-2.45)**	0.139	96
341	0.000281 (2.46)**	-0.0273 (-3.00)***	0.000130 (1.76)*	-0.344 (-2.06)**	0.199	96
342	0.000289 (2.60)**	-0.0153 (-1.89)*	0.0000748 (1.21)	-0.293 (-2.00)**	0.148	96
351+352	0.000517 (2.21)**	-0.0243 (-2.26)**	0.0000859 (1.42)	-0.284 (-2.03)**	0.129	96
353	0.000214 (1.61)	-0.0261 (-2.08)**	0.0000806 (1.25)	-0.240 (-1.58)	0.154	96
355	0.000304 (2.77)***	-0.0172 (-2.18)**	0.0000792 (1.24)	-0.279 (-1.85)*	0.135	96
356	0.000298 (2.81)***	-0.0180 (-2.24)**	0.0000875 (1.41)	-0.216 (-1.48)	0.145	96
361+362 +369	0.000388 (4.23)***	-0.0118 (-1.74)*	-0.0000242 (-0.63)	-0.0225 (-0.23)	0.348	96
371	0.000211 (2.21)**	-0.0168 (-2.18)**	0.000132 (1.97)*	-0.418 (-2.82)***	0.169	96
381	0.000298 (2.73)***	-0.0170 (-2.13)**	0.0000812 (1.33)	-0.339 (-2.33)**	0.146	96
382+383+ 384+385	0.000300 (2.87)***	-0.0171 (-1.78)*	0.0000802 (1.07)	-0.269 (-1.58)	0.129	96

Note: t-statistics in parentheses. Time dummies are included.

* significant at 10% level; ** significant at 5% level; *** significant at 1% level.

Table 2.7 The determinants of NETXva, employing SO_2 removed and dropping one sector at a time (random effects)

NETXva	RANDOM EFFECTS					
	SO_2rem	PCI	HCI	Constant	R^2	n
311 +313 +314	0.000295 (2.64) ***	-0.0188 (-2.69) ***	0.0000833 (1.42)	-0.318 (-1.11)	0.0185	96
321 +322	0.000253 (2.39) **	-0.0169 (-2.40) **	0.000111 (1.86) *	-0.0482 (-2.04) **	0.0553	96
323	0.000280 (2.48) **	-0.0160 (-2.23) **	0.0000805 (1.32)	-0.380 (-1.34)	0.0053	96
341	0.000281 (2.38) **	-0.0283 (-3.19) ***	0.000128 (1.76) *	-0.333 (-1.12)	0.0119	96
342	0.000287 (2.52) **	-0.0168 (-2.35) **	0.0000757 (1.30)	-0.289 (-1.00)	0.0096	96
351 +352	0.000527 (2.31) **	-0.0262 (-2.72) ***	0.000087 (1.54)	-0.280 (-0.99)	0.0403	96
353	0.000180 (1.47)	-0.0301 (-2.64) ***	0.0000793 (1.29)	-0.217 (-0.81)	0.152	96
355	0.000302 (2.66) ***	-0.0187 (-2.66) ***	0.0000798 (1.32)	-0.274 (-0.95)	0.0154	96
356	0.000286 (2.53) **	-0.0196 (-2.74) ***	0.0000858 (1.43)	-0.202 (-0.77)	0.0003	96
361 +362 +369	0.000388 (4.11) ***	-0.0123 (-2.08) **	-0.0000239 (-0.71)	-0.0216 (-0.09)	0.0448	96
371	0.000212 (2.21) **	-0.0183 (-2.66) ***	0.000131 (2.05) **	-0.410 (-1.40)	0.0042	96

Continued

NETXva	RANDOM EFFECTS					
	SO_2rem	PCI	HCI	Constant	R^2	n
381	0.000298 (2.68) ***	-0.0186 (-2.60) ***	0.0000823 (1.42)	-0.335 (-1.17)	0.0209	96
382 +383 + 384 +385	0.000297 (2.72) ***	-0.0193 (-2.24) **	0.0000838 (1.18)	-0.270 (-0.93)	0.0214	96

Note: z - statistics in parentheses. Time dummies are included.

* significant at 10% level; ** significant at 5% level; *** significant at 1% level.

Table 2.8 and 2.9 present estimates from sensitivity checks using SOOT removed per unit value added as the regulation variable. Following the same procedure of dropping one sector at a time, the estimate of SOOT removed remains negative and significant all the time, and the estimate of PCI also remains significantly negative throughout checks. The estimate of HCI is still insignificant most of the time, indicating that SOOT removed could be a good and reliable proxy for the stringency of environmental regulations in China.

Table 2.8 The determinants of NETXva, employing SOOT removed and dropping one sector at a time (fixed effects)

NETXva	FIXED EFFECTS					
	Sootrem	PCI	HCI	Constant	R^2	n
311 +313 +314	-0.0000896 (-3.11) ***	-0.0166 (-2.10) **	0.0000778 (1.35)	-0.0583 (-0.36)	0.200	96
321 +322	-0.0000859 (-3.18) ***	-0.0145 (-1.90) *	0.000103 (1.73) *	-0.225 (-1.32)	0.236	96
323	-0.0000894 (-3.17) ***	-0.0140 (-1.76) *	0.0000776 (1.28)	-0.121 (-0.71)	0.196	96

Continued

NETXva	FIXED EFFECTS					
	Sootrem	PCI	HCI	Constant	R^2	n
341	−0.0000855 (−2.34) **	−0.0258 (−2.38) **	0.000122 (1.73) *	−0.130 (−0.70)	0.225	96
342	−0.000092 (−3.13) ***	−0.0147 (−1.80) *	0.0000691 (1.20)	−0.0125 (−0.08)	0.206	96
351 +352	−0.000139 (−3.63) ***	−0.0189 (−2.26) **	0.0000681 (1.22)	0.0656 (0.40)	0.247	96
353	−0.0000985 (−2.62) **	−0.0355 (−3.00) ***	0.0000667 (1.13)	0.0789 (0.48)	0.239	96
355	−0.0000903 (−3.11) ***	−0.0163 (−2.03) **	0.0000738 (1.24)	−0.0181 (−0.11)	0.185	96
356	−0.0000948 (−3.23) ***	−0.0177 (−2.16) **	0.0000836 (1.45)	0.0686 (0.42)	0.207	96
361 +362 +369	−0.000042 (−2.09) **	−0.00583 (−0.86)	−0.0000141 (−0.34)	0.0670 (0.58)	0.200	96
371	−0.0000899 (−3.06) ***	−0.0171 (−2.39) **	0.000123 (2.19) **	−0.184 (−1.28)	0.238	96
381	−0.000092 (−3.16) ***	−0.0160 (−1.99) *	0.0000752 (1.31)	−0.0570 (−0.35)	0.201	96
382 +383 + 384 +385	−0.0000897 (−3.15) ***	−0.0157 (−1.59)	0.0000719 (1.01)	0.00917 (0.05)	0.180	96

Note: t – statistics in parentheses. Time dummies are included.

* significant at 10% level; ** significant at 5% level; *** significant at 1% level.

Table 2.9 The determinants of NETXva, employing SOOT removed and dropping one sector at a time (random effects)

NETXva	RANDOM EFFECTS					
	Sootrem	PCI	HCI	Constant	R^2	n
311 +313 +314	-0.0000933 (-3.76)***	-0.0175 (-2.45)**	0.0000767 (1.37)	-0.0427 (-0.15)	0.201	96
321 +322	-0.0000876 (-3.88)***	-0.0156 (-2.22)**	0.000105 (1.86)*	-0.223 (-0.92)	0.220	96
323	-0.0000907 (-3.80)***	-0.0145 (-2.06)**	0.0000759 (1.30)	-0.111 (-0.39)	0.144	96
341	-0.0000875 (-2.68)***	-0.0263 (-2.58)**	0.000120 (1.70)*	-0.117 (-0.39)	0.0978	96
342	-0.0000962 (-3.78)***	-0.0157 (-2.14)**	0.0000682 (1.22)	0.00452 (0.02)	0.211	96
351 +352	-0.000138 (-4.18)***	-0.0191 (-2.59)**	0.000067 (1.23)	0.0673 (0.24)	0.210	96
353	-0.000100 (-3.31)***	-0.0372 (-3.39)***	0.0000649 (1.14)	0.0939 (0.34)	0.255	96
355	-0.0000943 (-3.79)***	-0.0173 (-2.38)**	0.0000727 (1.25)	-0.00152 (-0.01)	0.211	96
356	-0.000109 (-4.40)***	-0.0193 (-2.60)***	0.0000757 (1.31)	0.133 (0.54)	0.434	96
361 +362 +369	-0.0000459 (-2.32)**	-0.00654 (-1.14)	-0.0000138 (-0.36)	0.0772 (0.33)	0.199	96

Continued

NETXva	RANDOM EFFECTS					
	Sootrem	PCI	HCI	Constant	R^2	n
371	-0. 000094 (-3. 73) ***	-0. 0180 (-2. 67) ***	0. 000120 (2. 17) **	-0. 163 (-0. 56)	0. 176	96
381	-0. 0000948 (-3. 79) ***	-0. 0167 (-2. 32) **	0. 0000743 (1. 34)	-0. 0443 (-0. 15)	0. 182	96
382 +383 + 384 +385	-0. 0000948 (-3. 85) ***	-0. 0172 (-1. 92) *	0. 0000733 (1. 07)	0. 0236 (0. 08)	0. 240	96

Note: z – statistics in parentheses. Time dummies are included.

* significant at 10% level; ** significant at 5% level; *** significant at 1% level.

Lastly, Table 2. 10 and 2. 11 present estimates from sensitivity checks using DUST removed per unit value added as the regulation variable. The estimate of DUST removed remains insignificantly negative always, however, after dropping the sector of Non – metallic mineral products (ISIC361 +362 +369), the estimate turns significant and positive, which is different from the expectation, however, this sector is one of the five dirtiest sectors and plays an important role in the industrial research, therefore, it is unreasonable to discuss the results without taking this industry into account. The estimate of PCI remains insignificant and negative most of the time while the estimate of HCI is insignificant all time. DUST removed is thus not expected to be an appropriate proxy for the environmental stringency.

Table 2.10 The determinants of NETXva, employing DUST removed and dropping one sector at a time (fixed effects)

NETXva	FIXED EFFECTS					
	Dustrem	PCI	HCI	Constant	R^2	n
311 +313 +314	-0.0000134 (-0.91)	-0.00835 (-0.97)	0.0000602 (0.87)	-0.185 (-0.82)	0.132	96
321 +322	-0.000011 (-0.79)	-0.00669 (-0.79)	0.0000886 (1.27)	-0.368 (-1.62)	0.159	96
323	-0.0000127 (-0.88)	-0.00556 (-0.63)	0.0000592 (0.81)	-0.259 (-1.10)	0.125	96
341	-0.0000134 (-0.95)	-0.0182 (-1.68) *	0.000104 (1.28)	-0.202 (-0.82)	0.184	96
342	-0.0000133 (-0.92)	-0.00681 (-0.77)	0.0000537 (0.78)	-0.160 (-0.71)	0.134	96
351 +352	-0.0000136 (-0.91)	-0.00711 (-0.83)	0.0000537 (0.77)	-0.152 (-0.67)	0.118	96
353	-0.0000182 (-1.19)	-0.0284 (-2.07) **	0.0000287 (0.37)	0.0302 (0.11)	0.191	96
355	-0.000013 (-0.88)	-0.00805 (-0.92)	0.0000574 (0.80)	-0.147 (-0.64)	0.113	96
356	-0.0000136 (-0.94)	-0.00895 (-1.01)	0.0000645 (0.93)	-0.0740 (-0.33)	0.127	96
361 +362 +369	0.0000447 (4.67) ***	-0.00307 (-0.48)	0.000023 (0.59)	-0.218 (-2.02) **	0.267	96

Continued

NETXva	FIXED EFFECTS					
	Dustrem	PCI	HCI	Constant	R^2	n
371	-0.0000208 (-1.50)	-0.0101 (-1.24)	0.000118 (1.84) *	-0.309 (-1.67)	0.216	96
381	-0.0000133 (-0.91)	-0.00790 (-0.90)	0.0000585 (0.85)	-0.201 (-0.89)	0.127	96
382 +383 +384 +385	-0.0000134 (-0.90)	-0.00612 (-0.54)	0.0000453 (0.50)	-0.103 (-0.38)	0.108	96

Note: t-statistics in parentheses. Time dummies are included.

* significant at 10% level; ** significant at 5% level; *** significant at 1% level.

Table 2.11 The determinants of NETXva, employing DUST removed and dropping one sector at a time (random effects)

NETXva	RANDOM EFFECTS					
	Dustrem	PCI	HCI	Constant	R^2	n
311 +313 +314	-0.0000131 (-1.16)	-0.00959 (-1.28)	0.0000604 (0.96)	-0.182 (-0.58)	0.0553	96
321 +322	-0.00001 (-0.95)	-0.00866 (-1.17)	0.0000935 (1.50)	-0.377	0.0603	96
323	-0.0000121 (-1.09)	-0.00658 (-0.88)	0.0000593 (0.90)	-0.257 (-0.82)	0.0323	96
341	-0.0000135 (-1.23)	-0.0188 (-1.84) *	0.000100 (1.29)	-0.188 (-0.58)	0.0749	96
342	-0.0000131 (-1.18)	-0.00824 (-1.07)	0.0000541 (0.86)	-0.156 (-0.51)	0.0538	96
351 +352	-0.0000134 (-1.16)	-0.00832 (-1.13)	0.0000538 (0.85)	-0.148 (-0.48)	0.0567	96

Continued

NETXva	RANDOM EFFECTS					
	Dustrem	PCI	HCI	Constant	R^2	n
353	-0.0000168 (-1.44)	-0.0307 (-2.58)**	0.0000319 (0.48)	0.0219 (0.07)	0.144	96
355	-0.0000129 (-1.14)	-0.00934 (-1.23)	0.0000572 (0.88)	-0.142 (-0.45)	0.0605	96
356	-0.000014 (-1.32)	-0.0105 (-1.37)	0.0000604 (0.95)	-0.0544 (-0.19)	0.110	96
361+362 +369	0.0000407 (3.85)***	-0.00340 (-0.63)	0.0000183 (0.53)	-0.196 (-0.70)	0.0031	96
371	-0.0000192 (-1.59)	-0.0112 (-1.58)	0.000117 (1.99)**	-0.306 (-1.01)	0.0359	96
381	-0.0000129 (-1.14)	-0.00914 (-1.20)	0.0000593 (0.95)	-0.200 (-0.64)	0.0492	96
382+383+ 384+385	-0.0000132 (-1.17)	-0.00806 (-0.82)	0.0000487 (0.60)	-0.107 (-0.33)	0.0629	96

Note: z-statistics in parentheses. Time dummies are included.

* significant at 10% level; ** significant at 5% level; *** significant at 1% level.

In addition to the above analysis, because early literature suggests that an industry's abatement costs may be endogenously determined by its net exports (Levinson and Taylor, 2004; Ederington and Minier, 2003), I also perform several sensitivity checks to deal with the potential endogeneity problems. The first step is to control for the potential endogeneity of the pollution abatement cost and the removal of pollution. In Table 2.12, the specifications regress NETXva on one year lagged values of pollution abatement operating cost, SO_2 removed, SOOT removed and DUST removed, leaving other variables unchanged. The results show that lagged pollution abatement operating cost turns positive though it is still an insignificant determinant of industrial specialization. The estimates of lagged SO_2 removed and SOOT removed are no different from those in the main results. However, for DUST removed, one year lagged DUST removed turns out to be a significant determinant of an industry's NETXva while the estimate of using its present value is insignificant. While using lagged values of the regulation proxies, the estimate of PCI turns insignificant and there is no obvious change to the estimate of HCI.

The specifications in Table 2. 13 regress NETXva on one year lagged values of pollution abatement operating cost and the removal of pollution (SO_2 rem, Sootrem and Dustrem), as well as one year lagged value of PCI and HCI, to remove any contemporaneous relationship between industry characteristics and net exports. There are three findings different from our prior expectations. First, the estimate of one year lagged SO_2 removed turns insignificant. Second, the estimate of one year lagged DUST removed is now significant. Third, one year lagged PCI becomes an insignificant determinant of net exports. Furthermore, I also perform sensitivity checks of dropping one sector at a time for regressions using lagged values of regulation variables, the results are reported in the appendix (Table A2. 2 – A2. 7 for detail). Generally, one year lagged values of PAOCva, PCI and HCI do not seem to perform better than their present values and I would like to focus on my main results.

Table 2.12 The determinants of NETXva, employing one year lagged value of pollution abatement operating cost and pollutants removed

NETXva	FIXED EFFECTS				RANDOM EFFECTS			
	(9)	(10)	(11)	(12)	(13)	(14)	(15)	(16)
PAOCva_1†	2.749 (1.12)				2.352 (0.84)			
SO_2rem_1		0.000220 (2.11)**				0.000221 (2.11)**		
Sootrem_1			-0.0000535 (-1.65)				-0.0000618 (-2.12)**	
Dustrem_1				-0.0000354 (-4.33)***				-0.0000327 (-3.34)***
PCI	0.00450 (0.50)	-0.00170 (-0.21)	0.00318 (0.35)	0.00983 (1.17)	0.00225 (0.27)	-0.00425 (-0.57)	0.00114 (0.14)	0.00821 (1.15)
HCI	0.0000227 (0.39)	0.0000248 (0.43)	0.0000102 (0.20)	-0.0000535 (-1.01)	0.0000219 (0.41)	0.0000279 (0.51)	9.84e-06 (0.21)	-0.0000471 (-1.01)

Continued

NETXva	FIXED EFFECTS				RANDOM EFFECTS			
	(9)	(10)	(11)	(12)	(13)	(14)	(15)	(16)
Constant	-0. 159 (-0. 97)	-0. 115 (-0. 79)	0. 0577 (0. 38)	0. 255 (1. 63)	-0. 140 (-0. 57)	-0. 113 (-0. 43)	0. 0872 (0. 34)	0. 230 (0. 95)
R^2	0. 130	0. 117	0. 136	0. 369	0. 051	0. 0097	0. 174	0. 0501
n	98	91	91	91	98	91	91	91

Note: t - statistics in parentheses for fixed effects and z - statistics in parentheses for random effects. Time dummies are included. †one year lagged value.
* significant at 10% level; ** significant at 5% level; *** significant at 1% level.

Table 2. 13 The determinants of NETXva, employing one year lagged values of pollution abatement cost, pollutants removed, PCI and HCI

NETXva	FIXED EFFECTS				RANDOM EFFECTS			
	(17)	(18)	(19)	(20)	(21)	(22)	(23)	(24)
PAOCva_1†	4. 388 (1. 65)				3. 742 (1. 36)			
SO_2rem_1		0. 000190 (1. 65)				0. 000188 (1. 65)		
Sootrem_1			-0. 0000488 (-1. 48)				-0. 000058 (-1. 96) **	
Dustrem_1				-0. 0000333 (-3. 96) ***				-0. 0000309 (-3. 17) ***
PCI_1	-0. 00215 (-0. 26)	-0. 00379 (-0. 53)	-0. 00169 (-0. 20)	0. 00614 (0. 83)	-0. 00318 (-0. 42)	-0. 00530 (-0. 79)	-0. 00327 (-0. 41)	0. 00507 (0. 80)
HCI_1	0. 000109 (1. 42)	0. 0000715 (0. 88)	0. 0000657 (0. 95)	-0. 0000175 (-0. 27)	0. 0000986 (1. 41)	0. 0000698 (0. 92)	0. 0000609 (0. 94)	-0. 0000129 (-0. 23)

Continued

NETXva	FIXED EFFECTS				RANDOM EFFECTS			
	(17)	(18)	(19)	(20)	(21)	(22)	(23)	(24)
Constant	-0.401 (-1.89)*	-0.239 (-1.16)	-0.0939 (-0.49)	0.153 (0.83)	-0.358 (-1.29)	-0.227 (-0.76)	-0.0524 (-0.19)	0.133
R^2	0.17	0.135	0.152	0.358	0.04	0.0125	0.150	0.0503
n	98	91	91	91	98	91	91	91

Note: t-statistics in parentheses for fixed effects and z-statistics in parentheses for random effects. Time dummies are included. †one year lagged value.

* significant at 10% level; ** significant at 5% level; *** significant at 1% level.

To conclude, the specifications dealing with endogeneity problems have produced some results different from previous expectations, which implies the existence of endogeneity. The proxy for environmental regulations (or pollution abatement costs) may not be treated as exogenous variables in the research of examining the relationship between a country's industry specialization and its stringency of environmental regulations, which needs further discussion in future work.

2.8 Conclusions

This research has introduced two specialization indices (RCA and NETXva) to investigate the industrial specialization patterns in China. Although the stringency of environmental regulations in China appears to be low relative to those of many developed countries, the specialization of 'dirty' industries is neither higher nor increasing more rapidly than other industries because industrial characteristics such as physical capital intensity plays significant roles in determining the specialization patterns in China. Using the Chinese industrial data, I found pollution intensive industries are more likely to use physical capital compared to clean industries, and physical capital intensity is a negative determinant of an industry's specialization. Therefore, dirty industries with high levels of physical capital intensity just have lower degree of specialization even though the stringency of environmental regulations in China is relatively weaker than that of developed economies. The human capital intensity is also found to be a significant determinant of the specialization in developed countries, but it is not true in China. The research found no evidence for a clear correlation between degree of specialization and human capital intensity across the Chinese industries. All in all, the most significant determinants of the industrial specialization in China are found to be an industry's pollution abatement cost and its physical capital intensity.

Appendix

Data Information:

Variable	Definition/Source
RCA:	As defined in section 2. 3, was calculated using Chinese HS export data and World Bank ISIC export data. All Chinese export data were concorded from HS two – digit sectors to ISIC three – digit sectors and RCA is available for nineteen ISIC three – digit sectors. Source: World Bank and China Statistical Yearbook.
NETXva:	Net exports per unit of value added, was calculated using Chinese trade data and industry data. Source: China Statistical Yearbook.
PAOCva:	Pollution abatement operating cost per unit of value added. Source: China Environment Yearbook.
SO_2rem:	The amount of SO_2 removed per unit of value added. Source: China Statistical Yearbook.
Sootrem:	The amount of SOOT removed per unit of value added. Source: see above.
Dustrem:	The amount of DUST removed per unit of value added. Source: see above.

Continued

Variable	Definition/Source
PCI:	Physical capital intensity was calculated using original value of fixed assets divided by the number of staff of an industry. Source: China Statistical Yearbook.
HCI:	Human capital intensity. Average wage of an industry is a proxy for HCI in this paper. Source: China labour Statistical Yearbook.

Table A2. 1 displays two different kinds of international classifications; one is International Standard Industrial Classification (ISIC) and the other is the Harmonized Commodity Description and Coding System (HS). In the table, all items are concorded to 3 – digit ISIC from 2 – digit HS.

Table A2. 1

2 – digit HS	3 – digit ISIC
02 meat and edible meat offal; 03 fish and crustaceans molluscs and other aquatic invertebrates; 04 diary products, bird eggs, honey, edible products of animal origin, not elsewhere specified or included; 07 edible vegetables and certain roots and tubers; 08 edible fruit and nuts, peel of citrus fruit or melons; 10 cereals; 11 products of the milling industry, malt, starches, inulin, wheat gluten; 15 animal or vegetable fats and oils and their cleavage products, prepared edible fats, animal or vegetable waxes; 16 preparations of meat, of fish or of crustaceans, mollusks or other aquatic invertebrates; 17 sugars and sugar confectionery; 18 cocoa and cocoa preparations; 19 preparation of cereals, flour, starch or milk, pastrycooks' products;	311 food products;

Continued

2 – digit HS	3 – digit ISIC
22 beverage, spirits and vinegar	313 beverages
24 tobacco and manufactured tobacco substitutes	314 tobacco
50 silk; 51 wool, fine or coarse animal hair, horsehair yarn and woven fabric; 52 cotton; 53 other vegetable textile fibres, paper yarn and woven fabrics of paper yarn; 54 man – made filaments; 55 man – made stape fibres; 56 wadding, felt and nonwovens, special yarns, twine, cordage, ropes and cables and articles thereof; 57 carpets and other textile floor coverings; 58 special woven fabrics, tufted textile fabrics, lace, tapestries, trimmings, embroidery; 59 impregnated, coated, covered or laminated textile fabrics, textile articles of a kind suitable for industrial use; 60 Knitted or crocheted fabrics; 63 other made up textile articles, sets, worn clothing and worn textile articles, rags articles, rags;	321 textiles
61 articles of apparel and clothing accessories, knitted or crocheted; 62 articles of apparel and clothing accessories, not knitted or crocheted;	322 wearing apparel except footwear
41 raw hides and skins (other than fur skins) and leather; 42 articles of leather, saddlery and harness, travel goods, handbags and similar containers, articles of animal gut (other than silk – worm gut); 43 furskins and artificial fur, manufactures thereof;	323 leather
64 footwear, gaiters and the like, parts of such articles;	324 footwear except rubber or plastic

Continued

2 – digit HS	3 – digit ISIC
44 wood and articles of wood, wood charcoal; 45 cork and articles of cork; 46 manufactures of straw, of esparto or of other plaiting materials, basket ware and wickerwork;	331 wood products except furniture
47 pulp of wood or of other fibrous cellulosic material, waste and scrap of paper or paperboard; 48 paper and paperboard, articles of paper pulp, of paper or of paperboard;	341 paper and products
49 printe books, newspapers, pictures and other products of the printing industry, manuscripts, typescripts and plans;	342 printing and publishing
28 inorganic chemicals, organic or inorganic compounds of precious metals, of rare – earth metals, of radioactive elements or of isotopes; 29 organic chemicals; 31 fertilizers;	351 industrial chemicals
30 pharmaceutical products; 32 tanning or dyeing extracts, tannins and their derivatives, dyes, pigments and other colouring matter, paints and varnishes, putty and other mastics, inks; 33 essential oils and resinoids, perfumery, cosmetic or toilet preparations; 34 soap, organic surface – active agents, washing preparations, lubricating preparations, artificial waxes, prepared waxes, polishing or scouring preparations, candles and similar articles, modeling pastes, dental waxes and dental preparations with a basis of plaster; 35 albuminoidal substances, modified starches, blues, enzymes; 36 explosives, pyrotechnic products, matches, pyrophoric alloys, certain combustible preparations; 37 photographic or cinematographic goods; 38 miscellaneous chemical products;	352 other chemicals

Continued

2 – digit HS	3 – digit ISIC
40 rubber and articles thereof;	355 rubber products
39 plastics and articles thereof;	356 plastic products
69 ceramic products;	361 pottery china earthenware
70 glass and glassware;	362 glass and products
25 salt, sulphur, earths and stone, plastering materials, lime and cement; 26 ores, slag and ash; 27 mineral fuels; 68 articles of stone, plaster, cement, asbestos, mica or similar materials	369 other non – metallic mineral products
72 iron and steel; 73 articles of iron or steel;	371 iron and steel
74 copper and articles thereof ; 75 nickel and articles thereof; 76 aluminium and articles thereof; 78 lead and articles thereof; 79 zinc and articles thereof; 80 tin and articles thereof;	372 non – ferrous metals
84 nuclear reactors, boilers, machinery and mechanical appliances, parts thereof;	382 machinery except electrical
85 electrical machinery and equipment and parts thereof, sound recorders and reproducers, television image and sound recorders and reproducers, and parts and accessories of such articles;	383 machinery electric

Continued

2 – digit HS	3 – digit ISIC
86 railway or tramway locomotives, rolling – stock and parts thereof, railway or tramway track fixtures and fittings and parts thereof, mechanical (including electro – mechanical) traffic signaling equipment of all kinds; 87 vehicles other than railway or tramway rolling – stock, and parts and accessories thereof; 88 aircraft, spacecraft, and parts thereof; 89 ships, boats and floating structures;	384 transport equipment
90 optical, photographic, cinemato – graphic, measuring, checking, precision medical or surgical instruments and apparatus, parts and accessories; 91 clocks and watches and parts thereof;	385 professional and scientific equipment
71 natural or cultured pearls, precious or semi – precious stones, precious metals, metals clad with precious metal and articles thereof, imitation jewellery, coin; 92 musical instruments, parts and accessories of such articles; 94 furniture, bedding, mattresses, mattress supports, cushions and similar stuffed furnishings, lamps and lighting fittings, not elsewhere specified or included, illuminated signs, illuminated; 95 toys, games and sports requisites, parts and accessories thereof; 96 miscellaneous manufactured articles;	390 other manufacturing products

Note: some of 2 – digit HS sectors (01, 05, 06, 12, 13, 14, 65, 66, 67, 93, 97, 98, 99) and some of 3 – digit ISIC sectors (353 and 354) are not included in the table due to the unmatched problem.

Table A2.2 The determinants of NETXva, employing one year lagged values of SO_2 removed, PCI and HCI, dropping one sector at a time (fixed effects)

NETXva	FIXED EFFECTS					
	SO_2rem_1	PCI_1	HCI_1	Constant	R^2	n
311 + 313 + 314	0.000186 (1.59)	−0.00350 (−0.48)	0.0000722 (0.88)	−0.252 (−1.21)	0.145	84
321 + 322	0.000142 (1.19)	−0.00161 (−0.22)	0.000102 (1.17)	−0.452 (−1.99)*	0.179	84
323	0.000171 (1.36)	−0.00103 (−0.14)	0.0000691 (0.82)	−0.331 (−1.51)	0.146	84
341	0.000139 (1.16)	−0.0163 (−1.86)*	0.000159 (1.65)	−0.377 (−1.54)	0.199	84
342	0.000186 (1.63)	0.000322 (0.05)	0.0000491 (0.61)	−0.184 (−0.90)	0.155	84
351 + 352	0.000197 (0.67)	−0.00381 (−0.35)	0.0000704 (0.86)	−0.221 (−1.04)	0.105	84
353	0.000162 (1.11)	−0.0109 (−0.79)	0.00007 (0.81)	−0.169 (−0.75)	0.130	84
355	0.000196 (1.63)	−0.00389 (−0.54)	0.0000678 (0.80)	−0.221 (−1.01)	0.127	84
356	0.000196 (1.70)*	−0.00482 (−0.64)	0.0000788 (0.96)	−0.160 (−0.76)	0.138	84
361 + 362 + 369	0.000363 (3.87)***	0.000132 (0.02)	−0.0000703 (−1.66)	0.159 (1.40)	0.307	84
371	0.000106 (0.89)	−0.00147 (−0.20)	0.000116 (1.35)	−0.353 (−1.72)*	0.166	84

Continued

NETXva	FIXED EFFECTS					
	SO_2 rem_1	PCI_1	HCI_1	Constant	R^2	n
381	0.000186 (1.58)	-0.00283 (-0.39)	0.0000678 (0.84)	-0.271 (-1.31)	0.143	84
382 +383 +384 +385	0.000190 (1.62)	-0.00571 (-0.57)	0.0000867 (0.79)	-0.266 (-0.97)	0.138	84

Note: t-statistics in parentheses. Time dummies are included.
* significant at 10% level; ** significant at 5% level; *** significant at 1% level.

Table A2.3 The determinants of NETXva, employing one year lagged values of SO_2 removed, PCI and HCI, dropping one sector at a time (random effects)

NETXva	RANDOM EFFECTS					
	SO_2 rem_1	PCI_1	HCI_1	Constant	R^2	n
311 +313 +314	0.000185 (1.59)	-0.00501 (-0.74)	0.0000707 (0.93)	-0.241	0.0112	84
321 +322	0.000142 (1.24)	-0.00440 (-0.62)	0.000106 (1.37)	-0.453 (-1.73)*	0.0054	84
323	0.000171 (1.41)	-0.00233 (-0.34)	0.0000668 (0.85)	-0.319 (-1.02)	0.0068	84
341	0.000141 (1.16)	-0.0171 (-2.00)**	0.000152 (1.62)	-0.352 (-1.04)	0.0127	84
342	0.000185 (1.63)	-0.00117 (-0.18)	0.0000482 (0.65)	-0.174 (-0.56)	0.0229	84
351 +352	0.000211 (0.71)	-0.00575 (-0.55)	0.0000688 (0.90)	-0.210 (-0.66)	0.0130	84
353	0.000125 (0.95)	-0.0156 (-1.20)	0.0000651 (0.78)	-0.133 (-0.42)	0.0576	84

Continued

NETXva	RANDOM EFFECTS					
	SO_2rem_1	PCI_1	HCI_1	Constant	R^2	n
355	0.000195 (1.64)	-0.00539 (-0.80)	0.0000661 (0.83)	-0.209 (-0.66)	0.0134	84
356	0.000185 (1.55)	-0.00634 (-0.90)	0.0000734 (0.95)	-0.136 (-0.46)	0.0576	84
361 +362 +369	0.000363 (3.72) ***	-0.000242 (-0.05)	-0.0000704 (-1.86) *	0.161 (0.68)	0.0002	84
371	0.000107 (0.95)	-0.00295 (-0.43)	0.000113 (1.42)	-0.340 (-1.07)	0.0125	84
381	0.000186 (1.61)	-0.00436 (-0.64)	0.0000669 (0.89)	-0.261 (-0.84)	0.0083	84
382 +383 +384 +385	0.000188 (1.60)	-0.00755 (-0.82)	0.0000863 (0.85)	-0.257 (-0.75)	0.0070	84

Note: z - statistics in parentheses. Time dummies are included.

* significant at 10% level; ** significant at 5% level; *** significant at 1% level.

Table A2.4 The determinants of NETXva, employing one year lagged values of SOOT removed, PCI and HCI, dropping one sector at a time (fixed effects)

NETXva	FIXED EFFECTS					
	Sootrem_1	PCI_1	HCI_1	Constant	R^2	n
311 +313 +314	-0.0000473 (-1.43)	-0.00146 (-0.17)	0.0000666 (0.95)	-0.105 (-0.53)	0.160	84
321 +322	-0.0000438 (-1.40)	-0.000410 (-0.05)	0.0000956 (1.29)	-0.314 (-1.48)	0.199	84
323	-0.0000481 (-1.48)	0.000861 (0.10)	0.0000636 (0.89)	-0.181 (-0.88)	0.168	84

Continued

NETXva	FIXED EFFECTS					
	Sootrem_1	PCI_1	HCI_1	Constant	R^2	n
341	-0.0000526 (-1.50)	-0.0158 (-1.41)	0.000151 (1.91) *	-0.240 (-1.11)	0.225	84
342	-0.0000494 (-1.50)	0.00242 (0.28)	0.0000422 (0.62)	-0.0242 (-0.13)	0.174	84
351 +352	-0.000079 (-1.46)	-0.00196 (-0.21)	0.0000495 (0.76)	0.00571 (0.03)	0.168	84
353	-0.0000702 (-1.66)	-0.0157 (-1.17)	0.0000502 (0.68)	0.0811 (0.41)	0.189	84
355	-0.0000496 (-1.47)	-0.00173 (-0.20)	0.0000618 (0.86)	-0.0712 (-0.35)	0.145	84
356	-0.0000517 (-1.54)	-0.00277 (-0.31)	0.000073 (1.04)	0.00376 (0.02)	0.160	84
361 +362 +369	3.58e -06 (0.16)	0.00884 (1.37)	-0.0000473 (-0.99)	0.0970 (0.64)	0.0902	84
371	-0.0000479 (-1.44)	-0.000428 (-0.05)	0.0001 (1.44)	-0.202 (-1.14)	0.195	84
381	-0.0000494 (-1.48)	-0.000602 (-0.07)	0.0000606 (0.88)	-0.111 (-0.56)	0.162	84
382 +383 + 384 +385	-0.0000487 (-1.46)	-0.00323 (-0.29)	0.0000781 (0.82)	-0.106 (-0.42)	0.155	84

Note: t - statistics in parentheses. Time dummies are included.

* significant at 10% level; ** significant at 5% level; *** significant at 1% level.

Table A2.5 The determinants of NETXva, employing one year lagged values of SOOT removed, PCI and HCI, dropping one sector at a time (random effects)

NETXva	RANDOM EFFECTS					
	Sootrem_1	PCI_1	HCI_1	Constant	R^2	n
311 +313 +314	-0.0000563 (-1.90)*	-0.00303 (-0.38)	0.000062 (0.94)	-0.0642 (-0.21)	0.142	84
321 +322	-0.0000537 (-1.95)*	-0.00289 (-0.36)	0.0000956 (1.46)	-0.280 (-1.14)	0.170	84
323	-0.000055 (-1.88)*	-0.000382 (-0.05)	0.0000588 (0.87)	-0.144 (-0.48)	0.102	84
341	-0.0000582 (-1.82)*	-0.0166 (-1.56)	0.000144 (1.83)*	-0.204 (-0.63)	0.0377	84
342	-0.0000584 (-1.97)**	0.000817 (0.10)	0.0000381 (0.60)	0.0169 (0.06)	0.148	84
351 +352	-0.0000879 (-1.85)*	-0.00322 (-0.37)	0.0000451 (0.73)	0.0414 (0.14)	0.184	84
353	-0.0000776 (-2.06)**	-0.0188 (-1.50)	0.0000451 (0.63)	0.123 (0.42)	0.236	84
355	-0.0000588 (-1.94)*	-0.00333 (-0.41)	0.000057 (0.84)	-0.0291 (-0.10)	0.158	84
356	-0.0000754 (-2.48)**	-0.00544 (-0.65)	0.0000561 (0.86)	0.122 (0.46)	0.392	84
361 +362 +369	-2.13e-06 (-0.11)	0.00793 (1.46)	-0.0000479 (-1.11)	0.115 (0.45)	0.0049	84
371	-0.0000572 (-1.89)*	-0.00177 (-0.23)	0.0000924 (1.41)	-0.157 (-0.53)	0.0984	84

Continued

NETXva	RANDOM EFFECTS					
	Sootrem_1	PCI_1	HCI_1	Constant	R^2	n
381	-0.0000573 (-1.91) *	-0.00207 (-0.26)	0.0000567 (0.88)	-0.0736 (-0.24)	0.129	84
382 + 383 + 384 + 385	-0.000059 (-1.96) *	-0.00510 (-0.49)	0.0000739 (0.84)	-0.0613 (-0.19)	0.173	84

Note: z - statistics in parentheses. Time dummies are included.

* significant at 10% level; ** significant at 5% level; *** significant at 1% level.

Table A2.6 The determinants of NETXva, employing one year lagged values of DUST removed, PCI and HCI, dropping one sector at a time (fixed effects)

NETXva	FIXED EFFECTS					
	Dustrem_1	PCI_1	HCI_1	Constant	R^2	n
311 + 313 + 314	-0.0000329 (-3.93) ***	0.00628 (0.84)	-0.0000164 (-0.25)	0.153 (0.81)	0.363	84
321 + 322	-0.0000313 (-3.68) ***	0.00668 (0.90)	9.07e-06 (0.13)	-0.0430 (-0.21)	0.387	84
323	-0.0000329 (-3.91) ***	0.00822 (1.08)	-0.0000207 (-0.31)	0.0759 (0.38)	0.370	84
341	-0.0000313 (-3.54) ***	-0.00347 (-0.40)	0.0000439 (0.60)	0.0796 (0.37)	0.408	84
342	-0.000033 (-3.93) ***	0.00917 (1.24)	-0.0000333 (-0.50)	0.206 (1.09)	0.378	84
351 + 352	-0.0000345 (-4.08) ***	0.00797 (1.10)	-0.0000314 (-0.48)	0.205 (1.10)	0.371	84

Continued

NETXva	FIXED EFFECTS					
	Dustrem_1	PCI_1	HCI_1	Constant	R^2	n
353	-0.0000376 (-4.76)***	-0.0148 (-1.14)	-0.00007 (-0.97)	0.437 (2.08)**	0.418	84
355	-0.0000336 (-3.96)***	0.00608 (0.83)	-0.0000229 (-0.34)	0.192 (0.99)	0.367	84
356	-0.0000334 (-3.85)***	0.00537 (0.70)	-0.0000105 (-0.16)	0.251 (1.31)	0.371	84
361+362 +369	0.0000501 (3.60)***	0.00920 (1.64)	-0.0000242 (-0.60)	-0.0469 (-0.42)	0.216	84
371	-0.0000391 (-4.69)***	0.00743 (1.21)	0.0000228 (0.41)	0.0172 (0.12)	0.499	84
381	-0.0000331 (-3.98)***	0.00709 (0.94)	-0.0000217 (-0.33)	0.138 (0.73)	0.366	84
382+383+ 384+385	-0.0000341 (-4.00)***	0.00926 (0.90)	-0.0000429 (-0.47)	0.241 (0.95)	0.364	84

Note: t-statistics in parentheses. Time dummies are included.

* significant at 10% level; ** significant at 5% level; *** significant at 1% level.

Table A2.7 The determinants of NETXva, employing one year lagged values of DUST removed, PCI and HCI, dropping one sector at a time (random effects)

NETXva	RANDOM EFFECTS					
	Dustrem_ 1	PCI_ 1	HCI_ 1	Constant	R^2	n
311+313 +314	-0.0000307 (-3.16)***	0.00526 (0.82)	-0.000012 (-0.21)	0.133 (0.48)	0.0478	84
321+322	-0.000027 (-2.77)***	0.00480 (0.74)	0.0000237 (0.41)	-0.0985 (-0.45)	0.0414	84

Continued

NETXva	RANDOM EFFECTS					
	Dustrem_ 1	PCI_ 1	HCI_ 1	Constant	R^2	n
323	-0. 00003 (-3. 07) ***	0. 00738 (1. 13)	-0. 0000152 (-0. 25)	0. 0501 (0. 18)	0. 0388	84
341	-0. 0000297 (-2. 97) ***	-0. 00406 (-0. 49)	0. 0000435 (0. 61)	0. 0739 (0. 25)	0. 0810	84
342	-0. 0000306 (-3. 14) ***	0. 008022 (1. 27)	-0. 0000284 (-0. 49)	0. 186 (0. 70)	0. 0473	84
351 +352	-0. 0000322 (-3. 29) ***	0. 00698 (1. 13)	-0. 0000266 (-0. 46)	0. 184 (0. 68)	0. 0530	84
353	-0. 0000339 (-3. 41) ***	-0. 0159 (-1. 42)	-0. 0000579 (-0. 92)	0. 388 (1. 41)	0. 0952	84
355	-0. 0000313 (-3. 19) ***	0. 00503 (0. 80)	-0. 0000183 (-0. 31)	0. 171 (0. 62)	0. 0540	84
356	-0. 0000309 (-3. 12) ***	0. 00425 (0. 65)	-9. 13e -06 (-0. 16)	0. 239 (0. 96)	0. 110	84
361 +362 +369	0. 0000439 (2. 74) ***	0. 00888 (1. 84) *	-0. 0000299 (-0. 79)	-0. 0172 (-0. 06)	0. 0187	84
371	-0. 0000369 (-3. 54) ***	0. 00662 (1. 27)	0. 0000242 (0. 51)	0. 00809 (0. 03)	0. 0399	84
381	-0. 0000307 (-3. 17) ***	0. 00605 (0. 93)	-0. 0000165 (-0. 29)	0. 115 (0. 41)	0. 0428	84
382 +383 + 384 +385	-0. 0000313 (-3. 18) ***	0. 00750 (0. 86)	-0. 0000328 (-0. 41)	0. 205 (0. 70)	0. 0516	84

Note: z - statistics in parentheses. Time dummies are included.

* significant at 10% level; ** significant at 5% level; *** significant at 1% level.

Table A2. 8 Test for the homogeneity of regression coefficients across sectors (reporting F – statistics in Chow test)

SECTOR	311 + 313 + 314 (1)	321 + 322 (2)	323 (3)	341 (4)	342 (5)	351 + 352 (6)	353 (7)	355 (8)	356 (9)	361 + 362 + 369 (10)	371 (11)	372 (12)	381 (13)
Sectors to be compared	2 – 14	3 – 14	4 – 14	5 – 14	6 – 14	7 – 14	8 – 14	9 – 14	10 – 14	11 – 14	12 – 14	13 – 14	14
PAOCva	0. 86 (0. 60)	0. 92 (0. 53)	1. 01 (0. 45)	0. 91 (0. 53)	0. 59 (0. 80)	0. 66 (0. 72)	0. 71 (0. 67)	0. 76 (0. 60)	0. 90 (0. 49)	0. 89 (0. 48)	0. 25 (0. 86)	0. 01 (0. 99)	0. 60 (0. 44)
PCI	0. 45 (0. 94)	0. 49 (0. 91)	0. 45 (0. 92)	0. 42 (0. 93)	0. 33 (0. 96)	0. 35 (0. 94)	0. 36 (0. 92)	0. 42 (0. 86)	0. 50 (0. 77)	0. 25 (0. 91)	0. 25 (0. 86)	0. 01 (0. 99)	0. 00 (0. 96)
HCI	0. 50 (0. 92)	0. 54 (0. 88)	0. 57 (0. 84)	0. 51 (0. 87)	0. 51 (0. 86)	0. 50 (0. 85)	0. 55 (0. 79)	0. 49 (0. 81)	0. 59 (0. 71)	0. 19 (0. 94)	0. 22 (0. 88)	0. 32 (0. 72)	0. 00 (0. 97)

Note: F – statistics are reported in the table, P – value in parentheses. Each sector is given a number from 1 to 14 for simplicity.

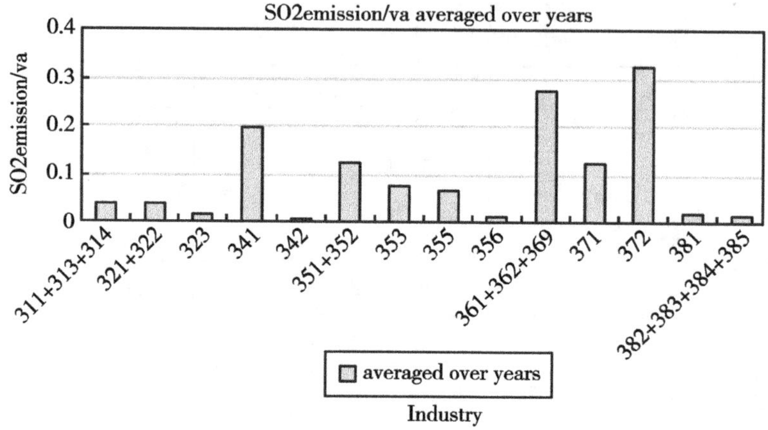

Figure A2.1 SO_2 emission per unit of value added for individual sectors in China

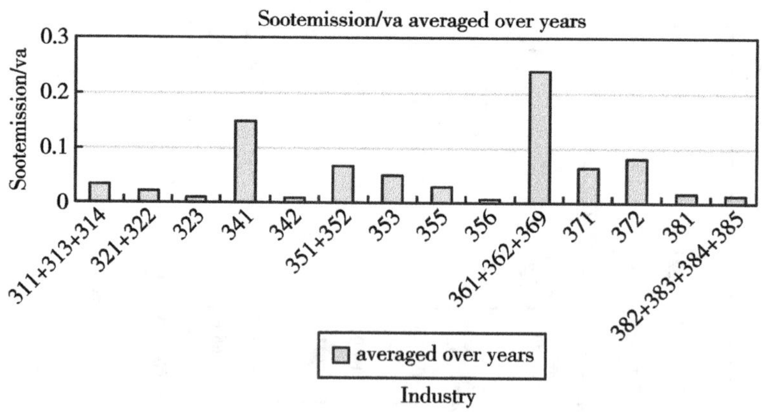

Figure A2.2 SOOT emission per unit of value added for individual sectors in China

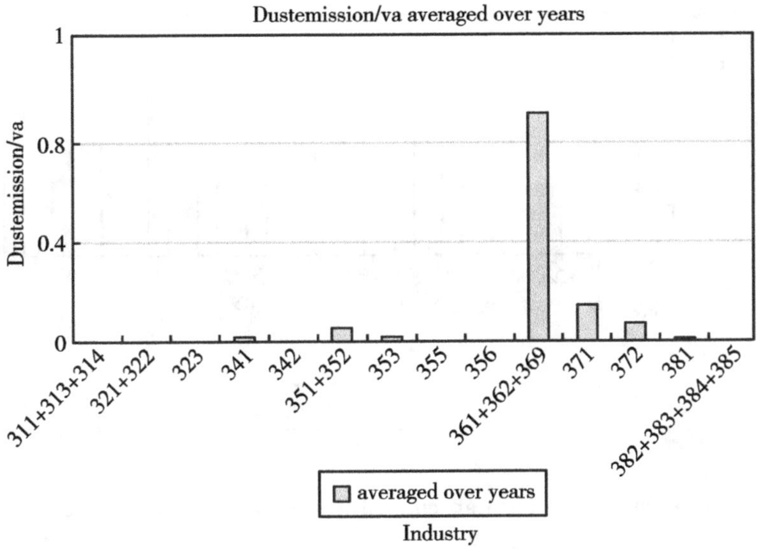

Figure A2. 3 DUST emission per unit of value added for individual sectors in China

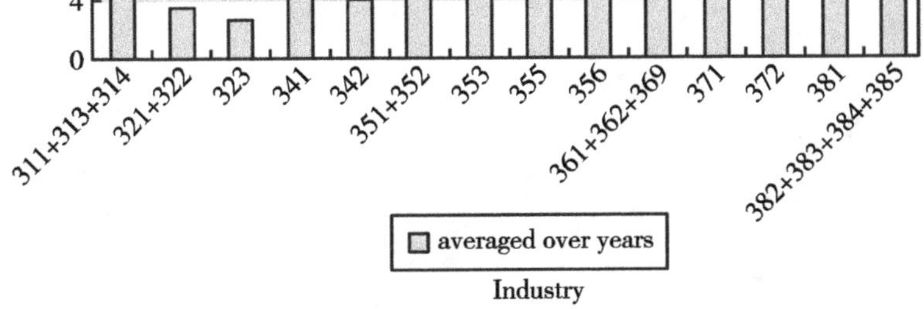

Figure A2. 4 Physical capital intensity for individual sectors in China

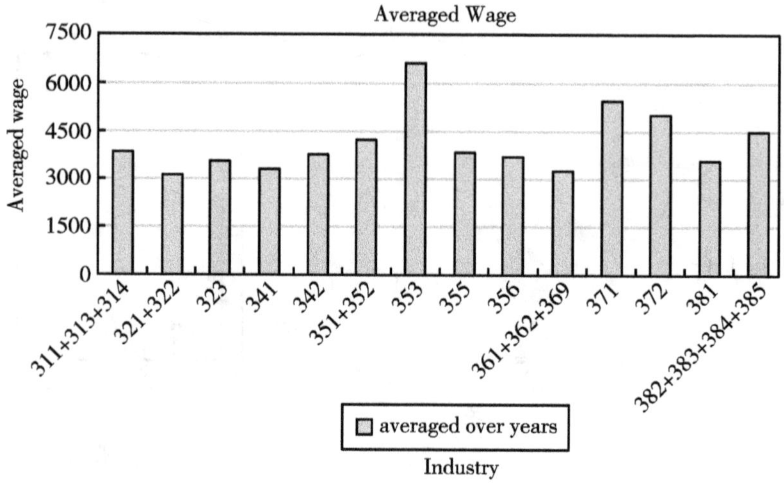

Figure A2. 5 Human capital intensity (average wage) for individual sectors in China

Chapter 3

Industrial Characteristics, Environmental Regulations and Air Pollution in A Developing Country: An Analysis of the Chinese Manufacturing Sector

3. 1 Introduction

The rapid industrial growth of China has placed increasing pressure on the country's environmental infrastructure. Such pressures have led to an increased awareness by policy makers and economists of the need to obtain a comprehensive understanding of the relationship between industrial activity, environmental regulations and pollution. The majority of work in this area has been undertaken for developed countries, primarily the

US (e. g. Kahn, 1999; Gray and Shadbegian, 1995, 2002, 2003 and 2004; Cole *et al.*, 2005 for a UK study). With the exception of Pargal and Wheeler (1996) in a study of Indonesia, similar studies for China or any other developing or newly industrialised country are also limited.

The lack of studies outside of the US is largely a consequence of a scarcity of data on pollution emissions at the sub – national level and particularly at the industry or plant level. I have been able to partly address this deficiency by the construction of an industry level panel for China. Although not as detailed as the US and UK datasets, my data do enable us to examine industry specific emissions of a number of pollutants for China between 1997 and 2003.

The existing US literature has tended to concentrate on the effects of regulations on plant location, productivity and pollution abatement expenditures, usually for selected industries. Gray and Shadbegian (2003), for example, examine measures of environmental regulatory activity and levels of air and water pollution in the Paper and Pulp industry, and they find emissions are affected both by the benefits from pollution abatement and the characteristics of the people exposed to the pollution. Similarly, Bartik (1988), Levinson (1996), Henderson (1996) and Gray and Shadbegian (2002) examine whether a firm's allocation of production across plants responds to the level of environmental regulation faced by individual plants. ①

In this research I concentrate on the determinants of pollution for a number of industries in China and endeavour to provide a greater understanding of the linkages between industrial characteristics, environmental regulations and pollution intensity. Such an analysis permits us to assess the relative importance of each determinant of pollution intensity and will indicate how pollution intensity is likely to be influenced by government policy (environmental or otherwise). The analysis is set within a framework of the demand for, and supply of, environmental services where the characteristics of an industry determine its demand for such services, whilst society, through environmental regulations, supplies environmental services at a price. The equilibrium level of emissions for a given industry will reflect both demand and supply – side considerations. The research provides us with a theoretical framework to explore the possible determinants of industry specific emissions intensity.

My dataset allows us to make the following contributions: first, I consider the role played by an industry's factor intensities and assess whether industries that have high physical and human capital intensities generate more pollution per unit of output. Several studies have suggested a positive relationship between physical capital and pollution

① In a related literature, Hamilton (1993), Kahn (1999) and Helland and Whitford (2003) provide estimates of the impact of political boundaries, demographics and political activism on the exposure to pollution. One strand of this literature has concentrated on the characteristics of the population affected by pollution, in particular whether ethnic minorities are adversely affected by pollution. The results to date are somewhat mixed once the time the plant was established is taken into account (for further discussion see e. g. Hamilton, 1995; Kreisel *et al.*, 1996; Arora and Cason, 1998; Jenkins *et al.*, 2002).

intensity in US industries (Antweiler *et al.*, 2001; Cole and Elliott, 2003), but the relationship has rarely been demonstrated for a developing newly industrialised economy. I also examine whether the size of the average firm within an industry affects pollution (do large firms benefit from economies of scale and hence emit less per unit of output than smaller firms?); whether productive firms are more resource efficient and hence less pollution intensive; and whether levels of innovation and the age of plant and machinery within an industry affect pollution intensity. I am also able to estimate the relative magnitude of these effects and the extent to which they vary across different pollutants.

Secondly, the research investigates the role of Chinese regulations. I argue, following Gianessi *et al.* (1979) and Pargal and Wheeler (1996), that there may be both a formal and an informal component to regional regulation levels with formal regulations defined as those that operate through national government or local authorities. Where formal regulations are weak or perceived to be insufficient however, it is argued that communities may informally regulate firms or industries through lobbying and petitioning. The results suggest that there may be an element of both forms of regulation in operation in China. ①

---

① Pargal and Wheeler (1996) investigate the role of informal regulations in plant level emissions of water pollution in Indonesia. They find water pollution to be an increasing function of output and state ownership and a decreasing function of productivity and local (informal) environmental regulations. Whilst interesting, Pargal and Wheeler's study differs from ours in that it examines a single pollutant for a developing country using cross – sectional data only. Nevertheless, some interesting commonalities are found between our results and those of Pargal and Wheeler.

The remainder of the paper is organised as follows: Section 2 reviews the literature, Section 3 provides some background information on the Chinese economy; Section 4 discusses the determinants of pollution while Section 5 outlines the econometric specification including data considerations; Section 6 provides results while Section 7 concludes.

3.2 Literature Review

There is a significant body of work that examines the interaction between industrial activity, pollution and environmental regulations. Certain studies concentrate on the effect of industrial activity on pollution while others examine on the effect of formal and informal regulations on pollution.

Gianessi *et al.* (1979) examines industry – specific determinants of air pollution emissions employing regional characteristics to take account of regional differences in the stringency of regulations. The paper begins by describing how to estimate damages sector – by – sector (or benefits) in a geographical area as a result of different types of pollution.

Gray and Shadbegian (2004) examine the determinants of environmental regulatory activity (inspections and enforcement actions) and levels of air and water pollution for US pulp and paper mills, focusing on the benefits to the surrounding population from pollution abatement. The number of inspections and enforcement actions, and the level of air pollution emissions and water pollution discharges are both estimated as dependent variables, the difference being that the former provides a direct measure of regulatory pressure whilst the latter can be treated as an indirect measure related to regulatory stringency. The independent variables capture the marginal benefits of pollution reduction at a given plant that depends heavily on the number of people in the area and the emissions that they are exposed to, and also capture differences in people's susceptibility to pollution exposure.

Plant characteristics affecting abatement costs are taken into account in their model as control variables that include plant capacity, plant age, firm financial condition, county attainment status (air only), major source and public health effects (water only), and a measure of state environmental attitudes. The key variables are those that influence the marginal benefits from pollution abatement, namely the expected benefits of pollution reduction in air and water respectively, groups with greater sensitivity to air pollution (population under the age of 6 and those 65 and over), poor and minority groups (the percentage of the nearby population living below the poverty line and the population that is non – white); voter activity indicating political pressure, and the effects of political boundaries indicating whether the plant is within 50 miles of another jurisdiction.

The results suggest that plants in areas with higher marginal benefits of pollution abatement have lower pollution levels. Demographics also matter as plants where nearby there are more children, more elderly, and fewer poor people, emit less pollution. Plants whose pollution affects residents of other states emit more pollution, with these boundary effects reduced if bordering states have more pro – environment Congressional delegations. Plants in areas with politically active populations that are also environmentally conscious tend to emit less pollution. However, the percentage of nonwhites near the plant, expected to reduce regulatory attention, is often associated with more regulatory activity and lower emissions.

Other US based studies have tended to concentrate on the effect of environmental regulations on plant location, productivity and pollution abatement expenditures, usually for a small number of selected industries. As indicated in Gianessi *et al.* (1997), policy – makers should evaluate the impact of environmental regulation on an industry – by – industry basis to avoid substantial under – (or over –) estimates. Gray and Shadbegian (1995) employ plant – level data from three industries, paper and pulp mills, oil refineries, and steel mills, to similarly investigate the impacts of environmental regulation on productivity. The results show that in a broad sense, plants with high compliance expenditures tend to have lower total factor productivity levels and plants with compliance expenditures tend to have slower productivity growth rates.

In a more detailed study of one industry, Gray and Shadbegian (2003) examine the impact of environmental regulation on productivity for the Paper and Pulp industry accounting for industrial characteristics such as plant vintage and technology. They focus their study on a panel of 116 pulp and paper mills making the distinction between integrated mills which incorporates a pulping process and non – pulping plants as the key technology difference across plants. Since integrated mills have higher abatement cost (twice as large as their non – pulping counterparts), the predicted impact of regulation on productivity for integrated mills is especially large. The reason for introducing plant vintage can be easily explained. Once a plant is in operation, it is very difficult to change the production process, thus, those plants designed before environmental concerns (older plants) are less productive and might have more difficulties meeting a given environmental standard, leading to higher abatement costs.

Focusing on the location decisions chosen by the new plants of Fortune 500 companies between 1972 and 1978, Bartik (1998) suggests that sizable increases in the stringency of state environmental regulation are unlikely to have a large effect on the location decisions of the average industry. Yet, there remains the possibility that these effects are large for heavily polluting industries. Levinson (1996) introduced a broad range of proxies for environmental standard stringency and found the coefficients of these proxies negative and significant only for the plants of very large firms, suggesting that the branch plants of large firms appear more sensitive to local conditions, including environmental regulations, than do all plants in general. One reason proposed is that large firms may have economies of scale in conducting site searches with individual plants being more footloose than those of independent manufacturers. The conclusion from examining the location choice model industry by industry is that few industries have negative and significant coefficients for the environmental stringency variables. Henderson (1996) investigates the effects of local regulatory effort on ground level ozone air quality and on industrial location. Local regulatory effort varies by annual air quality attainment status and by state attitudes towards the environment. A switch from attainment (less polluted) to non-attainment (polluted) status induces greater regulatory effort in a county, leading to an improvement in air quality, thus, polluting industries tend to relocate over time to areas with a record of staying in attainment, so as to avoid regulatory scrutiny.

Based on the earlier micro – level studies introduced above, Gray and Shadbegian (2002) use plant – level data from the paper and oil industries to look at a firm's allocation of production across its plants in different states, the allocation is defined by the share of its total production in each state. A firm can change the allocation by opening a new plant, or closing up one of its plants, or restructuring production of its existing plants. The model in Gray and Shadbegian (2002) includes several state – specific explanatory variables; these range from state – level regulatory variables to input cost and other factors expected to influence the production decision. Their regulatory stringency variables incorporate the support for environmental legislation in Congress; pollution abatement operating costs divided by total manufacturing shipments as a measure of pollution abatement intensity, 'Green Policies' index as a measure of the stringency of state environmental regulations, 'Green Conditions' index as a measure of environmental problems in each state, the number of members of three conservation groups (Sierra Club, Greenpeace, and National Wildlife Federation) to indicate support for environmental issues among the state's electorate, and the dollars per capita spent on the state's programs for the environment and natural resources.

In addition, variables of industry characteristics and several regional characteristics are included: a state – specific demand index by industry, a Herfindahl index, a measure of concentration of production, plants' shipments that indicate the size of an industry, variables of factor price that include the energy price, land price and staff wages, labour indicators that include percent of non - agricultural workforce unionised, unemployment rate and income, level of education, tax differences, percentage of votes for Democratic candidates, population density, and the state market share.

Gray and Shadbegian's (2002) find that, regulatory stringency and production allocation are significantly related in the paper industry. States with stricter regulations have smaller shares of production, and the regulatory stringency is more likely to impact on low - compliance firms, where firms with high compliance rates appear to have higher share of production in more stringent states. Yet, they find few significant interactions between regulatory stringency and industry characteristics within a state. The overall results are weaker for the oil industry in terms of statistical significance, but it is consistent with the paper and pulp industry in terms of one finding that the negative impacts of state regulatory stringency on production shares only work for low - compliance firms.

Other related studies include Hamilton (1993), Kahn (1999) and Helland and Whitford (2003) who provide estimation results for the impacts of, political boundaries, demographics and political activism, on the exposure to pollution.

Hamilton (1993) examines the probability of expanding processing capacity for commercial waste given the engagement in collective action in local regions. After controlling for location - specific characteristics, the paper finds that the greater the voter turnout in a given area, the less likely that area was to be slated for expansion of commercial waste processing capacity. Several alternative tests also suggest that the voter turnout rate is a good proxy for collective action. Kahn (1999) concentrates in the area of US Rust Belt counties and examines the impact of manufacturing activities on level of pollution. The results show that the air quality of this area has significantly improved due to a sharp decline in the manufacturing activities, and the decline is caused by an increasing competition. Other than that, there is significant cross – county spillover effect for pollution of this area and the effect may have changed quality of environment. The cross – border spillover effect is also found by Helland and Whitford (2003), who test a jurisdictional model using the Toxic Release Inventory (TRI) data from 1987 to 1996 and find production facilities located in counties border have higher levels of toxic releases into the air and water.

Only a few studies ever discussed informal regulations. In addition to Gianessi *et al.* (1979), Pargal and Wheeler (1996) investigate the effects of informal regulations on industrial pollution using manufacturing evidence from Indonesia. Based on an 'environmental supply/demand schedule', they have determined a number of variables that may impact pollution. These variables include income, education, level of civic activity, legal or political recourse, media coverage, presence of a nongovernmental organization, the efficiency of existing formal regulation, total pollution load of local community, sector specifics, output, manufacturing wage, prices of materials, capital and energy, equipment vintage, efficiency or productivity, and ownership. Their results suggest that pollution intensity declines with scale of plants. Characteristics of plant and firm have strong impacts on pollution intensity. Plants of the food and paper sectors or old factories are intensively polluted, but productive plants are relatively clean. Foreign participation is not significantly related to pollution intensity and public ownership, on the other hand, is strongly associated with 'dirty' production. From the perspective of informal regulations, the results show that pollution intensity of plants declines in local communities where income is increasing or level of education is high, and also declines in local communities with a low rate of unemployment or less densely populated.

Cole *et al.* (2005) uses a methodology similar to that of Pargal and Wheeler (1996) but employs industrial pollution data with observations on air pollution from the UK manufacturing sector. They find pollution intensity to be positively determined by energy use, physical capital and human capital intensities, and negatively determined by the average firm size of the industry, productivity and expenditure on capital and R&D. Their results also suggest that from the perspective of informal regulation, regional population density, unemployment rates, age structures and per capita incomes all have impacts on pollution intensities.

The methodology in my research is based on the study in Cole *et al.* (2005) but I use data from the Chinese manufacturing sectors. The regressions of my research have tested more variables than those in Cole *et al.*'s model. Before I start introducing the methodology and data, it is helpful to understand some background knowledge of the economic development and environmental regulations in China.

3.3 Background of the Chinese Economy

China's economy has grown remarkably since the late 1980s, but such a growth has caused negative effect on China's environment. In this section of the chapter I explore factors that may be linked to the industrial pollution in China.

3.3.1 Factors that Cause Industrial Pollution in China

Industrial pollution is almost an inevitable consequence of economic development. The industrial production in China heavily depends on the consumption of natural resources and raw materials, and energy efficiency is thus not high. China's Industrial Development Report (2005) suggests that the consumption of energy that produces one dollar of GDP is 4.3 times larger than US and 11.5 times larger than Japan, and the energy efficiency is 26.9% of that in US and 11.5% of that in Japan. The real efficiency of electricity generation is 6% - 11% lower than the international average. ①

The Report discusses several reasons why a growing economy may experience degradation on the environment, and two of which are noticeable. On the one hand, heavy industries still dominate the Chinses economy even after a substantial development of agriculture sector and light industry. Heavy industries have energy and mine products as ma-

① Data source: China's Industrial Development Report 2005.

jor raw materials and rely on primary sectors for these inputs,[①] it is a common sense that heavy industries are the primary source of industrial pollution.

On the other hand, the development of medium – and small – sized enterprises, especially the development of town and township enterprises, is another accomplishment of China's reform. However, such enterprises have also become the source of industrial pollution because of their features of disadvantage, such as old technologies, large input of energy and raw materials, inefficient distribution system, low – skilled workers and no abatement cost. From January 1996 to December 1997, the State Environmental Protection Administration, Ministry of Agriculture, Ministry of Finance, and National Bureau of Statistics jointly launched a campaign that put all town and township enterprises under regulatory scrutiny. They show statistics compared to the level in 1989 that, SO_2 emissions from town and township enterprises increased by 23%, industrial soot emissions increased by 56% and industrial dust emissions increased even by 182%.[②]

3.3.2 Industrial Pollution in China

Table 3.1 presents levels of emissions for the major industrial pollutants in China. A time trend of emissions can be found in Figure 3.1, 3.2 and 3.3. The levels of total SO_2 emissions as well as SO_2 emissions from industry remain stable in early years and then increase since 2002. The levels of total SOOT emissions and industrial

① Primary sectors refer to petroleum, coal, electric power, chemicals and smelting and pressing sectors.

② Data source: China's Industrial Development Report 2005.

SOOT emissions stay relatively high in early years of the sample time period and then slightly decline and remain stable after then, and DUST emissions from industry also stay at relatively high levels in early years and then slightly drop and remain stable.

Table 3.1 SO_2, SOOT, DUST annual emissions (10000 tons)

Year	Total emissions		Annual change (%)		Industrial emissions			Annual change (%)		
	SO_2	SOOT	SO_2	SOOT	SO_2	SOOT	DUST	SO_2	SOOT	DUST
1997	2266	1573			1772	1265	1505			
1998	2091.4	1455.1	-7.7	-7.5	1594.4	1178.5	1321.2	-10.0	-6.8	-12.2
1999	1857.5	1159	-11.2	-20.3	1460.1	953.4	1175.3	-8.4	-19.1	-11.0
2000	1995.1	1165.4	7.4	0.6	1612.5	953.3	1092	10.4	0	-7.1
2001	1947.8	1069.8	-2.4	-8.2	1566.6	851.9	990.6	-2.8	-10.6	-9.3
2002	1926.6	1012.7	-1.1	-5.3	1562	804.2	941	-0.3	-5.6	-5
2003	2158.7	1048.7	12	3.5	1791.4	846.2	1021	14.7	5.2	8.5
2004	2255	1095	4.5	4.4	1891	886	905	5.6	4.7	-11.4
2005	2549.3	1182.5	13.1	8.0	2168.4	948.9	911.2	14.7	7.1	0.7
2006	2588.8	1078.4	1.5	-8.8		854.8	807.5		-9.9	-11.4

Data source: Annual Environment Report for China. Data of total emission of DUST is not available; industrial emission of SO_2 is not available in 2006.

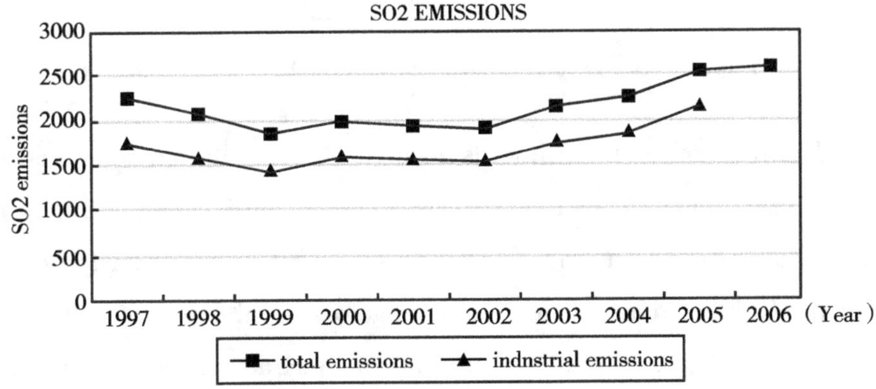

Figure 3.1 SO_2 Emissions (tonnes) 1997 – 2006

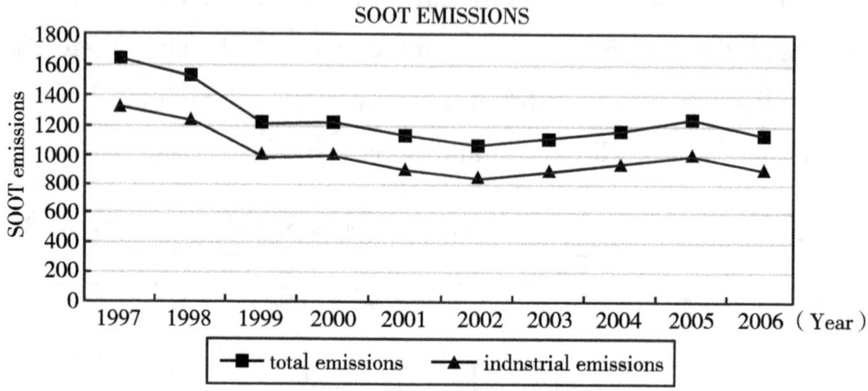

Figure 3.2 SOOT Emissions (tonnes) 1997 – 2006

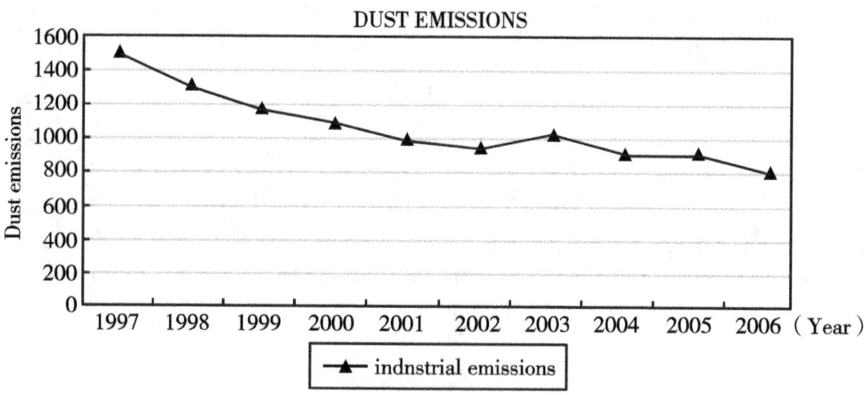

Figure 3.3 DUST Emissions (tonnes), 1997 – 2006

The research is more interested in studying pollution by industrial sectors. Industrial sectors are classified according to the International Standard of Industrial Classification (ISIC). In order to match with the Chinese data, I need to aggregate several 3 – digit ISIC sectors into one sector, such as food, beverages and tobacco (ISIC311 + 313 + 314), textiles and wearing apparel (ISIC321 + 322), non – metallic mineral products (ISIC361 + 362 + 369) and machinery except electrical and machinery electric, transport equipment, professional and scientific equipment (ISIC382 + 383 + 384 + 385). For comparison, total value added of each sector is also taken into account.

Figure 3.4 clearly depicts that industrial pollution intensity has been decreasing for all pollutants since 1998. Hence, although levels of total emissions have increased since 2002, industrial emissions per unit value added have continued to fall, suggesting that the growth of pollution is accompanied by an even greater growth of industrial production in the Chinese economy.

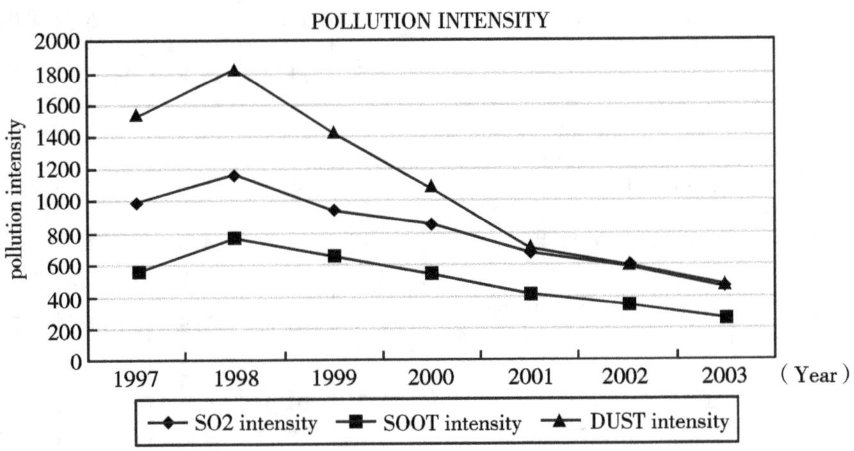

Figure 3.4 Pollution intensities (tons per million yuan of value added) for SO_2, SOOT and DUST, 1997 – 2003

Table 3.2 presents average pollution intensities of three air pollutants by sector from 1997 to 2003. Text in bold indicate sectors that rank top 5. In terms of total value added are food, beverages and tobacco, textiles and wearing apparel, industrial chemicals, iron and steel and the various machinery industries. The value added of the manufacturing sectors all grew rapidly in this time, in which iron and steel, non – ferrous metals, and machinery industries demonstrate particularly rapid growth of value added.

Table 3.2 Average Pollution Intensities and Share of Total Value Added, 1997 – 2003

ISIC	Industry	% VA	ΔVA (%)	SO_2	SOOT	DUST
311 + 313 + 314	Food, beverage and tobacco	**15.1**	10.8	2.6	2.0	0.1
321 + 322	Textiles and wearing apparel	**9.6**	9.8	2.7	1.3	0.02
323	Leather products	1.8	11.8	0.9	0.6	0.02
341	Paper and products	2.2	11.3	**15.8**	**11.2**	**2.8**
342	Printing and publishing	1.1	10.4	0.5	0.3	0.05
351	Industrial chemicals	**7.6**	11.5	**9.9**	**6.2**	**10.8**
352	Other chemicals	4.4	**13.6**	4.7	2.3	0.3
353	Petroleum processing and coking	4.0	**13.4**	7.9	5.1	2.1
355	Rubber products	1.2	10.4	4.0	1.6	0.09
356	Plastic products	2.5	13.2	0.6	0.3	0.3
361 + 362 + 369	Non – metallic mineral products	5.9	8.2	**29.8**	**30.0**	**124.7**
371	Iron and steel	**7.3**	**17.1**	**11.0**	**5.2**	**13.1**
372	Non – ferrous metals	2.6	**17.4**	**27.9**	**7.6**	**6.0**
381	Metal products	3.3	10.4	1.4	1.0	1.9

Continued

ISIC	Industry	% VA	ΔVA (%)	SO_2	SOOT	DUST
382 + 383 + 384 + 385	Machinery except electrical and machinery electric, transport equipment, professional and scientific equipment	**31.5**	**18.4**	0.8	0.5	0.2
Manufacturing overall		100	13.7	8.0	5.0	10.8

Note: % VA measures each industry's share of total value added. ΔVA provides the average annual growth rate of value added over the period 1997 – 2003. Pollution intensities are measured as tons per million yuan of value added. For each column, the industries with the five highest values are highlighted in bold.

The top 5 sectors defined in terms of pollution intensity are the same across all three pollutants, these sectors include Paper and Products, Industrial Chemicals, Non – Metallic Mineral Products, Iron and Steel and Non – Ferrous Metals, which are the dirtiest sectors in China. Two sectors, Iron and Steel and Non – Ferrous Metals, out of the five dirty sectors, also have their value added ranked in top 5. It has raised a concern that the Chinese manufacturing may grow towards more pollution intensive.

Figures 3.5, 3.6 and 3.7 plot pollution intensity of SO_2, SOOT and DUST for the five dirtiest industries. These five sectors have all turned to be cleaner in terms of pollution intensity from 1997 to 2003. The sector of Non – metallic mineral products (ISIC361 + 362 + 369) stands out as the largest polluter, however, it has reduced emissions by the highest amount at the same time. A 'spike' in pollution intensity for this sector seemed to exist in 1998, caused by a fall in production rather than an increase in pollution.

The next section extends the analysis to investigate the determinants of industrial pollution in China.

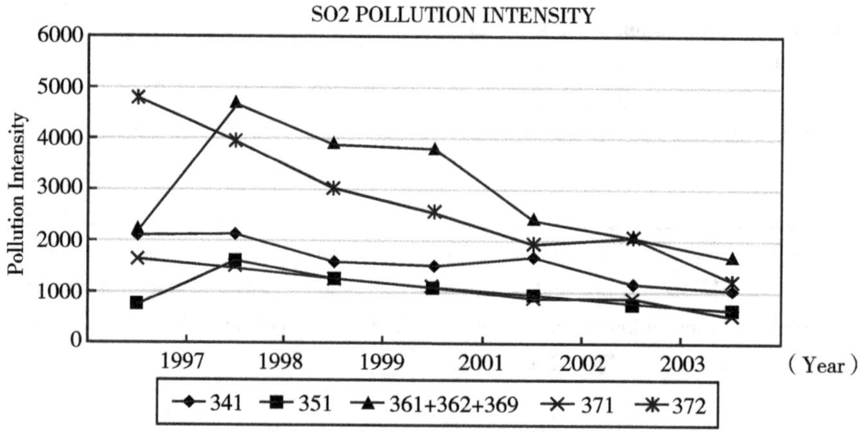

Figure 3. 5 Pollution intensity of SO_2 (tons per million yuan of value added) for the five dirtiest sectors in China

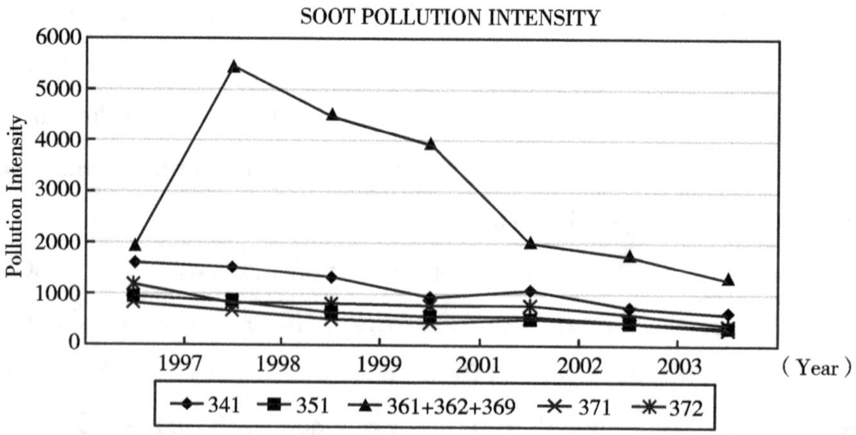

Figure 3. 6 Pollution intensity of SOOT (tons per million yuan of value added) for the five dirtiest sectors in China

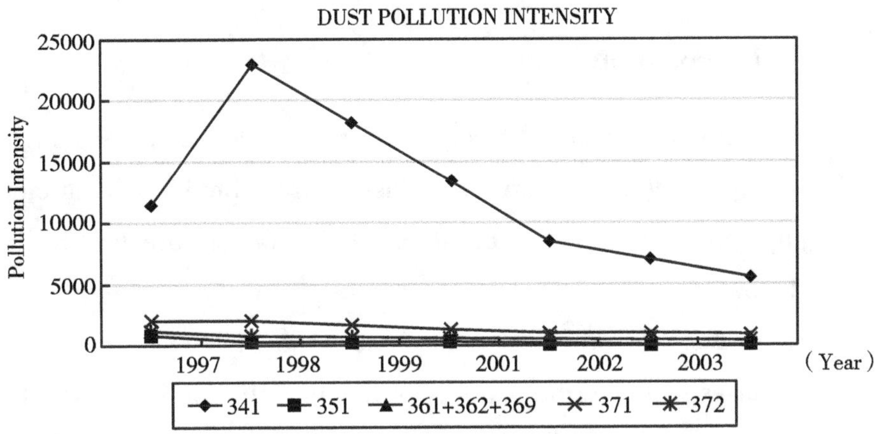

Figure 3.7 Pollution intensity of DUST (tons per million yuan of value added) for the five dirtiest sectors in China

3.4 The Determinants of Pollution

To investigate the determinants of pollution I use a 'pollution demand – supply schedule' methodology where emissions are considered as the use of an 'environmental service' and are thus included as an additional input in the production function. Pollution demand is defined as an industry's demand for environmental services, in other words, the level of emissions an industrial generates from production. Pollution supply is defined as the quantity that the society is prepared to supply, which refers to the amount of pollution that an industry is allowed to emit within a community. The implicit 'price' of pollution is the expected penalty or compensation exacted by the affected community. The greater the pollution generated by industries, the higher the costs that local communities impose on industries.

3.4.1 Pollution Demand

Potentially significant determinants of environmental demand include energy, factor intensities, industry size, production efficiency, equipment vintage and innovation. These factors are briefly discussed below.

Energy use: as previously discussed, the high energy – consuming industries generate the majority of the air pollution in China. The Chinese economy is broadly dependent on the production from heavy industry that tends to require high levels of raw material and energy inputs. Energy use is therefore likely to be a strong positive determinant of industrial air pollution, the more energy intensive production, the larger an industry's demand for pollution.

Factor Intensities: the pollution level of an industry may be influenced by its factor intensities that refer to physical and human capital intensity. Several studies have suggested a close relationship between pollution abatement costs and physical capital requirements (Antweiler *et al.*, 2001 and Cole and Elliott 2003). Physical capital – intensive industries are also energy intensive and they are more likely to become a polluter. Cole *et al.* (2005) find a positive relationship between physical capital use and pollution even after energy use is controlled for. The ambiguity of the relationship between human capital intensity and industrial pollution is also explained by Cole *et al.* (2005). They argue that, on one hand, human capital – intensive sectors with advanced technologies are more efficient and less energy intensive, therefore relatively clean. On the other hand, low –

skilled labour – intensive sectors could be clean because these sectors depend on less complex production process and produce low levels of pollution.

Size: it is measured by the value added per firm of the industry. Other things being equal, the relationship between a firm's total output and emissions is expected to be positive, although this relationship may be diminishing at the margin. The variable of Size should be controlled for in the regression because it is related to the dependent variable that is defined as pollution scaled by total output.

Efficiency: pollution intensity is likely to be a negative function of the efficiency. An industry that adopts advanced technologies, either in production or in management, is more productive. Thus, highly efficient industries are likely to produce less waste per unit of output, *ceteris paribus*. In addition, highly productive industries are supposed to respond relatively quickly to any change in pollution control incentives. It is argued that less productive industries may find it harder to abate pollution emissions and to comply with the requirement of environmental regulations. Productivity is therefore expected to be negatively related to the pollution intensity across industries. [①]The regression uses total factor productivity (*TFP*) as a measure of efficiency.

Vintage: also defined as the use of modern production processes. It is generally expected as a newer plant or one that uses cleaner

① Gray and Shadbegian (1995) and Gollop and Roberts (1983), for instance, find that plants with higher levels of abatement costs tend to have lower levels of productivity. However, since plants with high levels of abatement costs would tend to be those from pollution intensive industries, this finding may be driven by the explanation that unproductive industries generate more pollution.

modern production processes. Along with increasingly stringent environmental regulations, the utilization of modern production processes is more resource efficient and produces less waste per unit of output. Since opening the Chinese industries have more access to modern production processes and have improved technological capabilities thereafter. Plants set up after the economic reform in China are expected to be cleaner than old plants.

Innovation: the incentive of a firm's innovation is to improve efficiency. High efficiency means fewer inputs per unit of output and thus less depends on resources. Product or process innovations can be accomplished by research and development (R&D) activities. Except for improving efficiency, innovation of production process may also create new means of recycling that reduce waste and require fewer raw material inputs.

3.4.2 Pollution Supply

The 'environmental supply schedule' is determined by environmental regulations. Environmental regulations ensure that the greater the use of environmental services (i. e. the larger the emissions of pollution) and the higher the costs imposed on firms or industries. Environmental regulations can be defined in terms of formal and informal regulations. Under circumstances of formal regulations, the government (or local authority) regulates pollution on behalf of the community and measures of control generally include command and control, pollution taxes and tradable permits. Informal regulations are acted to complement weak, weakly enforced or even missing formal regulations, and they are taken in such a way that communities 'informally' regulate polluters through bargaining and lobbying. When local environmental quality fails to meet the preferences of local communities by means of taking formal regulations, local communities may report the environmental violations to the local authority or pressure regulators and firms to update environmental standards, strengthen scrutiny and take enforcement more seriously.

Here is an overview of the Chinese formal environmental regulations. The pollution charge system was formally established by the Chinese government in 1978, claiming that "the levy should be imposed on pollution discharges that exceed national pollution discharge standards and level of the levy is determined based on quantity and concentration of discharges as well as fee schedules established by the State Council." In 1979, the National People's Congress adopted the Environmental Protection Law (EPL), which was officially enacted in 1989. Regarding formal air pollution regulations, legislation on the prevention and control of air pollution in 2000 specifies that local authorities are responsible for the air quality in their own jurisdictions. As such, local authorities are required to take measures to ensure that the air quality in their own jurisdiction meets the prescribed national standard. The administrative department of environmental protection under the State Council establishes national standards for air quality, while local authorities have the power to establish local standards of their own for those items not specified by the national standards, and to report to the administrative department of environmental protection.

There are several policy strategies of air pollution control in China. One strategy is to restructure industrial production. Unbalanced structure of industrial production is one reason that has caused air quality to degrade. Coal mines and electricity generation are the primary sources of SO_2 and acid rain. China has closed down several coal mines with sulphur content more than 3% and small fire power stations with capability less than 50000 KW (kilowatt). By the end of 1999, the closure has significantly reduced SO_2 emissions and acid rain. The other strategy is to prohibit the use of leaded fuel since road transport is another important source of air pollution. The prohibition was successfully achieved on 1st July 2000. The Chinese Environmental Protection Agency and other official organizations jointly launched a project called "clean vehicle" that targets on vehicles using LPG (liquefied petroleum gas) and CNG (compressed natural gas), electric vehicles and some other vehicles of advanced technology. The prohibition of leaded fuel and promotion of clean vehicles are both widely practiced in the two controlled areas①.

Despite formal regulations, informal regulations somehow appear to be present in China. One example of informal regulations is the petition system. Every year the China Environment Yearbook reports statistics about number of environmental petitions that sent to the national or local authorities. Petitions are made by means of writing letters or visiting in person. Local communities often use this system to report environmental violations. Informal regulation may also be 'direct' when local communities directly lobby the firm.

3.4.3 Pollution Equilibrium

As discussed above, an industry's pollution demand is given by:

---

① SO_2 controlled region and acid – rain controlled region.

$$e_{it} = f(p_{it}, n_{it}, pci_{it}, hci_{it}, s_{it}, tfp_{it}, vin_{it}, innov_{it}) \quad (3-1)$$

where subscripts i and t denote industry and year, e denotes air emissions, p denotes the expected price of pollution as a result of environmental regulations, n denotes energy use, pci is physical capital intensity, hci is human capital intensity, s is the size of the average firm in the industry, tfp is an industry's total factor productivity, vin is a measure of the vintage of production process and $innov$ represents innovation. The next section will discuss variables in detail.

The expected price of pollution in equation (3 – 1) can be identified through the industry's pollution supply schedule. It is a function of the quantity of pollution and the stringency of formal and informal environmental regulations.

$$p_{it} = f(e_{it}, FRegs_{it}, IRegs_{it}) \quad (3-2)$$

where p and e are already defined, *FRegs* refers to formal environmental regulations, whilst *IRegs* refers to informal regulations.

In equilibrium, substituting p in equation (3 – 1) with equation (3 – 2) and then pollution can be defined as:

$$e_{it} = f(n_{it}, pci_{it}, hci_{it}, s_{it}, tfp_{it}, vin_{it}, innov_{it}, FRegs_{it}, IRegs_{it}) \quad (3-3)$$

3.5 Econometric Specification and Data Considerations

Our estimating equation is based closely on equation (3 – 3),

$$E_{it} = \alpha_i + \delta_t + \beta_1 N_{it} + \beta_2 PCI_{it} + \beta_3 HCI_{it} + \beta_4 SIZE_{it} + \beta_5 TFP_{it} + \beta_6 CAP_{it} + \beta_7 RD_{it} + \lambda REG + \varepsilon_{it} \quad (3-4)$$

our dependent variable, E_{it}, is pollution emissions expressed per unit of value added. We estimate equation (3 - 4) separately for three different types of air pollution, namely SO_2, SOOT and DUST. The variable α_i with subscript i denotes industry specific effects whilst δ_t with subscript t denotes year specific effects. Equation (3 - 4) is estimated for 15 three - digit ISIC manufacturing industries, and the period covers 7 years from 1997 to 2003. ①All related monetary variables are deflated to 1990 prices by a GDP deflator.

3.5.1 'Demand' Variable Considerations

Regarding 'demand' variables, N_{it} denotes total energy consumption per unit of value added, including consumption of coal, coke, crude oil, gasoline, kerosene, diesel oil, fuel oil, natural gas and electricity. PCI_{it}, physical capital intensity, is measured as non - wage value added per worker. HCI_{it}, human capital intensity, is defined as an average wage paid to staff in a specific industry. The size variable, $SIZE_{it}$, is defined as value added per firm, calculated as the ratio of an industry's value added to the number of enterprises in that industry. The variable total factor productivity, TFP_{it}, is defined in the next section. The variable CAP_{it} is an industry's capital expenditure per unit of value added, and capital expenditure use the data of investment in capital construction reported in China Statistical Yearbook including investments in new construction, expansion and

① Although we have data for 2004 for most of our variables, one important variable 'value added' is not reported in the yearbook 2005 which limits the sample time up to 2003.

reconstruction.[①] CAP_{it} is a good measure for the vintage of production processes since more investment implies newer equipment and machinery. The variable RD_{it} is an industry's research and development expenditure scaled by value added, and is measured by innovation investment in new construction projects, expansion projects and reconstruction projects.[②]

Total factor productivity, TFP_{it}, represents industry efficiency. Gray and Shadbegian (1995) define the productivity—TFP_{it} as the residuals from a three-input production function model that regresses output on three inputs: labour, capital and materials. It has raised a concern that inputs and unobserved firm-specific shocks to productivity may be correlated in the regression, for example, firms respond to a positive shock to productivity by using more inputs. If this is true, ordinary least squares (OLS) estimates of the production function could be biased, therefore, alternatives to the OLS estimates should be allowed. Olley and Pakes (1996) use firm-level instruments, input prices and lagged value of inputs to deal with such potential correlation. Levinsohn and Petrin (2003) suggest that including intermediate inputs, such as energy or materials, can manage the simultaneity problem.

---

① Capital construction refers to the new construction projects or extension projects, and related work of the enterprises, institutions or administrative units, only covering projects with a total investment of 500000 RMB yuan and over. The purpose of capital construction is mainly for expanding production capacity or improving project efficiency.

② Investment in innovation refers to the renewal of fixed assets and technologies innovation of the original facilities in enterprises and institutions. It also includes investment in the corresponding supplementary projects and the related work. This measure only covers projects with a total investment of 500000 RMB yuan and over.

The research use both fixed effects and random effects regressions to estimate productivity. There are two inputs, labour and capital, in the production function. The Hausman test suggests that simultaneity problem is not significant in our estimations. The Cobb – Douglas production function is therefore specified as follows:

$$Y = AK^{\alpha}L^{\beta} \quad \text{where } 0 < \alpha < 1 \text{ and } 0 < \beta < 1 \qquad (3-5)$$

Y denotes real GDP, A represents total factor productivity (TFP), K denotes total physical capital stock and L denotes total labour force. After scaling each variable by total labour force, equation (3 – 5) is converted to:

$$y = Ak^{\alpha}L^{\alpha+\beta-1} \qquad (3-6)$$

where y and k denote real GDP per worker and the physical capital stock per worker, respectively. The natural logarithms of equation (3 – 6) is given by:

$$\ln y = \ln A + \alpha \ln k + (\alpha + \beta - 1)\ln L \qquad (3-7)$$

The regression model is set up based on equation (3 – 7) and it is given by:

$$\ln y_{it} = \phi_i + \varphi_t + \alpha \ln k_{it} + (\alpha + \beta - 1)\ln L_{it} + \varepsilon_{it} \qquad (3-8)$$

where subscripts i and t denote industry and year, respectively. Total factor productivity is measured by $(\phi_i + \varphi_t + \varepsilon_{it})$ equivalent to lnA in equation (3 – 7). The sample of regression is a panel of 15 industries from 1996 to 2003. Real GDP per worker, y_{it}, is an industry's GDP per worker deflated to 1990 prices. I use the original value of fixed assets reported in China Statistical Yearbook as a proxy for physical capital stock, K, and total number of staff as a measure of total labour force, *L*. ① Table A3. 1 in the appendix provides more information about the data. Table 3. 3 presents estimates of fixed effects and random effects specifications. Since the Hausman tests do not reject the random effects estimates, I report estimates from both specifications and denote them by *TFPfe* and *TFPre*, respectively.

Table 3. 3 Production Function Estimates

Real GDP per worker (*lny*)	FE.	RE.
lnk	0. 550 (6. 31)***	0. 533 (7. 77)***
lnL	-0. 011 (-0. 10)	-0. 026 (-0. 32)
R^2	0. 983	0. 770
n	120	120
Hausman (*FE V. RE*)	0. 02 (1. 00)	

Note: Time dummies are included. *** denote significant at 1% levels, respectively. P-value in parentheses for the Hausman test.

Based on the estimates in Table 3. 3, I calculate *TFP* in such a way:

Fixed effects: $TFP_{it} = \ln y_{it} - 0.55 \ln k_{it} + 0.011 \ln L_{it}$ (3-9)

Random effects: $TFP_{it} = \ln y_{it} - 0.533 \ln k_{it} + 0.026 \ln L_{it}$ (3-10)

where 0. 55 and 0. 53 are the estimates of lnk_{it}, indicating the elasticity of output with respect to the physical capital stock (α). The esti-

---

① The original value of fixed assets refers to the total value of payments on a particular item of fixed asset, including payments on buildings, purchasing, installing, reconstructing, expanding, and payment on technology innovation. In general, it includes value of purchases, cost for packaging, transportation, installation, etc.

mate of lnL_{it} is $(\alpha + \beta - 1)$, indicating elasticity of output with respect to the labour force, and it is 0.44 in both regressions.

3.5.2 'Supply' Variable Considerations

REG in equation (3 – 4) denotes a vector of variables capturing formal and informal regulations. All variables are locally determined rather than using direct measures of formal and informal regulations. Since formal regulations are generally weaker or even absent in developing countries, local communities have to bargain with local factories for reducing pollution, therefore, characteristics of local communities have determined informal regulations. Without recourse to the existing formal regulations (if any), local communities rely on social pressure, adverse publicity, threat (or use) of violence, civil law, politicians, local administrators, or religious leaders to make bargain. The process is distinct from national or local formal regulations because it searches for channels by all means to push firms to maintain compliance with the community – determined standards.

Meantime, formal regulations are also likely to contain regional components. As previously discussed, the environmental legislation of China endows local authorities with the power to establish their own standards for those items that are not specified by the national standards. In this case, the enforcement of local authorities is relatively flexible, which allows local determinants to engage in.

Several local determinants have been taken into account in this research. One is the regional pollution prosecutions. I use number of environmental penalty cases scaled by a region's industry output as a proxy for pollution prosecutions. A large number of penalty cases imply strong enforcement of environmental regulations. Another determinant is unemployment rate. Local authorities in a region with high unemployment rate may allocate resources as many as possible to manage the issue of unemployment and certainly less resource would be available to pollution control, therefore, more pollution intensive industries may relocate to a region with high unemployment.

Informal regulations may also be determined by a region's population density. On one hand, a densely populated area may have more people adversely affected by pollution and hence opposition to a pollution intensive plant is larger. On the other hand, within a densely populated area a pollution intensive plant may be less 'visible' and hence less likely to be caught by local communities. Population density is estimated in terms of total population scaled by a region's geographic area.

Other local determinants include demographic factors such as a region's age structure and level of education. These factors determine the lobbying power of local communities. For example, a younger generation of population may be more concerned about pollution issues and better placed to lobby against polluters. Cole *et al.* (2005) use a share of population under age 44 as a proxy for younger population. Due to lack of data, I use the share of population under age 15, and I believe a region with more children must show great concerns on pollution issues.

The level of education is a local determinant because people without education have little ability to acquire information and often ignore pollution matters. They are also incapable of using available regulatory channels. Polluting plants are thus more likely to relocate to regions with a large percentage of poorly educated people. Level of education is measured by the share of population that have acquired a college degree or higher level of education.

All determinants discussed above are region specific, but data of pollution and industrial characteristics are both industry specific, following equation (3 - 11) I can convert region - specific variables into industry - specific variables:

$$REGpros_{it} = \sum_{r} (s_{irt} \times PROS_{rt}) \qquad (3-11)$$

where subscripts i, r, and t denote industry, region and year, respectively. s is the output of industry i in region r as a share of total national output of industry i, and $PROS_{rt}$ is pollution prosecutions in region r scaled by that region's total output. Therefore, industries that have a higher share of output in regions with larger pollution prosecutions will have higher values of *REGpros*. Equivalent variables for regional unemployment rate, population density, population under the age of 15 and level of education are also calculated in the same way and denoted by *REGunem*, *REGpd*, *REGagapop*, *REGedu*, respectively. The number of regions in this methodology include 22 provinces, 5 autonomous districts and 4 municipalities. [①]See Table A3. 1 in the appendix for detail.

Note that s_{irt} is a key variable in equation (3 - 11) that needs further explanation. s is the output of industry i in region r as a share of total national output of industry i. There is only one year of data (2004) for gross output (deflated to 1990 prices) by industry in

① Hong Kong, Macau and Taiwan are excluded due to lack of data.

Hebei and Gansu. In order to incorporate these two regions in the sample, I use equation (3 – 12) to calculate gross output of other years for two regions:

$$Y_{irt} = \frac{GDP_{rt}}{GDP_{r2004}} \times Y_{ir2004} \qquad (3-12)$$

where Y_{irt} denotes gross output of industry i in region r in year t, GDP_{rt} is one region's total gross output in year t and GDP_{r2004} is therefore one region's total gross output in 2004. Y_{ir2004} finally denotes one region's gross output of industry i in 2004. Y_{irt} is thus the gross output by industry for Hebei and Gansu available from 1997 to 2003.

Endogeneity of regulation variables is another issue that needs discussion. Regional pollution prosecutions, for example, could be endogenously determined by pollution rather than the other way around. It is possible that a region has many cases of prosecutions because it has been heavily polluted already. Regional unemployment rate could be endogenously determined by pollution because high – income individuals may choose not to live in a pollution intensive region and hence the region will be full of low – income and unemployed individuals. Population density may be determined by a region's pollution intensity because individuals may choose not to reside in close proximity to a pollution intensive plant and hence the surrounding population density is certainly lower. Regional level of education may have been determined by that region's pollution intensity because highly educated individuals are likely to be more aware of detrimental outcome of pollution. All of these concerns about endogeneity will be carefully examined in the sensitivity analysis.

Equation (3 –4) is estimated using both fixed effects and random effects specifications that include year dummies always. The estimations rely on industry specific fixed effects (α_i) to capture factors that are specific to individual industry but do not change over time, and rely on year specific fixed effects (δ_t) to capture factors that are common to all industries but change over time. As previously discussed, β_1 – the estimate of energy use per unit of value added and β_2 – the estimate of physical capital intensity, are expected to be positive. The estimate of human capital intensity, β_3, could be positive or negative. β_4 – the estimate of value added per firm of industry i (*SIZE*), β_5 – the estimate of total factor productivity (*TFP*), β_6 – the estimate of capital expenditure (*CAP*) and β_7 – the estimate of R&D expenditure (*RD*), all should be negative. The estimate of *REGpros* is expected to be negative and estimate of *REGunem* is to be positive. The estimate of *REGpd* may be negative or positive, and estimates of *REGagepop* and *REGedu* are both expected to be negative.

3.6 Estimation Results

3.6.1 Main Results

Table 3.4a presents the main results for both fixed and random effects estimates.[①] Table 3.4b reports estimates with standard errors that are clustered by industry. The dependent variable is defined by

① Econometric software STATA 9.0 is applied to run the regressions and the major syntaxes include *xtreg* with *fe* and *re robust*.

pollution intensity of three air pollutants, SO_2, SOOT and DUST. ① The Hausman specification test rejects the null hypothesis when using SO_2 as the dependent variable. The null hypothesis suggests that the estimator from random effects specification is consistently and efficiently estimate the true parameters, and a rejection of the null implies unreliable estimates, therefore, while considering the pollutant SO_2 more emphasis should be placed on the fixed effects estimates.

Table 3.4a Determinants of Industrial Pollution (Fixed and Random effects)

	FIXED EFFECTS			RANDOM EFFECTS		
	(1) SO_2	(2) SOOT	(3) DUST	(4) SO_2	(5) SOOT	(6) DUST
Energy	96.43 (2.61) **	96.60 (3.29) ***	542.44 (2.70) ***	95.205 (3.21) ***	68.640 (3.93) ***	327.04 (2.37) **
PCI	0.0110 (1.16)	0.0067 (0.48)	0.036 (0.99)	0.00631 (0.87)	0.00880 (0.78)	0.0363 (1.50)
HCI	0.0385 (0.24)	0.389 (1.86) *	1.585 (2.07) **	0.0700 (0.67)	0.212 (1.21)	0.741 (1.40)
SIZE	4485.291 (1.69) *	1489.81 (0.52)	4282.06 (0.39)	-771.07 (-0.43)	-1505.34 (-0.62)	-9814.72 (-1.21)
TFPfe	-2002.67 (-1.89) *	-1587.71 (-1.54)	-2557.59 (-0.78)	-898.19 (-1.80) *	-1132.91 (-1.95) *	-3898.71 (-2.15) **
CAP	-1213.19 (-0.97)	138.707 (0.10)	-3531.88 (-0.89)	-2209.53 (-0.98)	-437.457 (-0.34)	-7579.95 (-1.21)

① Estimations for SO2 and DUST use heteroscedastic robust standard errors. However, models fitted on data of SOOT fail to meet the asymptotic assumptions of the Hausman test, therefore only providing standard errors without the heteroscedastic robust test.

Continued

	FIXED EFFECTS			RANDOM EFFECTS		
	(1) SO_2	(2) SOOT	(3) DUST	(4) SO_2	(5) SOOT	(6) DUST
RD	-106.856 (-0.07)	-1463.01 (-0.77)	-6797.05 (-1.09)	-3112.74 (-2.21) **	-4149.11 (-2.45) **	-21487.81 (-2.27) **
REGpros	-347.12 (-0.95)	-169.92 (-0.41)	-845.88 (-0.84)	-131.27 (-0.42)	-114.75 (-0.29)	-870.491 (-0.95)
REGunem	204.472 (0.31)	-110.62 (-0.16)	939.041 (0.58)	1054.99 (1.30)	222.73 (0.42)	902.192 (0.69)
REGpd	5.910 (2.29) **	2.171 (0.73)	-2.418 (-0.29)	-0.381 (-0.57)	-0.0137 (-0.02)	-0.861 (-0.42)
REGagepop	-51.20 (-0.12)	137.88 (0.31)	550.906 (0.42)	84.444 (0.23)	323.89 (0.84)	1926.53 (1.46)
REGedu	6061.36 (1.64)	-1247.65 (-0.39)	-16783.5 (-1.60)	-2067.57 (-0.84)	-5340.64 (-2.42) **	-18514.08 (-2.09) **
R^2	0.604	0.393	0.422	0.588	0.502	0.473
Hausman (*FE. V RE.*)				140.75 (0.0000)	10.97 (0.7547)	0.39 (1.0000)
D-M Exog. (*REGpros*)	2.13 (0.15)	0.32 (0.57)	0.42 (0.52)			
D-M Exog. (*REGpd*)	0.20 (0.66)	0.61 (0.44)	0.14 (0.71)			
D-M Exog. (*REGunem*)	2.81 (0.10)	0.28 (0.60)	0.70 (0.40)			
n	105	105	105	105	105	105

Note: Our dependent variables are expressed in terms of pollution intensities, measured as emissions per unit of value added. t-statistics in parentheses for fixed effects and z-statistics in parentheses for random effects. Time dummies are included.

* significant at 10% level; ** significant at 5% level; *** significant at 1% level.

D-M Exog is the Davidson and Mackinnon test for exogeneity, this test cannot be performed for random effects estimations.

Table 3.4b Determinants of Industrial Pollution (Fixed and Random effects)

	FIXED EFFECTS			RANDOM EFFECTS		
	(1) SO_2	(2) SOOT	(3) DUST	(4) SO_2	(5) SOOT	(6) DUST
Energy	96.43 ** (45.9)	96.60 *** (55.8)	542.44 *** (269.6)	95.205 *** (40.4)	68.640 *** (44.0)	327.04 ** (205.4)
PCI	0.0110 (0.0)	0.0067 (0.0)	0.036 (0.1)	0.00631 (0.0)	0.00880 (0.0)	0.0363 (0.0)
HCI	0.0385 (0.2)	0.389 * (0.3)	1.585 ** (1.2)	0.0700 (0.1)	0.212 (0.2)	0.741 (0.8)
SIZE	4485.291 * (3147.7)	1489.81 (2705.6)	4282.06 (12132.2)	-771.07 (1943.9)	-1505.34 (2657.6)	-9814.72 (10821.5)
TFPfe	-2002.67 * (1566.6)	-1587.71 (1620.4)	-2557.59 (4953.0)	-898.19 * (573.7)	-1132.91 * (731.5)	-3898.71 ** (2928.6)
CAP	-1213.19 (1902.0)	138.707 (1388.0)	-3531.88 (6068.7)	-2209.53 (3124.9)	-437.457 (2067.9)	-7579.95 (7840.7)
RD	-106.856 (1776.6)	-1463.01 (1821.4)	-6797.05 (9622.1)	-3112.74 ** (1622.5)	-4149.11 ** (2958.5)	-21487.81 ** (15532.9)
REGpros	-347.12 (299.1)	-169.92 (156.6)	-845.88 (1156.0)	-131.27 (194.0)	-114.75 (158.4)	-870.491 (923.6)
REGunem	204.472 (442.9)	-110.62 (400.9)	939.041 (1605.8)	1054.99 (853.2)	222.73 (245.8)	902.192 (1195.4)
REGpd	5.910 ** (3.4)	2.171 (2.6)	-2.418 (10.1)	-0.381 (0.6)	-0.0137 (0.4)	-0.861 (1.8)
REGagepop	-51.20 (291.3)	137.88 (397.0)	550.906 (1490.3)	84.444 (295.7)	323.89 (376.1)	1926.53 (1512.7)

Continued

	FIXED EFFECTS			RANDOM EFFECTS		
	(1) SO_2	(2) SOOT	(3) DUST	(4) SO_2	(5) SOOT	(6) DUST
REGedu	6061. 36 (4089. 1)	-1247. 65 (1816. 4)	-16783. 5 (11343. 8)	-2067. 57 (2567. 0)	-5340. 64 ** (3075. 8)	-18514. 08 ** (14484. 7)
R^2	0. 604	0. 393	0. 422	0. 588	0. 502	0. 473
Hausman (*FE. V RE.*)				140. 75 (0. 0000)	10. 97 (0. 7547)	0. 39 (1. 0000)
n	105	105	105	105	105	105

Note: Our dependent variables are expressed in terms of pollution intensities, measured as emissions per unit of value added. Standard errors that are clustered by industry are reported in parentheses. Time dummies are included. * significant at 10% level; ** significant at 5% level; *** significant at 1% level.

I perform the Davidson - Mackinnon exogeneity test to check the potential endogeneity of *REGpros*, *REGpd* and *REGunem*. The null hypothesis of this test says OLS estimate is consistent and hence a rejection of the null indicates the presence of endogeneity, and thus instrumental variables should be employed. I use one year lagged *REGpros*, *REGpd* and *REGunem* as instruments to perform the test and find the null is not rejected, which implies that endogeneity is not a serious problem in the estimation (see Table 3. 4).

The first point to note is that, across all six models, energy intensity (*Energy*) is a positive and significant determinant of pollution intensity. Physical capital intensity (*PCI*) is found to be a positive determinant of pollution intensity across all six models though none of the estimates are significant. Given that energy intensity and physical capital intensity are potentially related (capital intensive industries use large energy input in the production process), Table A3.2 in the appendix reports estimates after dropping energy intensity in the regression, the estimates of *PCI* have changed to positive and significant in four of six models. The above suggests that energy intensity somehow captures the effect of physical capital intensity.

Table 3.4 shows that the estimate of human capital intensity (*HCI*) is consistently positive across all six models and significant in two fixed effects specifications with SOOT intensity and DUST intensity as the dependent variables. The finding indicates that high – skilled, human capital – intensive industries are more likely to be pollution intensive. To investigate further, of fifteen sectors in the sample I select seven ones that are most polluted in terms of pollution intensity of three pollutants and seven sectors with highest average wage, Table A3.3 in the appendix ranks these sectors in a descending order. Five sectors overlap and present in both rankings, they are Petroleum processing and coking (ISIC353), Iron and steel (ISIC371), Non – ferrous metals (ISIC372), Other chemicals (ISIC352) and Industrial chemicals (ISIC351). The result is the same to the regression results that high – skilled, human capital – intensive industries are more likely to be pollution intensive in China.

In the fixed effects specifications, the average size of a firm in an industry (*SIZE*) positively and significantly determines SO_2 intensity, but the estimate of the *SIZE* variable is negative (although insignificant) across all random effects specifications. The top 3 sectors with the largest firm size are Petroleum processing and coking (ISIC353), Iron and steel (ISIC371) and Other chemicals (ISIC352), and sectors whose firm size is the smallest are Printing and publishing

(ISC342), Plastic products (ISIC356), and Fabricated metal products (ISIC381).[①] Figure 3.8 plots the SO_2 intensity for these six sectors and Figure 3.9 and 3.10 plot SOOT intensity and DUST intensity, respectively.

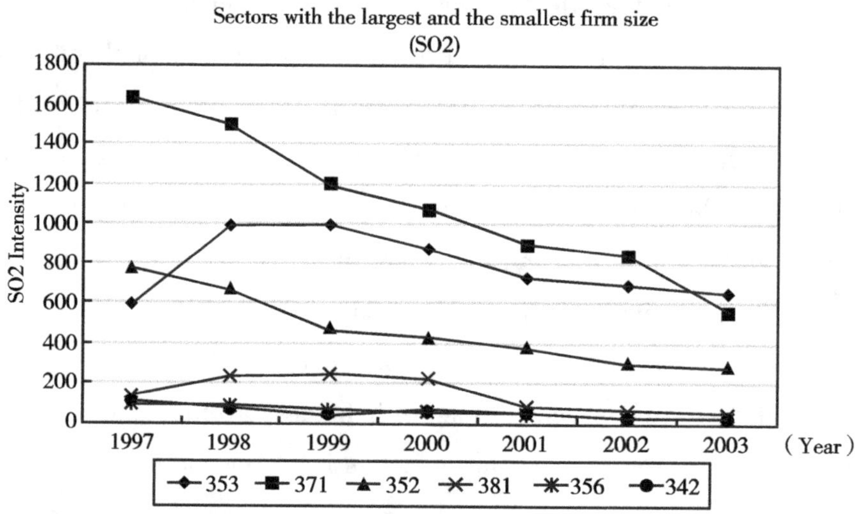

Figure 3.8 SO_2 intensity for the sectors with the largest and the smallest firm size

Figure 3.8, 3.9 and 3.10 all demonstrate a clear relationship between the average firm size of an industry and its pollution intensity. Industries with large firm size are more polluted relative to industries with small firm size, therefore, the economies of scale may be offset by relatively high levels of pollution in China. Back to Table 3.4, the estimate of total factor productivity (*TFPfe*) is negative and often statistically significant. Capital expenditure per unit of value added

① The selection of industries is based on average firm size of individual industry.

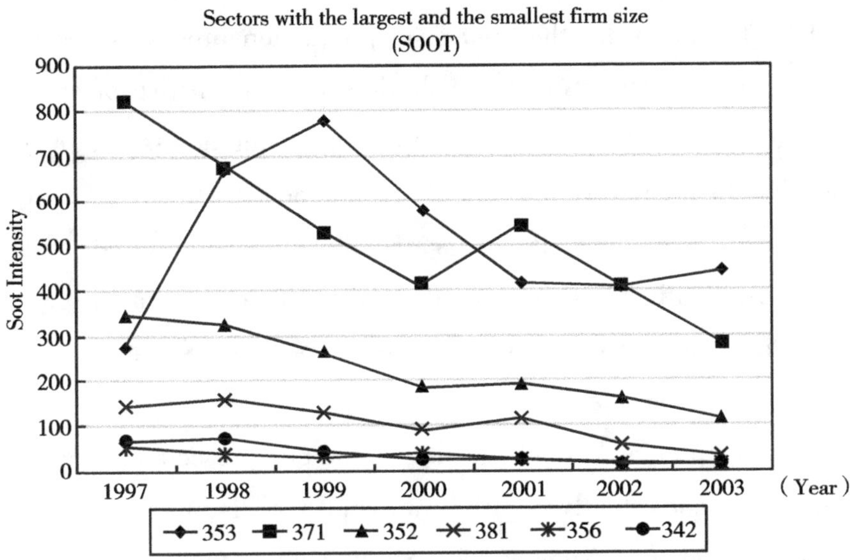

Figure 3.9 SOOT intensity for the sectors with the largest and the smallest firm size

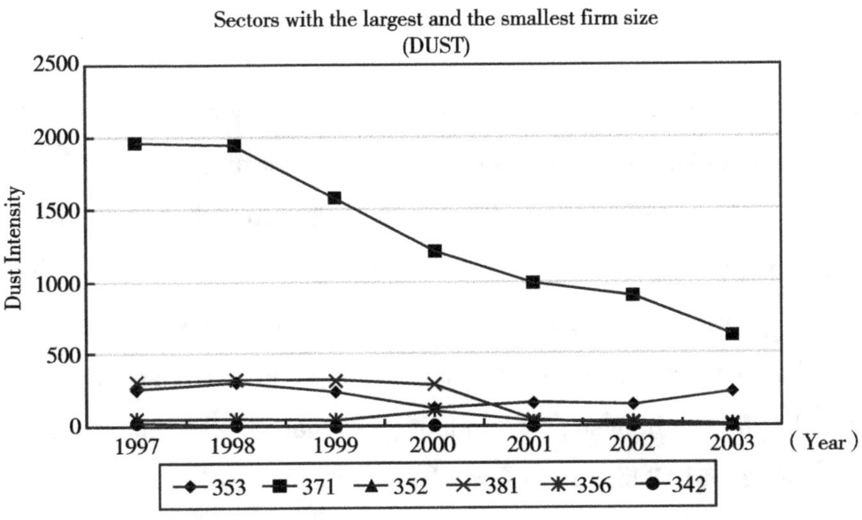

Figure 3.10 DUST intensity for the sectors with the largest and the smallest firm size

(*CAP*), the proxy for the vintage of production processes, is found to be a negative determinant of pollution intensity in five of six models, but not found to be statistically significant across all models. Last, R&D expenditure per unit of value added (*RD*) is consistently negative in all six models and statisticlly significant in all random effects specifications, suggesting that industries of innovation produce less pollution not only in developed countries like UK but also in developing countries like China. ①

For regulation variables, the pollution prosecution variable, *REGpros*, is consistently negative across all models, although not significant throughout. Number of environmental penalty cases is employed as a proxy for pollution prosecution and a negative estimate means pollution intensive industries are less likely to move to regions with a great number of environmental penalty cases.

In Table 3.4, the estimate of regional population density (*REGpd*) is positive in model (1) and (2), and negative in model (3) to (6). Population density is a significant determinant of SO_2 intensity in the fixed effects specification, suggesting that industries in densely populated area produce higher levels of SO_2 emissions. Figure 3.11 displays average population density of all provinces in China. Note that ten provinces that are largely populated (Shanghai, Tianjin, Beijing, Jiangsu, Shandong, Henan, Zhejiang, Anhui, Guangdong and Chongqing) are also the major destinations of inward

① This finding, to a certain extent, supports the Porter Hypothesis and suggests that while innovation can reduce pollution, the benefits of innovation may partially or more than fully offset the costs of complying with environmental regulations.

direct investment. Moreover, almost all of these largely populated provinces are located within ' SO_2 controlled region' where emissions of SO_2 remain at a quite high level and the Chinese government has placed a great effort on the control of SO_2 emissions. It turns out, for China, there is a positive relationship between regional population density and pollution intensity, but only for the pollutant of SO_2.

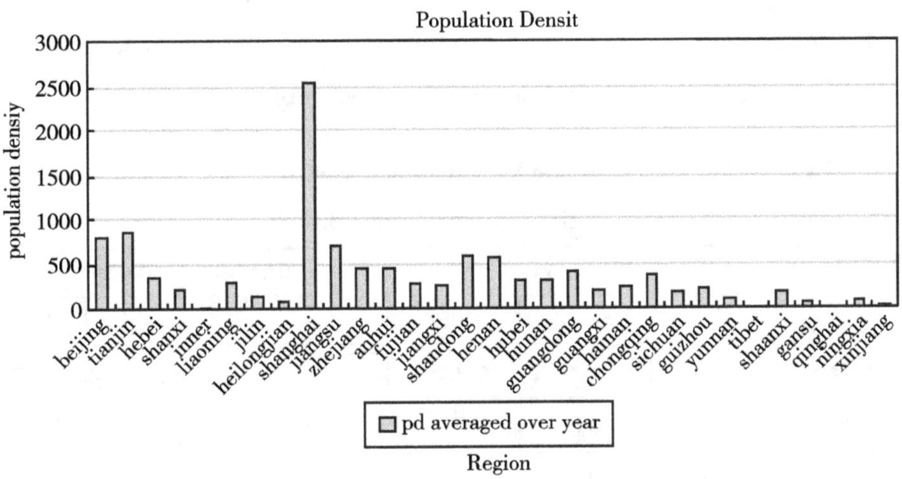

Figure 3. 11 Population density for 31 regions in China

The estimate of regional unemployment rate (*REGunem*) is positive across all models except for the fixed effects specification of SOOT, however, it is never significant. *REGagepop*, the regulation variable that captures the effect of younger population, is found to be positive in many models, but statistically insignificant. Finally, *REGedu*, which captures regional effect of highly educated population, negatively determines the pollution intensity in five of six models and is significant for SOOT and DUST in the random effects specifications. It turns out that regional level of education works the best as a proxy for the informal regulation that has impacts on regional pollution. ①

To explain the economic significance of the results, Table 3.5 presents the estimated elasticities based on the estimates in Table 3.4. Among those statistically significant variables, *Energy* and *TFP* perhaps exent the largest impact on pollution intensity. Taking the fixed SO_2 model as an example, the estimate indicates that a 1% increase in energy use results in a 1.04% increase in SO_2 intensity, while a 1% increase in *TFP* reduce SO_2 intensity by 3.5%. The magnitude of elasticity is also high for other significant variable.

Table 3.5 Estimated Elasticities based on estimates from Table 3.4

	FIXED EFFECTS			RANDOM EFFECTS		
	SO_2	SOOT	DUST	SO_2	SOOT	DUST
Energy	1.040 ***	1.600 ***	4.335 ***	1.027 ***	1.186 ***	2.613 ***
PCI	0.452	0.441	1.097	0.259	0.578	1.096
HCI	0.236	3.814 **	7.119 **	0.428	2.078 *	3.325
SIZE	0.516 *	0.274	0.364	-0.0887	-0.277	-0.834
TFP	-3.498 *	-4.442 *	-3.289	-1.569 *	-3.170 ***	-5.012 ***
CAP	-0.132	0.0242	-0.282	-0.240	-0.0763	-0.606
RD	-0.0180	-0.395	-0.842	-0.525 **	-1.120 ***	-2.660 ***
REGpros	-0.514	-0.403	-0.920	-0.194	-0.272	-0.946

① When comparing the results of regulation variables in China with those in Cole, Elliott and Shimamoto (2005) from UK, it is more significant in UK. One reason might be that UK regions are much smaller than Chinese regions. Ideally we would have within province regulation variables such as at city, county or village level, but the data is not yet available.

Continued

	FIXED EFFECTS			RANDOM EFFECTS		
	SO_2	SOOT	DUST	SO_2	SOOT	DUST
REGunem	0.545	-0.472	1.833	2.813	0.951	1.761
REGpd	3.439 **	2.024	-1.032	-0.222	-0.0128	-0.368
REGagepop	-0.132	0.569	1.043	0.217	1.336	3.646
REGedu	3.319	-1.094	-6.722	-1.132	-4.685 ***	-7.413 **

* significant at 10% level; ** significant at 5% level; *** significant at 1% level.

3.6.2 Sensitivity Analysis

To check the sensitivity of the main results, I perform a number of robustness checks, including using alternative measures of *PCI*, *HCI* and *TFP*, as well as testing the endogeneity of regional regulation variables.

Model (13) to (18) in Table A3.4 in the appendix estimate an alternative measure of *PCI*. The original measure of *PCI* is defined as non-wage value added per worker, while *PCIasset*, is simply measured as an industry's deflated value of fixed assets per worker. It is found to be inconsistently signed and insignificant across models. Model (19) to (24) in Table A3.5 replaces the original measure of *HCI* with a measure of *HCImanf*, defined as a sector's average wage relative to the average wage of the overall manufacturing sector. *HCImanf* is found to be insignificant across all models. Model (25) to (30) in Table A3.6 replace the original measure of total factor productivity (*TFP*) with a simpler measure of labour productivity, defined as gross output per worker (*TFPoutput*). It remains consistently negative but insignificant always.

The research concerns more on the endogeneity of the regional variable that proxy for informal regulation. Table 3.6 presents estimates of sensitivity checks in terms of using fixed effects specifications. Models (31), (32) and (33) begin by dropping all the regulation variables out of the estimated equation, and rely on industry and year effects to capture the effect of environmental policy. The estimates of other determinants are identical to the estimates in the main results. The following models in Table 3.6 add each regulation variable in turn in the regression. Models (34) to (36) add in pollution prosecution (*REGpros*) and the estimate of pollution prosecution is consistently negative for three air pollutants, other determinants also remain the same. The result implies that the endogeneity of pollution prosecution is not a critical issue when taking it as a regulation determinant.

Models (37), (38) and (39) add in regional unemployment rate that has no significant impact on other determinants, and then population density (*REGpd*) is added in (40) to (42), the share of population under the age of 15 (*REGagepop*) is added in (43) to (45), and level of education (*REGedu*) is added in (46) to (48). None of them have significant impact on other determinants either in sign or in magnitude. ① Overall, I can conclude that the potential endogeneity of regional regulation variables is not a serious problem in the regression and have no impact on other non – regulation variables.

① This exercise is repeated in the random effects specifications. The changes are similar to those with the fixed effects specifications in Table 3.6.

Table 3.6 **Sensitivity Analysis (FIXD EFFECTS)**

FIXED EFFECTS	(31) SO_2	(32) SOOT	(33) DUST	(34) SO_2	(35) SOOT	(36) DUST	(37) SO_2	(38) SOOT	(39) DUST
Energy	123.858 (2.95)***	97.730 (3.91)***	515.951 (2.73)***	122.379 (2.98)***	96.252 (3.81)***	508.993 (2.72)***	123.303 (3.13)***	96.410 (3.79)***	509.326 (2.70)***
PCI	-0.00212 (-0.37)	0.000366 (0.03)	0.0204 (0.76)	-0.000362 (-0.05)	0.00212 (0.18)	0.0285 (0.96)	0.00450 (0.54)	0.00295 (0.24)	0.0306 (0.98)
HCI	0.209 (1.45)	0.458 (2.44)**	1.680 (2.06)**	0.203 (1.41)	0.452 (2.39)**	1.664 (2.05)**	0.138 (0.94)	0.441 (2.29)**	1.636 (2.02)**
SIZE	1441.992 (0.67)	657.609 (0.28)	3220.517 (0.32)	2135.368 (0.83)	1350.593 (0.50)	6614.106 (0.62)	3073.391 (1.12)	1510.682 (0.55)	6995.388 (0.64)
TFPfe	-630.735 (-0.89)	-1207.695 (-1.39)	-2094.003 (-0.76)	-840.916 (-1.14)	-1417.757 (-1.49)	-3137.209 (-1.04)	-1424.333 (-1.53)	-1517.327 (-1.52)	-3372.277 (-1.04)
CAP	-1894.534 (-1.14)	31.870 (0.03)	-3230.145 (-0.83)	-1821.751 (-1.10)	104.611 (0.08)	-2857.475 (-0.74)	-1648.212 (-1.07)	134.228 (0.11)	-2789.479 (-0.72)
RD	-1935.71 (-1.27)	-1771.04 (-1.04)	-4380.648 (-0.70)	-1972.797 (-1.32)	-1808.107 (-1.05)	-4606.032 (-0.73)	-2109.224 (-1.50)	-1831.39 (-1.06)	-4654.621 (-0.73)

Continued

FIXED EFFECTS	(31) SO_2	(32) SOOT	(33) DUST	(34) SO_2	(35) SOOT	(36) DUST	(37) SO_2	(38) SOOT	(39) DUST
REGpros				-209.154 (-0.71)	-209.036 (-0.55)	-1041.708 (-1.24)	-366.821 (-1.07)	-235.944 (-0.60)	-1102.854 (-1.18)
REGunem							1058.737 (1.44)	180.691 (0.35)	431.117 (0.34)
REGpd									
REGagepop									
REGedu									
R^2	0.506	0.385	0.402	0.508	0.387	0.406	0.538	0.388	0.406
n	105	105	105	105	105	105	105	105	105

Continued

FIXED EFFECTS	(40) SO_2	(41) SOOT	(42) DUST	(43) SO_2	(44) SOOT	(45) DUST	(46) SO_2	(47) SOOT	(48) DUST
Energy	101.028 (2.61)**	90.309 (3.32)***	526.761 (2.70)***	102.320 (2.66)**	91.388 (3.29)***	527.44 (2.64)**	96.429 (2.61)**	96.600 (3.29)***	542.443 (2.70)***
PCI	0.0170 (1.73)*	0.00637 (0.48)	0.0207 (0.61)	0.0161 (1.57)	0.00566 (0.41)	0.0202 (0.61)	0.0110 (1.16)	0.00672 (0.48)	0.0363 (0.99)
HCI	0.0148 (0.10)	0.407 (2.03)**	1.736 (2.15)**	0.00205 (0.01)	0.396 (1.92)*	1.729 (2.15)**	0.0385 (0.24)	0.389 (1.86)*	1.585 (2.07)**
SIZE	3726.75 (1.46)	1689.626 (0.61)	6484.17 (0.60)	3684.767 (1.42)	1654.588 (0.59)	6462.099 (0.59)	4485.291 (1.69)*	1489.81 (0.52)	4282.056 (0.39)
TFPfe	−1848.646 (−1.81)*	−1633.539 (−1.61)	−3044.091 (−0.92)	−1835.067 (−1.78)*	−1622.206 (−1.58)	−3036.905 (−0.92)	−2002.667 (−1.89)*	−1587.708 (−1.54)	−2557.589 (−0.78)
CAP	−1227.308 (−1.00)	249.507 (0.19)	−3113.269 (−0.86)	−1331.012 (−1.00)	162.929 (0.12)	−3168.012 (−0.80)	−1213.19 (−0.97)	138.707 (0.10)	−3531.88 (−0.89)
RD	−466.508 (−0.33)	−1381.478 (−0.74)	−5946.958 (−0.96)	−473.716 (−0.33)	−1387.494 (−0.74)	−5950.461 (−0.96)	−106.856 (−0.07)	−1463.007 (−0.77)	−6797.046 (−1.09)

Continued

FIXED EFFECTS	(40) SO_2	(41) SOOT	(42) DUST	(43) SO_2	(44) SOOT	(45) DUST	(46) SO_2	(47) SOOT	(48) DUST
REGpros	-283. 684 (-0. 84)	-213. 174 (-0. 54)	-1172. 628 (-1. 27)	-254. 659 (-0. 70)	-188. 951 (-0. 46)	-1157. 228 (-1. 20)	-347. 124 (-0. 95)	-169. 918 (-0. 41)	-845. 880 (-0. 84)
REGunem	234. 620 (0. 35)	-45. 020 (-0. 07)	1069. 668 (0. 68)	165. 605 (0. 23)	-102. 619 (-0. 15)	1033. 303 (0. 63)	204. 472 (0. 31)	-110. 619 (-0. 16)	939. 041 (0. 58)
REGpd	6. 450 (2. 41) **	1. 767 (0. 64)	-5. 027 (-0. 62)	6. 732 (2. 54) **	2. 002 (0. 68)	-4. 878 (-0. 60)	5. 910 (2. 29) **	2. 171 (0. 73)	-2. 418 (-0. 29)
REGagepop				122. 387 (0. 30)	102. 141 (0. 24)	64. 538 (0. 05)	-51. 197 (-0. 12)	137. 871 (0. 31)	550. 906 (0. 42)
REGedu							6061. 36 (1. 64)	-1247. 652 (-0. 39)	-16783. 5 (-1. 60)
R^2	0. 578	0. 391	0. 408	0. 579	0. 392	0. 408	0. 604	0. 393	0. 422
n	105	105	105	105	105	105	105	105	105

Note: Our dependent variables are expressed in terms of pollution intensities, measured as emissions per unit of value added. t-statistics in parentheses.

Time dummies are included. * significant at 10% level; ** significant at 5% level; *** significant at 1% level.

Lastly, all regional regulation variables are replaced by regional per capita income that is even more directly related to environmental regulations. Table 3.7 presents results. Regional per capita income (*REGpcY*) is significant in one of six models [model (49)] and it is positive. The estimate is different from the one found by Cole *et al.* (2005) using UK data that concludes regional per capita income in their research is a negative, statistically significant determinant of pollution intensity. Figure 3.12 allows us to investigate the reason for raising such a difference.

Table 3.7 Sensitivity Analysis (Fixed and Random Effects)

	FIXED EFFECTS			RANDOM EFFECTS		
	(49) SO_2	(50) SOOT	(51) DUST	(52) SO_2	(53) SOOT	(54) DUST
Energy	78.926 (2.00)**	89.195 (2.93)***	546.637 (2.76)***	83.948 (3.09)***	61.998 (3.45)***	296.622 (2.15)**
PCI	0.00370 (0.51)	0.00147 (0.13)	0.0165 (0.59)	0.00629 (1.12)	0.00764 (0.71)	0.0378 (1.54)
HCI	0.281 (1.88)*	0.471 (2.47)**	1.631 (2.01)**	0.136 (1.42)	0.174 (1.04)	0.773 (1.61)
SIZE	1693.343 (0.75)	705.359 (0.30)	3051.211 (0.30)	-124.878 (-0.09)	-1575.353 (-0.74)	-11924.11 (-1.62)
TFPfe	-1711.963 (-1.77)*	-1413.098 (-1.47)	-1355.344 (-0.43)	-1073.529 (-2.38)**	-895.969 (-1.52)	-2472.552 (-1.49)
CAP	-1609.631 (-1.02)	85.993 (0.07)	-3425.235 (-0.89)	-2150.828 (-1.01)	-497.835 (-0.39)	-7090.221 (-1.16)

Continued

	FIXED EFFECTS			RANDOM EFFECTS		
	(49) SO_2	(50) SOOT	(51) DUST	(52) SO_2	(53) SOOT	(54) DUST
RD	-1226.224 (-0.79)	-1636.258 (-0.94)	-4863.782 (-0.77)	-1625.126 (-1.06)	-3117.453 (-1.85)*	-14450.34 (-1.98)**
REGpcy	1.022 (2.25)**	0.194 (0.50)	-0.698 (-0.74)	0.532 (1.56)	-0.0476 (-0.15)	-0.268 (-0.33)
R^2	0.554	0.138	0.404	0.350	0.329	0.328
n	105	105	105	105	105	105

Note: Our dependent variables are expressed in terms of pollution intensities, measured as emissions per unit of value added. t-statistics in parentheses for fixed effects and z-statistics in parentheses for random effects. Time dummies are included. * significant at 10% level; ** significant at 5% level; *** significant at 1% level.

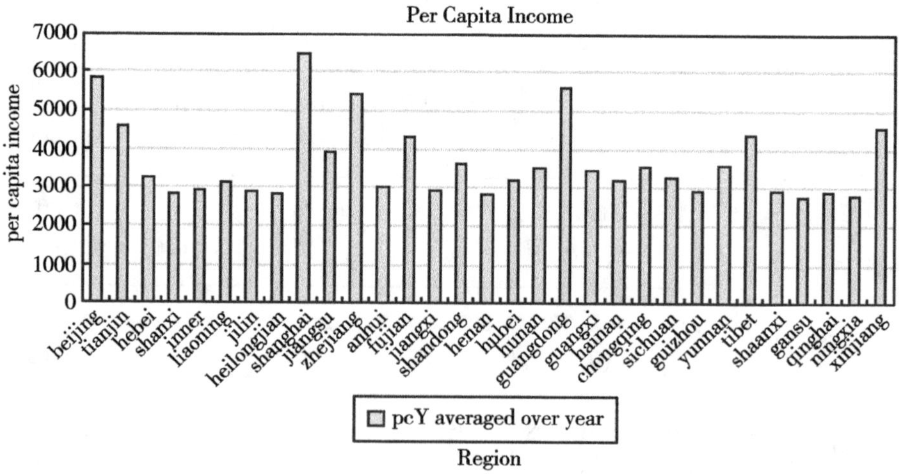

Figure 3.12 Income per capita for the 31 regions in China

Figure 3. 12 shows that, of 31 provinces in China, there are 8 provinces that have per capita income over RMB4000. Ruling out 2 less populated provinces in the West China (Tibet and Xinjiang), other provinces all locate in coastal regions (Shanghai, Guangdong, Zhejiang, Tianjing and Fujian) and Beijing (the capital of China). These high – income provinces are the centers of the Chinese economy and most developed, where all industries are likely to move to, therefore, it is not surprising these provinces are also pollution intensive. Meantime, according to the Environmental Kuznets Curve, income per capita in UK may have passed the turning point and pollution thus decreases along with an increase in income, but most provinces in China still remain on the left to the turning point and their pollution levels still increase along with an increase in income that explains why the estimate of per capita income in this research is different from the UK study.

Table 3. 8 reports the simultaneous estimations for three pollutants. A simple regression without fixed or random effects is performed through seemingly unrelated regression. There are a lot more significant estimates compared to the main results, but they are based on estimations that do not account for sector specific effects, which limits the reliability. The equality of estimates across pollutants are tested too. The hypothesis that the estimates are equal is rejected, therefore, it is reasonable to run regressions for each of pollutants, respectively.

Table 3.8 Simultaneous Estimation Results for Three Pollutants via Seemingly Unrelated Estimations (SUEST results)

	(55) SO_2	(56) SOOT	(57) DUST
Energy	93.4 (5.9)***	83.0 (3.65)***	412.6 (4.05)***
PCI	0.003 (0.46)	0.01 (2.35)**	0.05 (1.95)*
HCI	0.14 (1.17)	-0.23 (-2.10)**	-0.56 (-1.04)
SIZE	-5593.5 (-3.00)***	-491.8 (-0.31)	-7898.6 (-1.11)
TFPfe	-767.7 (-2.53)**	-1194.1 (-3.15)***	-4880.9 (-2.96)***
CAP	-1127.3 (-0.67)	564.8 (0.48)	-8000.1 (-1.69)*
RD	-4817.3 (-3.08)***	-7551.3 (-3.02)***	-39659.1 (-3.59)***
REGpros	592.0 (1.95)*	-51.1 (-0.17)	-968.9 (-0.73)
REGunem	2281.9 (2.99)***	1537.9 (4.06)***	5678.6 (3.19)***
REGpd	-1.0 (-3.75)***	-1.13 (-4.37)***	-4.9 (-3.78)***
REGagepop	404.1 (1.30)	278.2 (0.82)	1529.0 (0.94)
REGedu	-7193.8 (-5.75)***	-3179.3 (-2.52)**	-4650.1 (-0.78)

Continued

	(55) SO_2	(56) SOOT	(57) DUST
SO_2 & SOOT (*coefficients compared*)	140.1 (0.0)		
SO_2 & DUST (*coefficients compared*)	48.6 (0.0)		
SOOT & DUST (*coefficients compared*)	60.4 (0.0)		
n	105	105	105

Note: Seemingly unrelated estimation results are reported in the table using the STATA command 'SUEST'; Coefficients of estimations across pollutants are compared using the STATA command 'test'. Time dummies are included. * significant at 10% level; ** significant at 5% level; *** significant at 1% level.

3.7 Conclusions

This research carefully examines the possible factors that may impact on industrial pollution intensity in China. The results are expected to provide advices for both firms and regulators while they are seeking for a better environment in China.

A panel data of 15 industries from 1997 to 2003 has been employed to test the determinants of industrial pollution intensity. I find energy use, physical capital intensity and human capital intensity a positive determinant of pollution intensity, while productivity, the vintage of plants and expenditure on innovation are negative determinants. For three air pollutants, SO_2, SOOT and DUST, the average firm size of an industry is positively related to SO_2 intensity only.

The research captures the impact of environmental regulations using several regional characteristics that are likely to determine informal regulations. However, informal regulation variables do not work well using the Chinses data. Majority of regional variables are not statistically significant, but level of education is a significant determinant of SOOT and DUST intensity.

I conclude that, for both firms and pollution regulators in China, the best way to abate industry pollution is to save energy since energy use is a significant determinant of pollution intensity for all three pollutants. A firm can increase its productivity and improve energy efficiency. R&D expenditure also contributes to industry innovation because it improves energy efficiency. Overall, we have to acknowledge that China is in the middle of development and shall make remarkable improvement on all the determinants discussed above in near future.

Appendix

Table A3. 1 Data definitions and sources

Variable	Definition/Source
Pollution intensity	Emissions divided by gross value added (tons per 100 million yuan). Source: Industry section, China Statistical Yearbook.
Energy consumption	Total energy consumption per unit of value added, including consumption of coal, coke, crude oil, gasoline, kerosene, diesel oil, fuel oil, natural gas and electricity. Source: as above.

Continued

Variable	Definition/Source
Energy	Energy consumption divided by gross value added (10000 tons per 100 million yuan). Source: see individual sources for energy consumption and gross value added.
Gross value added	Gross value added by industry. 100 million yuan (1990 price). Source: Industry section, China Statistical Yearbook.
PCI	Physical capital intensity: Non – wage value added per worker ((VA – total wage)/number of staff). Source: wage and number of staff data from China Labour Statistical Yearbook.
PCIasset	Original value of fixed assets per worker. Source: Industry section, China Statistical Yearbook.
HCI	Human capital intensity: average wage by industry. Source: China Labour Statistical Yearbook.
HCImanf	An industry's average wage relative to the average manufacturing sector's wage. Source: as above.
SIZE	Value added per firm. 100 million yuan (1990 price). Source: as gross value added.
TFP	Total factor productivity. Source: data required to calculate TFP is from Industry section, China Statistical Yearbook.
TFPoutput	Gross output per worker. Source: as above.
CAP	Capital expenditure: investment in capital construction per unit of value added (100 million yuan of investment per 100 million yuan of value added). Source: as above.
RD	Research and development expenditure: investment in innovation per unit of value added, including innovation investment in new construction projects, expansion projects and reconstruction projects within an industry (100 million yuan of investment per 100 million yuan of value added). Source: as above.
REGpros	Regional pollution prosecution: administrative penalty case on pollution divided by region's GDP (1990 price). Source: China Environment Yearbook.

Continued

Variable	Definition/Source
REGunem	Regional unemployment rate. Source: China Labour Statistical Yearbook.
REGpd	Regional population density: total population divided by region's area. Source: Population section, China statistical Yearbook; area data from http://www.usacn.com.
REGagepop	Share of population under the age of 15: population under 15 divided by region's total population. Source: China Labour Statistical Yearbook.
REGedu	Regional level of education: population having acquired college or higher level of education divided by total population. Source: as above.
K	Physical capital stock: original value of fixed assets. Source: Industry section, China Statistical Yearbook.
L	Total labour force: total number of staff. Source: see above.

Table A3.2 The Determinants of Industrial Pollution with Energy dropped (Fixed and Random Effects)

	FIXED EFFECTS			RANDOM EFFECTS		
	(7) SO_2	(8) SOOT	(9) DUST	(10) SO_2	(11) SOOT	(12) DUST
PCI	0.0224 (1.91)*	0.0177 (1.22)	0.102 (1.96)*	0.0178 (2.13)**	0.0169 (1.41)	0.0781 (2.01)**
HCI	0.0614 (0.32)	0.411 (1.85)*	1.696 (1.79)*	0.118 (0.84)	0.231 (1.22)	1.201 (1.81)*
SIZE	2445.81 (0.98)	-468.69 (-0.16)	-7207.79 (-0.89)	-978.717 (-0.51)	-964.35 (-0.37)	-8315.22 (-1.06)

Continued

	FIXED EFFECTS			RANDOM EFFECTS		
	(7) SO_2	(8) SOOT	(9) DUST	(10) SO_2	(11) SOOT	(12) DUST
TFPfe	-2920.97 (-2.42)**	-2469.55 (-2.32)**	-7707.56 (-1.78)*	-2010.02 (-2.79)***	-1937.43 (-3.36)***	-7338.11 (-1.89)*
CAP	-35.710 (-0.04)	1269.43 (0.91)	3069.02 (0.64)	47.084 (0.03)	1271.73 (0.95)	1157.49 (0.27)
RD	208.15 (0.13)	-1160.51 (-0.57)	-4977.10 (-1.03)	-1308.86 (-0.87)	-2716.03 (-1.52)	-11322.74 (-1.72)*
REGpros	-506.20 (-1.13)	-322.68 (-0.74)	-1714.79 (-1.43)	-172.93 (-0.51)	-191.90 (-0.45)	-1257.50 (-1.52)
REGunem	-100.81 (-0.14)	-403.78 (-0.57)	-774.11 (-0.41)	1523.56 (1.44)	495.03 (0.86)	1485.74 (0.92)
REGpd	8.468 (2.81)***	4.627 (1.50)	12.070 (1.03)	-0.526 (-0.82)	0.0266 (0.03)	0.588 (0.20)
REGagepop	-323.17 (-0.81)	-123.31 (-0.27)	-968.28 (-0.75)	-460.28 (-1.67)*	-117.39 (-0.30)	-425.54 (-0.57)
REGedu	7299.50 (1.76)*	-58.67 (-0.02)	-10096.64 (-1.11)	-3063.54 (-1.31)	-4962.06 (-2.11)**	-18280.78 (-1.91)*
R^2	0.518	0.302	0.224	0.415	0.315	0.171
n	105	105	105	105	105	105

Note: Our dependent variables are expressed in terms of pollution intensities, measured as emissions per unit of value added t - statistics in parentheses for fixed effects and z - statistics in parentheses for random effects. Time dummies are included. * means significant at 10% level; ** means significant at 5% level; *** means significant at 1% level.

Table A3.3 Sector ranking for pollution intensity and average wage

Sector Rank	SO_2	SOOT	DUST	Average wage
1	361 + 362 + 369 Non – metallic mineral products	361 + 362 + 369 Non – metallic mineral products	361 + 362 + 369 Non – metallic mineral products	353 Petroleum processing and coking
2	372 Non – ferrous metals	341 Paper and products	371 Iron and steel	371 Iron and steel
3	341 Paper and products	372 Non – ferrous metals	351 Industrial chemicals	372 Non – ferrous metals
4	371 Iron and steel	351 Industrial chemicals	372 Non – ferrous metals	352 Other chemicals
5	351 Industrial chemicals	371 Iron and steel	341 Paper and products	382 + 383 + 384 + 385 Machinery except electrical and machinery electric, Transport equipment, and Professional and scientific equipment
6	353 Petroleum processing and coking	353 Petroleum processing and coking	353 Petroleum processing and coking	351 Industrial chemicals
7	352 Other chemicals	352 Other chemicals	381 Fabricated metal products	342 Printing and publishing

Note: Rank is in a descending order. SO_2, SOOT and DUST denote emissions per unit of value added for SO_2, SOOT and DUST respectively.

Table A3.4 Sensitivity Analysis (PCI is defined as original value of fixed assets)

	FIXED EFFECTS			RANDOM EFFECTS		
	(13) SO_2	(14) SOOT	(15) DUST	(16) SO_2	(17) SOOT	(18) DUST
Energy	98.79 (2.58)**	91.71 (3.21)***	576.95 (2.73)***	97.088 (3.84)***	72.376 (4.31)***	345.16 (2.49)**
PCIasset	-15.946 (-0.55)	-22.59 (-0.49)	95.97 (0.76)	3.937 (0.18)	-19.95 (-0.60)	-114.48 (-1.47)
HCI	0.0921 (0.57)	0.428 (2.12)**	1.707 (2.09)**	0.0993 (0.89)	0.204 (1.18)	0.611 (1.12)
SIZE	4817.01 (1.85)*	1947.93 (0.65)	2445.51 (0.21)	-2617 (-1.26)	-495.56 (-0.18)	-3549.26 (-0.43)
TFPfe	-1683.90 (-1.77)*	-1425.16 (-1.52)	-1190.89 (-0.38)	-753.14 (-2.01)**	-947.85 (-1.94)*	-3295.34 (-2.11)**
CAP	-1668.76 (-1.19)	-342.54 (-0.23)	-2640.66 (-0.59)	-2342.35 (-0.99)	-731.83 (-0.54)	-8753.48 (-1.37)
RD	-676.59 (-0.45)	-1843.55 (-1.03)	-8296.25 (-1.26)	-3844.49 (-2.38)**	-4489.06 (-2.67)***	-23394.53 (-2.32)**
REGpros	-236.79 (-0.67)	-78.38 (-0.19)	-800.09 (-0.76)	85.564 (0.32)	14.299 (0.04)	-263.38 (-0.27)
REGunem	193.52 (0.30)	-126.89 (-0.19)	1009.58 (0.64)	1304.48 (1.55)	246.33 (0.46)	1279.30 (0.99)
REGpd	5.156 (2.33)**	1.704 (0.60)	-4.879 (-0.65)	-0.857 (-1.78)*	-0.255 (-0.36)	-1.990 (-1.08)
REGagapop	9.503 (0.02)	177.27 (0.41)	705.88 (0.54)	299.210 (0.90)	418.46 (1.13)	2268.23 (1.73)*

Continued

	FIXED EFFECTS			RANDOM EFFECTS		
	(13) SO_2	(14) SOOT	(15) DUST	(16) SO_2	(17) SOOT	(18) DUST
REGedu	6728.855 (1.76)*	-702.46 (-0.22)	-15908.17 (-1.54)	-5086.32 (-2.60)**	-5134.78 (-2.40)**	-16115.01 (-1.95)*
R^2	0.600	0.393	0.421	0.735	0.500	0.494
n	105	105	105	105	105	105

Note: Our dependent variables are expressed in terms of pollution intensities, measured as emissions per unit of value added t-statistics in parentheses for fixed effects and z-statistics in parentheses for random effects. Time dummies are included. * means significant at 10% level; ** means significant at 5% level; *** means significant at 1% level.

Table A3.5 Sensitivity Analysis (HCI is defined as an industry's wage relative to the average manufacturing sector's wage)

	FIXED EFFECTS			RANDOM EFFECTS		
	(19) SO_2	(20) SOOT	(21) DUST	(22) SO_2	(23) SOOT	(24) DUST
Energy	93.138 (2.52)**	89.914 (3.11)***	535.753 (2.60)**	97.683 (3.22)***	75.662 (4.08)***	362.826 (2.42)**
PCI	0.00867 (0.85)	0.0101 (0.71)	0.0565 (1.20)	0.00754 (0.99)	0.0120 (1.07)	0.0476 (1.66)*
HCImanf	1155.95 (0.94)	1457.56 (1.02)	4238.17 (1.00)	-276.37 (-0.32)	-920.42 (-0.91)	-5551.99 (-1.65)
SIZE	4236.04 (1.85)*	3618.4 (1.43)	13335.62 (1.20)	102.15 (0.05)	1371.41 (0.62)	3241.98 (0.66)

Continued

	FIXED EFFECTS			RANDOM EFFECTS		
	(19) SO_2	(20) SOOT	(21) DUST	(22) SO_2	(23) SOOT	(24) DUST
TFPfe	-2173.28 (-1.92)*	-1507.67 (-1.42)	-1936.12 (-0.60)	-813.63 (-1.76)*	-878.39 (-1.48)	-2491.05 (-1.72)*
CAP	-1177.06 (-0.95)	265.74 (0.19)	-3117.42 (-0.78)	-2177.33 (-0.97)	-315.50 (-0.24)	-7030.94 (-1.22)
RD	-374.52 (-0.28)	-1119.21 (-0.58)	-4853.82 (-0.81)	-2884.25 (-2.40)**	-3401.08 (-1.98)**	-17193.73 (-2.09)**
REGpros	-258.22 (-0.80)	-52.34 (-0.12)	-430.05 (-0.41)	-178.19 (-0.58)	-277.24 (-0.67)	-1633.12 (-1.75)*
REGunem	198.84 (0.31)	-225.08 (-0.33)	486.74 (0.30)	1134.26 (1.47)	490.03 (0.90)	2251.44 (1.53)
REGpd	5.480 (2.07)**	3.201 (1.08)	2.742 (0.28)	-0.479 (-0.74)	-0.385 (-0.49)	-2.839 (-1.18)
REGagapop	-49.71 (-0.13)	303.08 (0.70)	1253.31 (0.94)	88.48 (0.24)	316.36 (0.81)	1735.49 (1.37)
REGedu	5934.97 (1.65)	-1897.27 (-0.58)	-19984.18 (-1.72)*	-1729.28 (-0.86)	-3726.84 (-1.57)	-9334.15 (-1.35)
R^2	0.609	0.373	0.397	0.597	0.579	0.532
n	105	105	105	105	105	105

Note: Our dependent variables are expressed in terms of pollution intensities, measured as emissions per unit of value added t-statistics in parentheses for fixed effects and z-statistics in parentheses for random effects. Time dummies are included. * means significant at 10% level; ** means significant at 5% level; *** means significant at 1% level.

Table A3.6 Sensitivity Analysis (TFP is defined as gross output per worker)

	FIXED EFFECTS			RANDOM EFFECTS		
	(25) SO_2	(26) SOOT	(27) DUST	(28) SO_2	(29) SOOT	(30) DUST
Energy	116.849 (2.96) ***	109.13 (3.90) ***	581.599 (2.80) ***	105.098 (3.37) ***	81.559 (5.13) ***	375.311 (2.22) **
PCI	0.0143 (0.97)	0.0101 (0.55)	0.0711 (1.30)	0.00076 (0.06)	0.00293 (0.18)	0.0445 (1.33)
HCI	-0.0192 (-0.12)	0.344 (1.65)	1.546 (2.07) **	0.0347 (0.34)	0.0951 (0.54)	1.016 (1.91) *
SIZE	5640.15 (1.72) *	2497.78 (0.78)	9270.73 (0.81)	-798.68 (-0.40)	-1447.77 (-0.55)	-7706.11 (-0.93)
TFPoutput	-46.38 (-1.39)	-39.27 (-0.98)	-154.17 (-1.36)	-6.109 (-0.21)	-13.359 (-0.36)	-90.15 (-0.89)
CAP	-1759.30 (-1.24)	-305.16 (-0.22)	-4636.10 (-1.06)	-2522.42 (-1.06)	-948.97 (-0.71)	-7755.31 (-1.15)
RD	-1211.16 (-0.89)	-2366.86 (-1.21)	-9305.54 (-1.41)	-2978.94 (-2.04) **	-3973.43 (-2.19) **	-16844.54 (-2.09) **
REGpros	-71.49 (-0.20)	45.62 (0.12)	-616.67 (-0.62)	65.274 (0.21)	175.23 (0.46)	-108.76 (-0.11)
REGunem	232.13 (0.32)	-77.44 (-0.11)	1399.51 (0.81)	981.13 (1.17)	296.13 (0.51)	191.26 (0.16)
REGpd	5.106 (2.21) **	1.533 (0.51)	-3.512 (-0.45)	-0.488 (-0.73)	-0.325 (-0.48)	0.568 (0.21)
REGagapop	-18.93 (-0.05)	162.31 (0.37)	544.49 (0.44)	157.46 (0.43)	473.31 (1.21)	1842.66 (1.29)

Continued

	FIXED EFFECTS			RANDOM EFFECTS		
	(25) SO_2	(26) SOOT	(27) DUST	(28) SO_2	(29) SOOT	(30) DUST
REGedu	5972.17 (1.57)	-1294.05 (-0.40)	-15862.34 (-1.57)	-1645.13 (-0.68)	-4379.88 (-2.10) **	1842.66 (1.29)
R^2	0.587	0.382	0.427	0.561	0.471	0.300
n	105	105	105	105	105	105

Note: Our dependent variables are expressed in terms of pollution intensities, measured as emissions per unit of value added t - statistics in parentheses for fixed effects and z - statistics in parentheses for random effects. Time dummies are included. * means significant at 10% level; ** means significant at 5% level; *** means significant at 1% level.

Chapter 4

The Relationship Between Environmental Specialization and Industrial Specialization in China

4.1 Introduction

Since environmental quality in terms of pollution levels has improved in developed countries such as the United States, some US scholars have began to investigate other related environmental problems. Environmental specialization is an issue that has emerged thereafter and has been discussed by some US scholars (e.g. Millimet and Slottje, 2003). If pollution levels continue to decline, the *composition* of the remaining pollution may be as important in the determination of environmental risks as the *level* of pollution, in other words, given a decreasing level of total pollution, exposure to a certain amount of pollution of similar type or category may cause more health risks than exposure to the same amount of pollution of a large number of types or categories. The composition of pollution thus can be measured in terms of environmental specialization. Considering two regions both with a decreasing level of total pollution, in one region the composition of the remaining pollution is of similar type whilst in the other region the composition of the remaining pollution is of several different types, environmental specialization in the former region is therefore greater than that in the latter one and the former region is more likely to suffer detrimental health effects.

I aim to examine the environmental specialization in China although the aggregate level of pollution in China has not declined so far. Since an increase in industrial specialization may result in an increase in environmental specialization (e. g. Millimet and Slottje, 2003) and the evidence in this research shows an increasing level of industrial specialization in China, the environmental specialization may be therefore increasing along with a rising level of aggregate pollution.

Chapter Four begins with an explanation from a scientific perspective on why environmental specialization is worth investigating. A recently updated (global update 2005) summary of risk assessment from WHO (World Health Organization) provides the air guidelines for several air pollutants. The WHO air quality guidelines are designed to offer guidance for reducing the health impacts of air pollution. Based on a review of the accumulated scientific evidence, the revised guideline for the most common air pollutants are presented in this summary. These guidelines are applicable across all WHO regions and provide policy – makers with the targets of air quality and various options of air quality management in different parts of the world. These guidelines are one of the motives that I may undertake research on environmental specialization.

Other literatures also demonstrate two scientific reasons why environmental specialization is important. The first reason is the threshold effect that refers to the minimum level of toxins to which humans may be exposed before suffering side effects (e. g. Dohll, 1996; Chestnut *et al.*, 1991). The second one refers to the non – linear damage functions that indicate a relationship between harmful outcomes and exposure levels. Such a relationship is assumed to follow an S – shaped curve and individuals in the US are likely confined to the bottom of the *S* (Chay and Greenstone, 2003; Doull, 1996; Chestnut *et al.*, 1991), however, it is unknown so far if individuals in developing countries are also confined to the bottom of the *S*. For all of these reasons, any exposure to a similar type of pollutant may increase the risk of harm to health.

The existing literature also argues that the most likely contributor to environmental specialization is industrial specialization, and there has been evidence suggesting a strong positive relationship between environmental and industrial specialization in the US (Millimet and Slottje, 2003). Many studies on regional specialization and national economic integration provide evidence that industrial specialization has been rising in China over time (Lu and Tao, 2005; Liang and Xu, 2004; Naughton, 2000; Brun and Renard, 2001), but whether such a rising industrial specialization results in an increase in environmental specialization in China needs further studies.

This chapter uses the Chinese provincial level data to estimate both environmental and industrial specialization. There are one major data sample of 28 provinces and two sub - samples, one covers 10 East coast provinces and the other one covers the remaining 18 provinces. The sample period is from 1997 to 2003. I employ four specialization measures: two relative measures, index 1 and index 2, and two absolute measures, the Herfindahl index and the Coefficient of Absolute Regional Specialization (CARS). The environmental specialization index is estimated using emissions of five pollutants including wastewater discharges, solid waste discharges, sulphur dioxide (SO_2) emissions, SOOT emissions, and DUST emissions, whilst the industrial specialization index is estimated using output of 15 three - digit ISIC manufacturing sectors in China. Regressions employ environmental specialization indices as dependent variables and industrial specialization indices and several other control variables as explanatory variables, and focus on the linkage between industrial and environmental specialization. Results suggest that although no strong relationship between environmental specialization and industrial specialization is found using sample of all provinces, it is found to be significant using a sample of 10 East coast provinces as well as a sample of the remaining 18 provinces.

The remainder of this chapter is organized as follows: Section 2 reviews the literature; Section 3 provides methodologies of estimating the specialization index; Section 4 examines the status of environmental specialization and industrial specialization in China through both graphical and empirical analysis; Section 5 explains econometric specifications including data considerations; Section 6 and Section 7 provide the main results and results of sensitivity checks and Section 8 concludes.

4.2 Literature Review

This research reviews relevant literature in three aspects: pollution and health, industrial specialization and environmental specialization.

4.2.1 Pollution & Health

Clean air is one of the basics for human health and well – being. However, air pollution continues to increase and pose a significant threat to the health worldwide. According to WHO assessment on the disease consequences caused by air pollution, every year more than 2 million premature deaths are caused by urban outdoor and indoor air pollution (from burning solid fuels). Population of developing countries have taken a burden of more than half of the disease consequences.

There is new evidence of health impacts available for particular matter (PM), ozone (O_3), nitrogen dioxide (NO_2) and sulfur dioxide (SO_2) in updated WHO air quality guidelines. Air borne particulate matter (PM) has shown side effects of health on urban populations in both developed and developing countries. The risk of exposure may vary with the health conditions or age, and there is little evidence of the threshold below which no side effects occur. In fact, the concentration that may cause side effects is estimated to be smaller than 2. 5μm for $PM_{2.5}$ and it is around 3 – 5μg/m^3 in US and Western Europe.

Moreover, the epidemiological research finds evidence for side effects of PM as a consequence of both short – term and long – term exposure. It is an annual average concentration of 10μg/m^3 as the long – term guideline value for $PM_{2.5}$, which is based on the long – term exposure studies using ACS and Harvard Six – Cities data (Dockery et al. , 1993; Pope et al. , 1995; HEI, 2000, Pope et al. , 2002, Jerrett, 2005). The short – term exposure studies report that mortality rate is 0. 62% per 10μg/m^3 of PM_{10} (24 – hour mean) in Europe and 0. 46% per 10μg/m^3 of PM_{10} in US, and a meta – analysis out of Europe and US shows a mortality rate of 0. 5% per 10μg/m^3, similar to Asian cities where it is 0. 49% per 10μg/m^3.

The second edition of the WHO air quality guidelines for Europe sets a guideline value of 120μg/m^3 on an 8 – hour daily average for ozone, but has little information about the health impact of ozone from chamber studies or field studies. Rather, more significant evidence come from epidemiological time – series studies, which suggest positive, small though convincing, associations between daily mortality and ozone levels and the guideline value of ozone concentration should be lower than 120μg/m^3. And evidence from both chamber and field studies suggest reducing the WHO air quality guideline value of ozone from the current level of 120μg/m^3 to 100μg/m^3 (daily maximum 8 – hour mean).

The current WHO guideline value of NO_2 concentration is set to be 40μg/m^3 (annual mean). Epidemiological studies find that bronchitic symptoms of asthmatic children have increased in association with annual NO_2 concentration, and the growth of children's lung function has been stunted due to elevated NO_2 concentration. However, there is not enough scientific evidence available to revise WHO current long – term guideline value for annual NO_2 concentrations.

Early epidemiological studies provide estimates of day – to – day changes in mortality, morbidity or lung function in relation to 24 – hour average concentrations of SO_2. It is difficult to separate impacts of individual pollutants on observed health outcomes, prior to 1987, the guideline value of SO_2 concentration was correlated to the value of PM and it was set to be 125μg/m^3 on a 24 – hour average, but in the second edition of the WHO air quality guidelines for Europe (WHO, 2000), the guideline value was separated and set to be 125μg/m^3 (24 – hour mean) for SO_2. One study in Hong Kong (Hedley et al., 2002) finds a reduction in the sulfur content of fuels has been achieved in a very short time of period and it has substantially relieved the side impact of diseases on health, such as childhood respiratory disease and all – age mortality. Time – series studies about hospital admissions for cardiac diseases in Hong Kong and London find no threshold effect of 24 – hour SO_2 concentrations (Wong et al., 2002). Burnett et al. (2004) find an association between 24 – hour SO_2 concentration of 5μg/m^3 and daily mortality rates in 12 Canadian cities. The American Cancer Society (ACS) study finds a significant association between SO_2 concentration of 18μg/m^3 and mortality for the 1982 – 1998 cohort in 126 US metropolitan areas (Pope et al., 2002).

Scientific evidence shows no clear threshold effect on health for classical air pollutants. If there were a threshold effect, it would have to be very low levels of concentration. However, WHO suggests guideline values for each pollutant to protect the public health, which motivates the research in this chapter. A specialization in one type of pollutant may cause the level of concentration higher than the suggested guideline values, whilst a mixture of pollution is less likely to go over the guideline values of concentration. Therefore, it is expected that environmental specialization would be more detrimental than emissions of mixed pollutants.

There are, on the other hand, some early scientific literatures that have found strong evidence of threshold effect. The word 'threshold' appears in Doull (1996) for the first time, and the scientific article uses the science of toxicology to improve our understanding of several environmental diseases such as multiple chemical sensitivity, the Gulf War or Desert Storm syndrome, and sick or tight building effects. Toxicology helps identify all possible side effects after exposure to a chemical in a biological system. Because certain chemicals may generate side health effect at high - dose exposures, toxicologists thus have to understand the full range of dose - responses and characterize all side effects of a chemical.

One cardinal principle proposed in Doull (1996) is that no such a thing like a non - toxic chemical exists, but the other side of the rule is that no chemical that cannot be used safely. All have to do is to reduce the exposure to the point at which the side effect can no longer be distinguished from background effects and the point is referred to as the threshold. The traditional toxicological approach to risk assessment is based on dose response and uses thresholds and safety factors to establish tolerances and acceptable levels of chemical exposure. The use of this approach has been and continues to be the major practical application of the risk assessment paradigm for regulating environmental exposure to chemicals in the workplace as well as in food, air, water, and elsewhere. Many regulatory groups in US and other countries such as FDA (Food and Drug Administration), EPA (Environmental Protection Agency), and OSHA (The Occupational Safety and Health Administration) and professional groups such as the Committee on Toxicology of the National Academy of Sciences, the TLV (Threshold Limit Value) committee of the American Conference of Governmental Hygienists, and other groups have adopted and validated this process.

Chestnut *et al.* (1991) is another valuable scientific study that examines the relationship between the level of ambient particulate matter and pulmonary function in adults across 49 cities in US using epidemiological evidence from NHANES I. (First National Health and Nutrition Examination Survey). Pulmonary function is an index specific to respiratory health and two measures of this function are defined as the forced vital capacity (FVC) and forced expiratory volume at one second (FEV. sub. 1. 0), respectively both measures are found to decrease for individuals who have restrictive or obstructive lung diseases. A graphical technique shows a smoothed curve of the linear relationship between FVC and level of TSP in never – smokers, after controlling for covariates, which clearly indicate a nonlinear relationship, a similar curve is obtained [FEV. sub. 1. 0]. It also shows no relationship between FVC and level of TSP when TSP levels are low and a negative relationship between FVC and level of TSP when TSP levels are high enough to reach the specific point called threshold point. Following the curve that indicates an S – shaped relationship, a nonlinear regression where the relationship between the log of FVC/ [FEV. sub. 1.0] and TSP is estimated, and the estimate of TSP are statistically significant, suggesting a non – linear damage functions and providing another scientific reason for a study on the environmental specialization.

Chay and Greenstone (2003) also examine the threshold and nonlinearities in the pollution – infant mortality relationship in US. They observed the impact of year 1981 – 1982 recession on reducing suspended particulates pollution in heavily industrialized sites, such as Pittsburgh, PA, where many manufacturing plants were shut down. Regions without pollution – intensive manufacturing or without such manufacturing nearby experienced minimal pollution changes. The variety of pollution improvement allows researchers to take nonlinear or threshold studies on the relationship between pollution and infant mortality, and researchers find quite obvious discontinuities and thresholds for health effects of particulates pollution.

4.2.2 Industrial Specialization

Given the possible relationship between industrial specialization and environmental specialization, several literatures on industrial specialization need discussion. Kalemi – Ozcan *et al.* (2003) test an important theoretical proposition that risk sharing enhances specialization of production. A great specialization of production can be accomplished by spreading risk of production, and is more easily achieved in regions where financial markets are developed and reliable. Previous studies find that if risk sharing is important for specialization, one would expect states in US, regions of Spain, Italy, and UK, Canadian provinces, and Japanese prefectures to be more specialized than EC, OECD, or Latin American countries. The empirical work in this article confirmed the above hypothesis. Researchers use a large data set that combines all the above countries and regions and find risk sharing and industrial specialization are positively correlated. According to a new report from IIF (The Institute of International Finance, Inc.), due in part to improvements in corporate governance in China, foreign direct investment continues to flow into China and it has been joined by rising levels of international portfolio equity investments, which may cause higher specialization of production in China.

Wren and Taylor (1999) examine the regional specialization of UK employment using an absolute regional specialization index (CARS). A large value of this index indicates a narrow spread of employment across industries and hence great absolute specialization is necessary. The estimates show that UK has become more specialized over time. The index could also be applied to estimate the specialization in developing countries such as China.

The Chinese specialization studies have been focusing on industrial agglomeration and regional specializations. Lu and Tao (2005) use firm level data with more than 160000 industrial firms from 1998 to 2003 to investigate regional specialization in China. Output of these firms accounts for a large percentage of total industrial output in China. They find the specialization pattern of coastal region is quite different from the that in the inland and West China, and there has been an increase of regional specialization in most Chinese provinces from

1998 to 2003, in which the greatest specialization presents in coastal provinces. Lu and Tao (2006) use the same data to estimate the spatial concentration of manufacturing industries in China. They use a very important specialization index, namely Herfindahl index, in which Table 4.1 reports their estimates of Herfindahl index across 29 manufacturing sectors in 1998 and 2003. By comparison, it has seen an increase in the specialization of 14 sectors and a decrease of the other sectors. Sectors that have changed most significantly in their specialization are highlighted in bold, and most of them are machinery and equipment related, there are some dirty sectors as well such as Paper and paper products and Medicine. Lu and Tao (2006) suggests that the Chinese industry is experiencing a deepening specialization in most high – tech manufacturing sectors and a few pollution – intensive sectors.

Table 4.1 Herfindahl Index for 29 industry sectors in China (1998 and 2003)

Industry	H_i 1998	H_i 2003	Change
Communication equipment and computers	0.0080	0.0057	-0.0024
Culture, education and sport activity goods	0.0031	0.0023	-0.0009
Leather, fur, feather and related products	0.0022	0.0020	-0.0002
Chemical fibres	0.0234	0.0147	-0.0086
Textile	0.0005	0.0009	0.0004
Transportation equipment	**0.0089**	**0.0100**	**0.0010**
Furniture	0.0028	0.0025	-0.0004

Continued

Industry	H_i 1998	H_i 2003	Change
Measuring instruments and machinery for office work	**0.0089**	**0.0094**	**0.0005**
Electrical machinery and equipment	0.0037	0.0041	0.0004
Rubber	**0.0077**	**0.0082**	**0.0005**
Apparel, footwear and caps	0.0010	0.0008	-0.0002
Timber, wood, bamboo, rattan, palm, and straw	0.0034	0.0018	-0.0016
Other manufacturing	0.0018	0.0017	-0.0001
Smelting and pressing of ferrous metals	0.0129	0.0092	-0.0037
Processing of food from agricultural products	0.0009	0.0012	0.0004
Smelting and pressing of non-ferrous metals	0.0044	0.0035	-0.0009
Paper and paper products	**0.0014**	**0.0029**	**0.0016**
Non-metallic mineral products	0.0004	0.0005	0.0001
Foods	**0.0020**	**0.0034**	**0.0014**
Printing, and preproduction of reproducing media	0.0022	0.0020	-0.0001
Plastics	0.0009	0.0010	0.0001
General purpose machinery	**0.0013**	**0.0018**	**0.0005**
Special purpose machinery	0.0018	0.0021	0.0003
Medicines	**0.0028**	**0.0033**	**0.0006**
beverage	**0.0035**	**0.0071**	**0.0036**
Mental products	0.0008	0.0007	-0.0001
Raw chemical materials and chemical products	0.0025	0.0023	-0.0002
Processing of petroleum, coking	0.0262	0.0183	-0.0079
Tobacco	0.0330	0.0230	-0.0100

Note: sectors with the largest value of change in specialization are highlighted in bold.

Liang and Xu (2004) specifically examine a region's comparative advantage as a determinant of regional specialization using a panel data of 20 major industrial sectors across 29 Chinese provinces from 1988 to 2001. They find an increasing level of industrial specialization due to China's economic openness, and level of specialization is positively related to the sector's technical efficiency. They also find that, the industrial specialization is likely to remain at high levels in regions that present an increasing return to scale. Their research therefore concludes that industries with high value – added and up – graded technologies are highly specialized in coastal regions, while inland regions, originally less industrialized, contain more energy intensive sectors as well as production sectors of energy and raw materials.

Some other studies focus on the national economic integration in China. Using input – output tables from the Chinese provinces, Naughton (2000) shows that inter – provincial trade in 1992 was in fact larger than that of 1987. Moreover, Naughton (2000) reports a rise in regional level of specialization in 1992 compared to that in 1987 because the growth of inter – provincial trade from 1987 to 1992 is greater than the growth of provincial GDP as well as the growth of foreign trade. Brun and Renard (2001) examine the effect of international openness on regional specialization in China. They construct an Isard coefficient, a simple type of Krugman specialization index, to measure the specialization of provinces. Using data from 1988 to 1994, they find an increasing specialization for most of the Chinese provinces. Their empirical results show that China's openness raises the level of specialization across regions, that is, along with a growing opening, regions in China are more encouraged to exploit economies of scale and engage in specialized production.

4.2.3 Environmental Specialization

To the best of my knowledge, there has been only one paper that has investigated the relationship between environmental specialization and industrial specialization so far. Millimet and Slottje (2003) proposed that environmental specialization is important due to the threshold effect and convex damage functions, both of which imply that given a decreasing level of total pollution, the composition of the remaining pollution may be as important as total pollution in determining health outcomes. They also argue that industrial specialization is the most likely contributor to the environmental specialization. They use four specialization indices to measure environmental specialization and industrial specialization. In their models, environmental specialization, the dependent variable, is regressed on industrial specialization, the independent variable, keeping per capita income and per capita income square, population and population squared, and manufacturing sector size as control variables. Using US data, they find, regardless of the index used, an increase of industrial specialization significantly raises the environmental specialization.

4.3 Measurement of Specialization

Jackson (1984) briefly review several diversity measures, including three diversity measures that are widely applied. First, it is the national average that refers to a sum of the regional deviations from the national average for individual industry, the larger the sum of these deviations, the greater the industrial specialization is, or the lower the industrial diversity is. Secondly, it is the ogive measure that assumes, for a region to be diverse, there should be an equal percentage of regional employment for individual industry. Deviations from equal percentage are interpreted as specialization. Thirdly, it is the percentage of employment in durable goods production that could indicate region's reliance on export income, hence, it is sensitive to the fluctuation of the national economy. ①

Jackson (1984) states that each of these measures is normative, every region, regardless of resource advantages, development of infrastructure, agglomeration of economy, or factor endowments, should conform to that norm. The reference scenario of the national average measure is that, if the national economy is diverse across industries, the diversity of employment across industries in a region should replicate the national pattern. The reference scenario of the ogive technique is that, the concentration of employment is equal across industries in a given region. Lastly, the percentage of production of durable goods as a measure of diversity indicates that there is an optimal concentration of employment for production of durable goods in every region.

However, it is argued that the national average, ogive, and durable goods measures are overly simplistic and naive. It is clearly a

① Durable goods are characterized by a high – income elasticity of demand. In economic downturn, consumers are less likely to purchase such goods.

naive assumption (e. g. Thirlwall, A. P, 1966; Hewings, G. J. D, 1982) that each industry (or set of industries) is equally important to a given economy. Therefore, Jackson (1984) proposed the fourth measure of industry diversity, the portfolio theoretic approach, which represents a departure from normative measures through accounting for intraregional - intersectoral employment relationships that consider regional factor endowments. Empirical results contradict each other in terms of different measures, therefore, using a variety of measures literally complicates the issue of industrial diversity.

Given the arguments in Jackson (1984) and others, a concern has been raised about the robustness of various specialization measures. In this research I employ several specialization indices for comparison as well as for checking robustness.

4. 3. 1 Industrial Specialization Measures

The research estimates four specialization indices and the first two are quoted from Kalemli - Ozcan *et al.* (2003). The first measure, the squared deviation index, is given by:

$$I - spec_{it}^{1} = \sum_{s=1}^{S} \left(\frac{GDP_{it}^{S}}{GDP_{it}^{M}} - \frac{1}{J-1} \sum_{j \neq 1} \frac{GDP_{jt}^{S}}{GDP_{jt}^{M}} \right)^2 \qquad (4-1)$$

where S is total number of sectors and J is total number of regions in the group. GDP_{it}^{S} denotes the GDP of sector s in region i at time t, and GDP_{it}^{M} denotes the total manufacturing GDP of the given region. Industrial specialization of a region is therefore measured by the distance between the vector of sector shares in region i's manufacturing GDP, $GDP_{it}^{S}/GDP_{it}^{M}$, and the vector of average sector shares across the regions other than i. The larger the sum of these deviations, the greater is the industrial specialization, or the lower is the industrial diversity.

The second index is the absolute deviation index, given by:

$$I - spec_{it}^{2} = \sum_{s=1}^{S} \left| \frac{GDP_{it}^{S}}{GDP_{it}^{M}} - \frac{1}{J-1} \sum_{j \neq 1} \frac{GDP_{jt}^{S}}{GDP_{jt}^{M}} \right|^{2} \qquad (4-2)$$

where it measures the absolute deviation between a vector of output shares and a vector of mean output shares averaged on all regions except for region*i*. In this index, extreme values are less weighted.

Index (4 - 1) and (4 - 2) compare a region's shares of industries to the share in the whole nation, and the estimates range from 0 to 1, where 0 indicates equal share of industries in the region and 1 indicates that there is only one industry in the region. Wren and Taylor (1999) point out, one default of these two measures is that they both discuss how regional economy changes relative to the national pattern, but do not discuss how regional economy changes by itself (i. e. in absolute terms). Therefore, I use another two absolute measures of specialization to complement the study.

The first absolute measure is a Herfindahl - type index. According to the definition of OECD, the Herfindahl Index is a measure of industrial concentration. The index is valued by the sum of the squares of the market shares of all firms in an industry. Higher values indicate greater concentration. For instance, there are two industries, one industry whose four firms have equal share and the other industry in which one firm has 70 percent share and three others 10 percent each. The former, which is more competitive, would have a lower Herfindahl Index. However, in this research, I compute the Herfindahl index at regional level. A given region with equal shares of industrial output across sectors has lower values of Herfindahl index while another region with highly unequal shares of industrial output across sectors has much larger Herfindahl index. The Herdindahl Index is given by equation (3) and a large value indicate greater industrial specialization in the region:

$$I-spec_{it}^{H}=\sum_{s=1}^{S}\left(\frac{GDP_{it}^{S}}{GDP_{it}^{M}}\right)^{2} \tag{4-3}$$

where GDP_{it}^{S} denotes the GDP of sector s in region i at time t, and GDP_{it}^{M} denotes the total manufacturing GDP of this region.

The second absolute measure, the Coefficient of Absolute Regional Specialization (CARS), is derived from Wren and Taylor (1999). It is based on the coefficient of variation and has an advantage over the absolute deviations because it allows a decomposition of the index. The coefficient of variation is estimated in terms of the standard deviation divided by the mean, and the CARS is therefore given by:

$$I-spec_{it}^{CARS}=\frac{\sqrt{\frac{1}{S-1}\sum_{s=1}^{S}\left\{GDP_{it}^{S}-\sum_{S=1}^{S}\left(\frac{GDP_{it}^{S}}{S}\right)\right\}^{2}}}{\sum_{s=1}^{S}\left(\frac{GDP_{it}^{S}}{S}\right)}\equiv\frac{\sigma_{it}}{\mu_{it}} \tag{4-4}$$

where the numerator is the standard deviation of the output of all industries and the denominator is the mean output level averaged on all industries.

To conclude, I estimate each index of industrial specialization at regional level, and a large value of each index indicates less industrial diversity in the region, in other words, a given region that is more likely to specialize in fewer industrial sectors would have large values of specialization indices and vice versa.

4.3.2 Environmental Specialization Measures

I use the same four specialization indices to measure environmental specialization as well. However, when applying these indices to estimate environmental specialization, the key variable involved has become a region's level of pollution. The first index, the squared deviation index, is defined as:

$$P - spec_{it}^{1} = \sum_{p=1}^{P}\left(\frac{E_{it}^{P}}{E_{it}} - \frac{1}{J-1}\sum_{j\neq i}\frac{E_{jt}^{P}}{E_{jt}}\right)^{2} \tag{4-5}$$

where P is total number of pollutants, E_{it}^{P} is the level of emissions of pollutant p in region i at time t, and E_{it} is total emissions in region i at time t. The index indicates the squared distance between a vector of pollution shares and a vector of mean pollution shares averaged on all regions except for region i.

The second index is the absolute deviation index:

$$P - spec_{it}^{2} = \sum_{p=1}^{P}\left|\frac{E_{it}^{p}}{E_{it}} - \frac{1}{J-1}\sum_{j\neq i}\frac{E_{jt}^{p}}{E_{jt}}\right| \tag{4-6}$$

where it indicates the absolute deviation between a vector of pollution shares and a vector of mean pollution shares averaged on all regions except for region i. Both relative specialization indices vary from 0 to 1, where 0 means the region has emitted equal share of pollutants and 1 means there is only one pollutant emitted in the region.

Two absolute measures of specialization, the Herfindahl Index and CARS, are employed as well. The Herfindahl Index is the sum of the squared share of each pollutant:

$$P - spec_{it}^{H} = \sum_{p=1}^{P}\left(\frac{E_{it}^{p}}{E_{it}}\right)^{2} \tag{4-7}$$

where E_{it}^{P} is the level of emissions of pollutant p in region i at time t, and E_{it} is total emissions in region i at time t.

The CARS (Coefficient of Absolute Regional Specialization) is given by:

$$P - spec_{it}^{CARS} = \frac{\sqrt{\frac{1}{P-1}\sum_{p=1}^{P}\left\{E_{it}^{P} - \sum_{p=1}^{P}\left(\frac{E_{it}^{P}}{P}\right)\right\}^{2}}}{\sum_{s=1}^{S}\left(\frac{E_{it}^{P}}{P}\right)} \equiv \frac{\sigma_{it}}{\mu_{it}} \quad (4-8)$$

where the numerator is the standard deviation of levels of pollution across pollutants and the denominator is the mean level of pollution averaged on all pollutants.

To conclude, each index of environmental specialization is measured at regional level, and a large value of index indicates less diversity of pollutants, in other words, a region that is more likely to specialize in emissions of similar type would have a large value of index and vice versa.

4.3.3 Data

I use the Chinese provincial level data to estimate the specialization indices discussed above, however, I acknowledge that it is not ideal to use provincial level data, particularly the provincial data in China. The geographic area of one province in China is comparable in size with a country in Europe, the provincial data therefore could be highly aggregated. Certainly, I would like to perform the analysis at city or county level, but data is not easily available or reliable at smaller region level, therefore, I stick to the provincial – level analysis and cautiously interpret the results.

Based on 3 – digit ISIC classification, I define 15 manufacturing sectors in China and set up a sample with each sector's level of output in 28 provinces from 1997 to 2003. ① Output data is available in a series of provincial statistical yearbooks.

Pollution data of 28 Chinese provinces is available in the China Statistical Yearbook. Five pollutants can be found in the yearbook, including wastewater, solid waste, sulphur dioxide (SO_2), SOOT and DUST (see the appendix for detail). It is argued that assigning equal weight to the toxicity of every chemical in the pollutant is not accurate, and some studies start weighting chemicals in terms of their toxicity (e. g. Brooks and Sethi, 1997; Arora and Cason, 1998). Pollution in this research is measured in terms of tons, and one ton of a given pollutant may be different from one ton of the other. For example, one ton of wastewater contains several chemicals like *COD* or NO_x, while one ton of other pollutant contains only one chemical, the toxicity of wastewater thus could be larger compared to other pollutant. On the other hand, soot and dust are both particles but differ in terms of size. The diameter of soot particles is less than 0. 1μm (often referred to as pm10) whilst the diameter of dust particles is more than 0. 1μm, which implies that soot particles are more dangerous and damaging to health particularly to respiratory function. However, the specialization measure in this research may not be able to capture the concern discussed above because there is even no scientific evidence of the accuracy of toxicity for each pollutant, therefore, I leave the issue of weighting pollutants by toxicity to future research.

① There are 31 provinces in total in China, but we drop three provinces Hebei, Gansu and Tibet due to lack of data.

4.4 Background and Empirical Analysis

4.4.1 Environmental Specialization

4.4.1.1 Environmental specialization in the country

The following four figures observe the time trend of environmental specialization from 1997 to 2003 in China. The estimate of the index in a given region is scaled by that region's total population, and the observation of each year is calculated through averaging the population – weighted estimates of index across all regions. The mean level of total pollution averaged over all regions is also plotted in each figure for comparison.

Figures 4.1 and 4.2 plot index 1 and index 2, respectively. In terms of both measures, there is a significant increase in pollution specialization. Index 1 has increased by 2557% from 1997 to 2003, and index 2 has increased by 372% at the same time, which demonstrate a deepening specialization on pollution and a less diversity of pollutants in the country. Figure 4.3 and 4.4 plot two absolute measures of pollution specialization, the Herfindahl index and CARS. Both show a decreasing time trend of pollution specialization from 1997 to 2003, which is entirely opposite to the trends shown by index 1 and 2. The Herfindahl index slightly declines by an average rate of 23.9% and the CARS decreases by 70.1% on average. As suggested by previous literatures (Thirlwall, A. P, 1966; Jackson, 1984; Hewings, G. J. D, 1982), different measures of specialization may produce inconsistent results, therefore, the estimate should be cautiously interpreted while employing different measures.

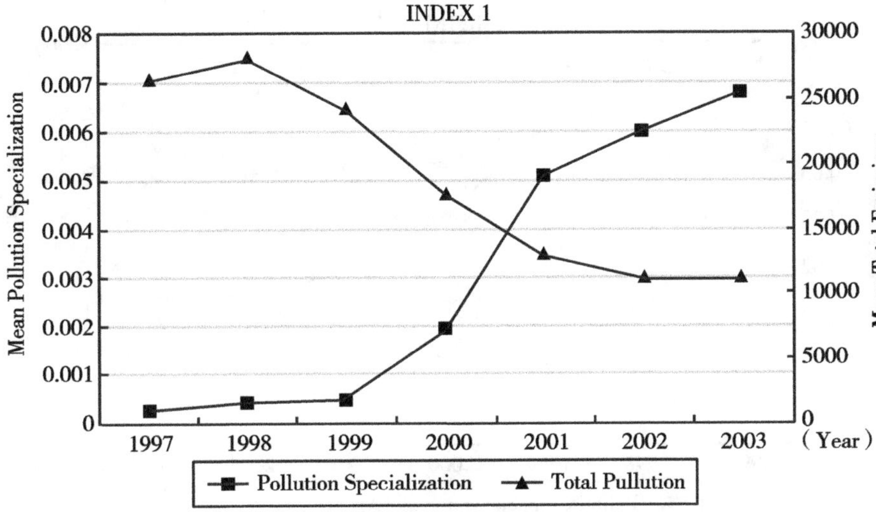

Figure 4.1 Pollution Specialization (Index 1) and Total Pollution, 1997 – 2003

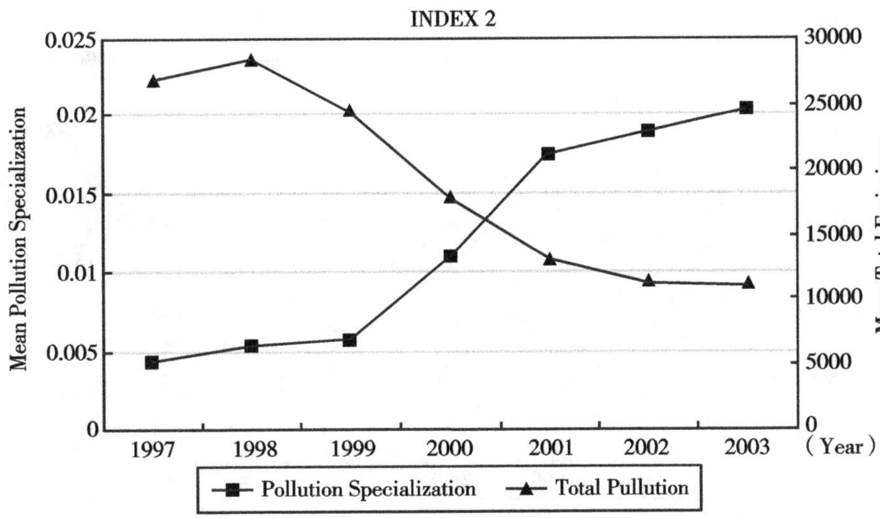

Figure 4.2 Pollution Specialization (Index 2) and Total Pollution, 1997 – 2003

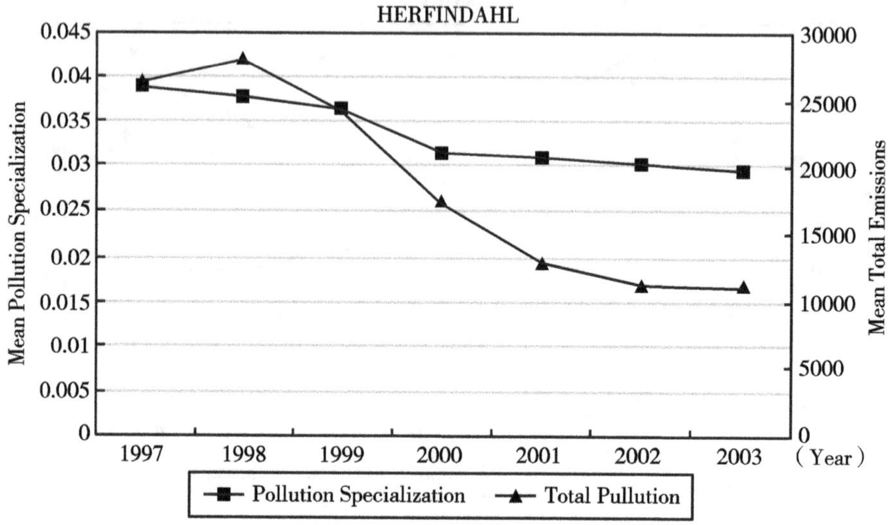

Figure 4. 3 Pollution Specialization (Herfindahl) and Total Pollution, 1997 – 2003

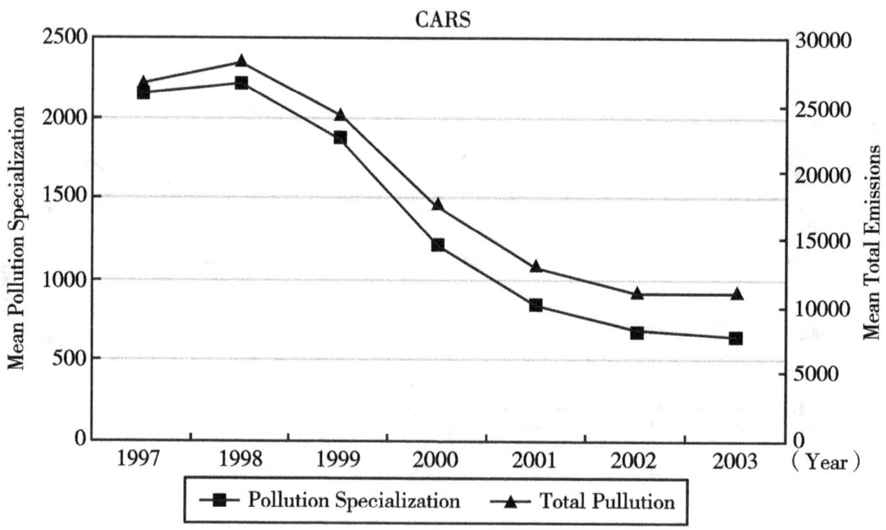

Figure 4. 4 Pollution Specialization (CARS) and Total Pollution, 1997 – 2003

Environmental specialization in terms of index 1 and 2 and specialization in terms of two absolute measures are found to move in opposite directions because of the definition of measures showed by equations. The specialization declines in terms of absolute measure because the share of each pollutant in total pollution converges and regions thus become more diverse in pollution. At the same time, the diversity of pollution may spread quicker in certain regions than in any other region, such as Tianjin, Beijing and Shanxi, the distance from the diversity of pollution in other regions is therefore growing over time. Since index 1 and 2 are estimated exactly in terms of this distance, it is not surprising that these two indices demonstrate an increasing specialization on the environment.

To check robustness of previous findings, I run a simple regression that regress each index in natural logarithm on a linear time trend and province fixed effects. In addition, I regress total level of pollution in natural logarithm on the same explanatory variables as well. Table 4. 2 reports estimates.

The estimate of time dummies increases for index 1 and index 2, with an annual average growth rate of 9. 8% for index 1 and 11. 6% for index 2. The estimate of time dummies declines for Herfindahl index and CARS, with an annual average rate of 18. 2% for Herfindahl index and 2. 1% for CARS. These findings are consistent with the graphical analysis. The last column of Table 4. 2 reports estimates for total pollution. It shows a falling time trend of total pollution from 1997 to 2003, which is also found in the Statistical Annual Report on Environment in China. The Report (1997 – 2003) states that there is a decreasing trend annually over 1997 – 2003 for major pollutants such as wastewater, sulphur dioxide

(SO_2), TSP and solid waste. [1]

Table 4.2 The Time Trend of Environmental Specialization Indices and Total Pollution

year	Index 1	Index 2	Herfindahl	CARS	Total Pollution
T2	0.048 (0.08)	0.0459 (0.17)	-0.0284 (-1.18)	0.0102 (0.09)	0.0483 (0.51)
T3	0.558 (1.14)	0.283 (1.20)	-0.0570 (-2.75)***	-0.181 (-1.80)*	-0.104 (-1.27)
T4	1.694 (3.32)***	0.842 (3.43)***	-0.173 (-5.82)***	-0.731 (-6.47)***	-0.488 (-5.99)***
T5	2.712 (5.33)***	1.342 (5.49)***	-0.250 (-9.76)***	-1.139 (-9.93)***	-0.785 (-8.83)***
T6	2.780 (5.63)***	1.381 (5.84)***	-0.280 (-11.61)***	-1.300 (-12.57)***	-0.905 (-10.91)***
T7	2.981 (6.30)***	1.481 (6.51)***	-0.295 (-9.46)***	-1.352 (-11.88)***	-0.931 (-10.34)***
Constant	-6.235 (-14.63)***	-2.733 (-13.36)***	-0.183 (-10.34)***	11.050 (125.93)***	9.900 (140.89)***
Observation	196	196	196	196	196

Table 4.3 provides evidence for the sensitivity of the time trend to types of specialization indices. Each index at provincial level is population weighted. Table 4.3 displays mean value and median value of all provinces for each index in 1997 and 2003, as well as the average growth rate of mean and median values. Index 1 and 2 are found to be increasing either in terms of mean value or in terms of median value, and two absolute measures, the Herfindahl index and CARS,

① Source: China Environment Yearbook.

are found to be decreasing both in terms of mean and median values. The fact again suggests that the environmental specialization in China depends on the type of specialization measure utilized, therefore, more thoroughly investigation on specialization measures should be taken before we can apply them widespread.

Table 4. 3 Average Growth Rate in Environmental Specialization 1997 – 2003

	Index 1	Index 2	Herfindhl	CARS
1997 Mean	0. 00026	0. 0043	0. 039	2140. 6
2003 Mean	0. 0068	0. 020	0. 030	640. 5
Average Growth Rate	102%	33%	–4. 3%	–17. 1%
1997 Median	0. 000083	0. 0021	0. 021	2032. 0
2003 Median	0. 0015	0. 0077	0. 014	541. 3
Average Growth Rate	68. 6%	25. 9%	–6. 3%	–17. 6%

Note: Mean and Median specialization value for 1997 and 2003 multiplied by 100. All values are weighted by provincial population.

4. 4. 1. 2 Environmental Specialization in the 10 East coast Provinces

I also set up a sub – sample of 10 East coast provinces. ① These regions are the most affluent regions with a high level of per capita income, geographic concentration as well as concentration on industrial production. It is expected that the outcome of analysis in these regions may reveal new findings that are different from those observed in the entire country.

Figure 4. 5 to 4. 8 plot pollution specialization in terms of each index over years, respectively. Time trend of total levels of pollution

① 10 East coast provinces (from North to South) are Liaoning, Beijing, Tianjin, Shandong, Jiangsu, Shanghai, Zhejiang, Fujian, Guangdong and Hainan.

is also displayed in each figure for comparison. The estimate of each index is scaled by regional population.

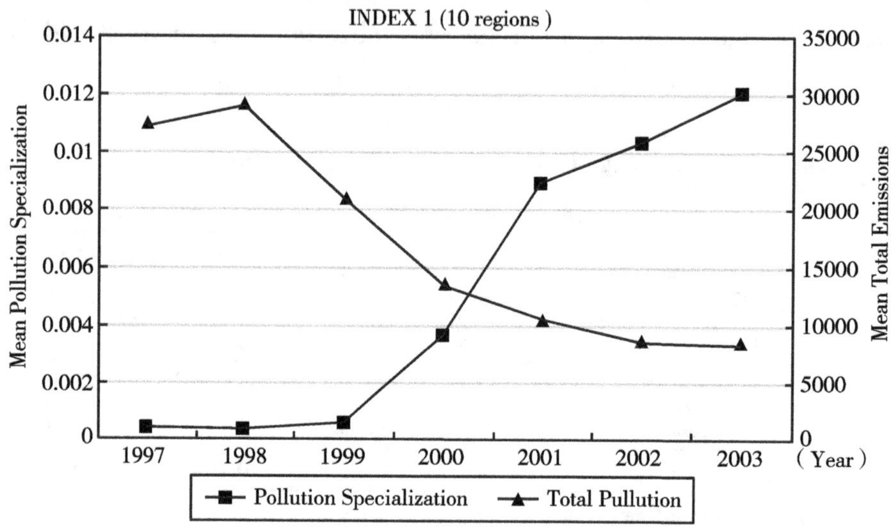

Figure 4.5 Pollution Specialization (Index 1) and Total Pollution, 1997 – 2003

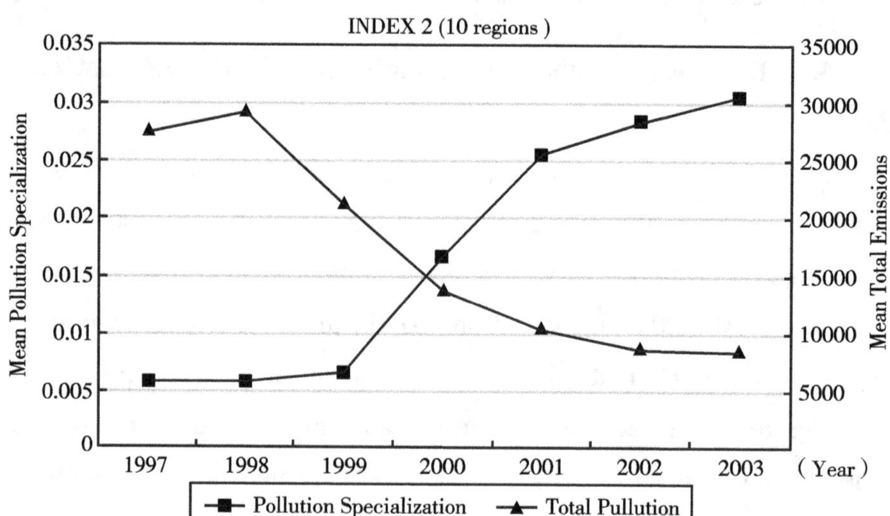

Figure 4.6 Pollution Specialization (Index 2) and Total Pollution, 1997 – 2003

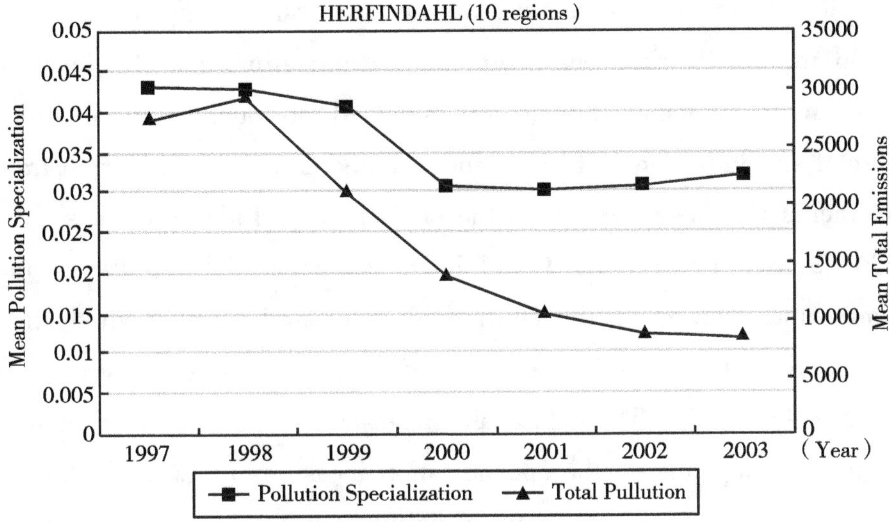

Figure 4.7 Pollution Specialization (Herfindahl) and Total Pollution, 1997 – 2003

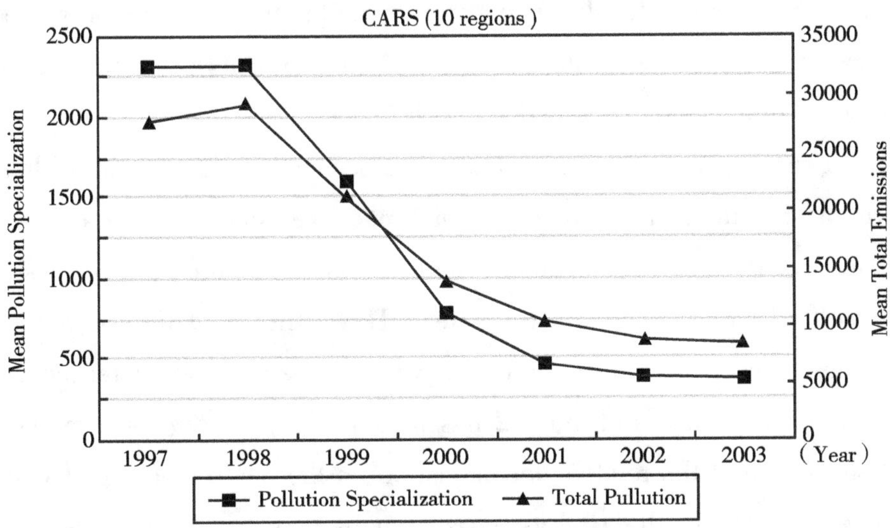

Figure 4.8 Pollution Specialization (CARS) and Total Pollution, 1997 – 2003

The estimate of specialization measures shows very similar time trend in the 10 East coast provinces, indicating that the level of economic development has not yet impacted too much on the environmental specialization in China. Index 1 and 2 apparently demonstrate an increasing specialization on the environment. Index 1 increased by 3364% from 1997 to 2003 and Index 2 increased by 449% at the same time. However, the Herfindahl index and CARS both decline with a decrease of 26% for the Herfindal index and a decrease of 69.5% for CARS. The data again suggests that the time trend of specialization depends on the specialization measures utilized. In the 10 East coast provinces, the share of pollutant in total pollution declines across provinces, which has resulted in a decreasing trend in terms of the Herfindahl and CARS, but the decreasing rate may not keep pace across provinces, the distance between pollution shares in provinces therefore turns to be greater over time, which results in an increasing trend in terms of index 1 and index 2.

I run a simply regression that regresses each index in natural logarithm on a linear time trend and province fixed effects using a sub – sample of 10 East coast regions, total levels of pollution are regressed as well. Table 4.4 reports estimates. The estimate of time dummies increases for both index 1 and 2, where index 1 has increased by 10.4% on average and index 2 has increased by 12.6% on average. It suggests that the relative specialization on the environment is deepening over time in the 10 East coast regions. As for the two absolute measures, the Herfindahl index has decreased by 23.4% per year and CARS has decreased by 3.0% per year, both of which suggest that the absolute specialization on the environment decreases in the 10

East coast provinces over time. These regression results strongly support the findings from previous graphical analysis.

Table 4. 4 The Time Trend of Environmental Specialization Indices and Total Pollution (10 provinces)

year	Index 1	Index 2	Herfindahl	CARS	Total Pollution
T2	0. 121 (0. 18)	0. 0653 (0. 20)	-0. 0107 (-0. 27)	0. 0308 (0. 21)	0. 0449 (0. 34)
T3	0. 0862 (0. 12)	0. 0578 (0. 16)	-0. 0726 (-1. 90) *	-0. 371 (-2. 66) **	-0. 274 (-2. 15) **
T4	1. 893 (2. 97) ***	0. 967 (3. 12) ***	-0. 261 (-3. 87) ***	-1. 245 (-6. 22) ***	-0. 873 (-6. 61) ***
T5	2. 630 (4. 23) ***	1. 323 (4. 36) ***	-0. 338 (-7. 64) ***	-1. 705 (-11. 19) ***	-1. 227 (-8. 94) ***
T6	2. 976 (4. 39) ***	1. 498 (4. 58) ***	-0. 333 (-7. 07) ***	-1. 822 (-13. 58) ***	-1. 353 (-11. 17) ***
T7	2. 876 (4. 26) ***	1. 450 (4. 42) ***	-0. 325 (-4. 38) ***	-1. 893 (-10. 44) ***	-1. 428 (-10. 34) ***
Constant	-5. 635 (-10. 51) ***	-2. 450 (-9. 38) ***	-0. 159 (-5. 06) ***	11. 042 (92. 31) ***	9. 861 (94. 65) ***
Observation	70	70	70	70	70

The sensitivity of the estimate to the type of specialization measures is also tested. Table 4. 5 presents the population – weighted mean and median values of each index for 10 East coast provinces in 1997 and 2003. The average growth rate of mean and median value of each index is estimated as well. It shows that index 1 and 2 have both increased in terms of mean value or median value. The Herfindahl index and CARS have both declined in terms of mean and median value. Again, results of the sensitivity test find consistency with previous analysis.

Table 4.5 Average Growth Rate in Environmental Specialization, 1997 – 2003 (10 provinces)

	Index 1	Index 2	Herfindhl	CARS
1997 Mean	0.00035	0.006	0.043	2307.7
2003 Mean	0.012	0.03	0.032	370.5
Average Growth Rate	135%	41.1%	-4.4%	-23.6%
1997 Median	0.00012	0.003	0.025	2416.6
2003 Median	0.0023	0.010	0.013	252.4
Average Growth Rate	104%	27.8%	-9.5%	-28.5%

Note: Mean and Median specialization value for 1997 and 2003 multiplied by 100. All values are weighted by provincial population.

To compare estimates in Table 4.3 and in Table 4.5, the absolute specialization measures of the 10 provinces decrease faster than the measures of the whole country. It implies that the share of pollution in total pollution drops more quickly in the 10 provinces than in the whole country. As a result, the distance between pollution shares in the 10 provinces turns to become larger than the distance in the whole country, and such an increase has been evident by the estimate of index 1 and 2 in Table 4.3 and 4.5 where the average growth rate of relative specialization measures in the 10 provinces is higher than that in the whole country.

Of course, I take exactly the same analysis using a sample of the remaining 18 provinces. The results are similar to the ones of the whole country. Two relative measures of specialization, index 1 and 2, present an increasing time trend of pollution specialization, whilst two absolute measures of specialization, the Herfindahl index and CARS, present a decreasing time trend of pollution specialization (see Figure A4.1 – A4.4 in the appendix). Therefore, I can conclude that across the whole country, either in the 10 East coast provinces or in the remaining 18 provinces, environmental specialization is rising in terms of index 1 and 2 but declining in terms of the Herfindahl and CARS.

At last to conclude, while examining the environmental specialization in China, I mainly employ two data samples, one is with the whole country of 28 provinces, and the other one concentrates on the richest regions of 10 East coast provinces. Both graphical and empirical analysis suggest that, relative measures show an increase in the degree of environmental specialization and absolute measures show that levels of pollution and environmental specialization both decline. Given the results, I presume absolute measures more relevant for advising on health outcomes because their estimation is based on the absolute exposure levels.

4.4.2 Industrial Specialization

4.4.2.1 Industrial specialization in the country

Millimet and Slottje (2003) find a strongly positive link between industrial specialization and environmental specialization using US data. They proposed that industrial specialization may be a major contributor to environmental specialization and their empirical work has found evidence to support such an argument. My research examines the industrial specialization in China and test whether it could be a possible determinant of environmental specialization.

I follow the same procedure as I previously did for analyzing environmental specialization. Figure 4.9 – 4.12 plot the mean value of each index averaged on all regions for industrial specialization. Industrial specialization in terms of each index all demonstrates a sharp increase over the sample period. Comparing the mean values in 1997 and in 2003, index 1 and index 2 have increased by 38.4% and 15.6%, respectively. The Herfindahl index and CARS have increased by 19.3% and 176%, respectively. Unlike specialization measures that show mixed trends of environmental specialization, the relative and absolute measures both consistently show a significant increase of industrial specialization over time. It is believed that the share of each sector's output in total output significantly increases in all regions, and at the same time, due to the imbalanced development, the distance of shares between regions is widened as well, both cause an increasing specialization on industry both in terms of absolute measures and relative measures.

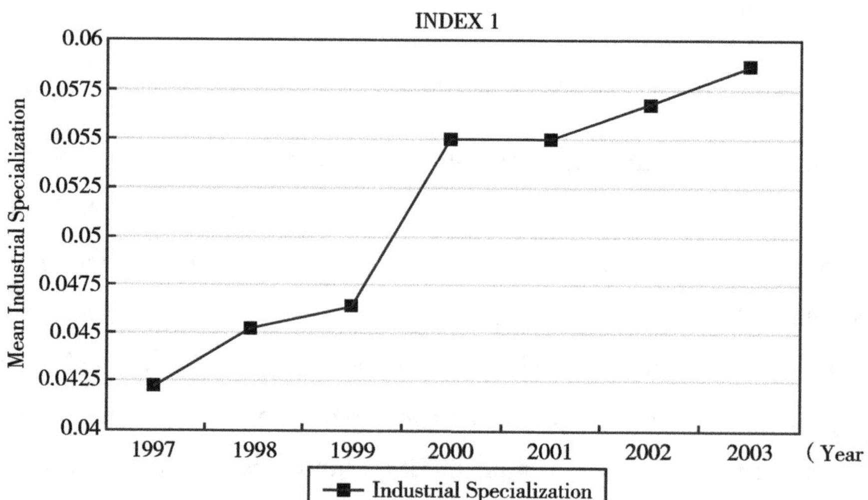

Figure 4.9 Industrial Specialization (Index 1) 1997 – 2003

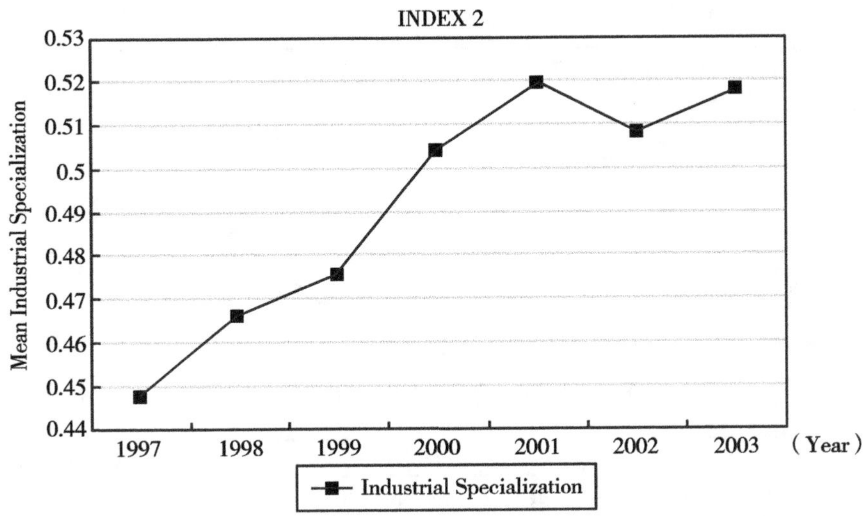

Figure 4. 10 Industrial Specialization (Index 2) 1997 – 2003

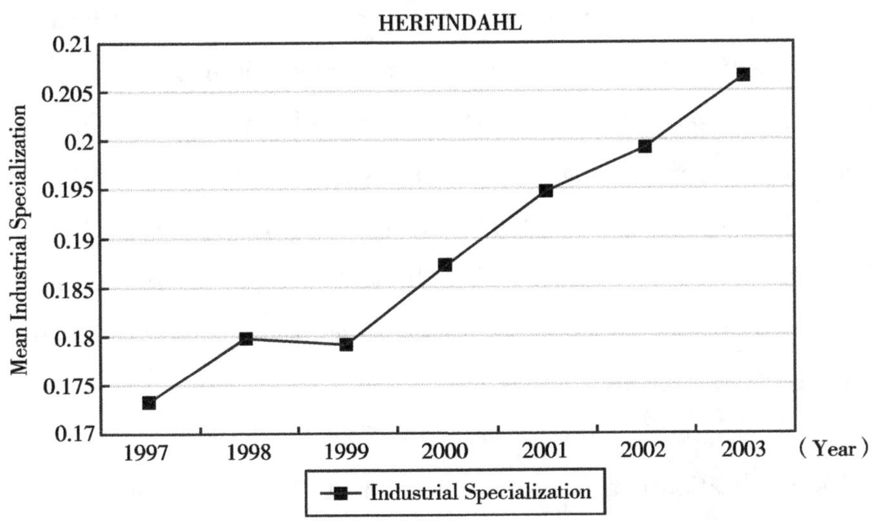

Figure 4. 11 Industrial Specialization (Herfindahl) 1997 – 2003

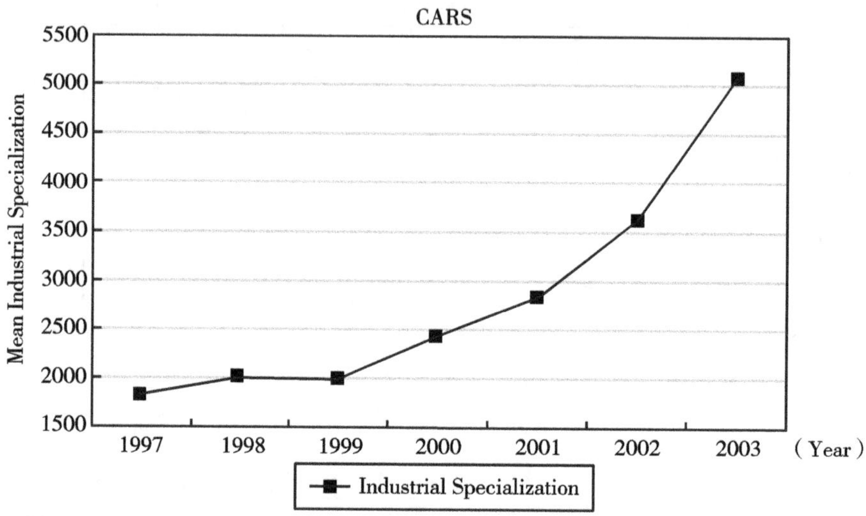

Figure 4.12 Industrial Specialization (CARS) 1997 - 2003

A simple regression that regresses each index in natural logarithm on a linear time trend and province fixed effects is estimated as well. Table 4.6 presents estimates. All measures of industrial specialization have shown an increasing time trend, with an annual average growth rate of 1.5% for index 1, 2.9% for index 2, 1.7% for the Herfindahl index and 2.1% for CARS. Although the growth rate is not as high as expected, it has strengthened findings of graphical analysis that industrial specialization is deepening over time in China.

The research is more interested in identifying whether the industrial specialization is a potential determinant of environmental specialization in China. Therefore, I move the analysis to the examination of the relationship between environmental specialization and industrial specialization across regions. Based on the estimate of specialization measures, 28 provinces could be ranked in a descending order, and three provinces of the largest industrial specialization and three provinces of the lowest industrial specialization could be selected out.

Table 4.6 The Time Trend of Industrial Specialization Indices

year	Index 1	Index 2	Herfindahl	CARS
T2	0.0696 (0.68)	0.0355 (0.91)	0.0491 (1.53)	0.0683 (1.07)
T3	0.0770 (0.86)	0.0537 (1.52)	0.0499 (1.74) *	0.140 (2.52) **
T4	0.211 (2.25) **	0.0998 (2.63) ***	0.0860 (2.88) ***	0.341 (5.96) ***
T5	0.272 (2.98) ***	0.144 (3.95) ***	0.121 (3.91) ***	0.441 (7.58) ***
T6	0.258 (2.88) ***	0.117 (3.14) ***	0.146 (5.23) ***	0.649 (11.81) ***
T7	0.315 (2.84) ***	0.143 (3.18) ***	0.175 (5.32) ***	0.918 (13.51) ***
Constant	-3.603 (-43.76) ***	-0.886 (-26.43) ***	-1.802 (-73.51) ***	6.760 (144.33) ***
Observation	196	196	196	196

Figure 4.13 – 4.16 plot environmental specialization of six selected provinces, it is noted that the selection of six provinces is not the same across specialization measures. Figure 4.13 plots the environmental specialization in terms of index 1. Three provinces with the largest industrial specialization are Inner Mongolia, Shanxi and Jilin, all located in the north China, and three provinces with the least industrial specialization are Hubei, Jiangxi and Anhui, all located in the South China. However, it does not demonstrate a clear

relationship between environmental and industrial specialization for these six provinces. Figure 4. 14 plots the environmental specialization in terms of index 2. Top three provinces are Ningxia, Shanxi and Guangdong, where Guangdong locates in the East coast China. The other three provinces with the least degree of industrial specialization are Hubei, Anhui and Jiangxi. Again, the relationship between environmental and industrial specialization cannot be obviously observed, but Shanxi that is one of top three provinces in industrial specialization also has a higher degree of environmental specialization than other provinces.

Figure 4. 15 plots environmental specialization in terms of the Herfindahl index. Three provinces with a high degree of industrial specialization are Jilin, Yunnan and Beijing, where Jilin locates in the Northeast China and Yunnan locates in the West China. The other three provinces with the least industrial specialization are Jiangxi, Henan and Ningxia. Estimates of the Herfindahl index do not show a clear relationship between industrial and environmental specialization, even worse, time trends of six selected provinces are mixed together. Figure 4. 16 plots the environmental specialization in terms of CARS for the six selected provinces, where the top three provinces are Guangdong, Jiangsu and Shanghai, all located in the East coast China, and the other three provinces are Hainan, Qinghai and Ningxia. It has not seen any relationship between regional industrial specialization and environmental specialization using the measure of CARS.

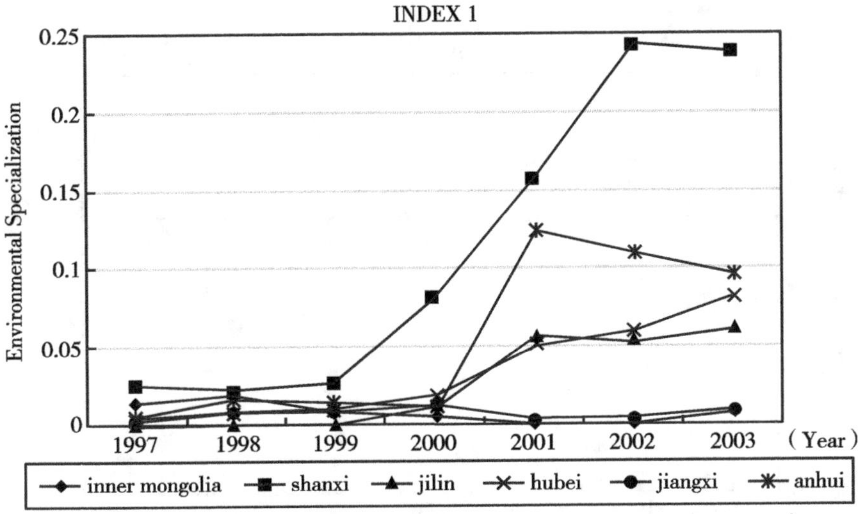

Figure 4.13 Environmental Specialization (index 1) for Regions with the Highest and Lowest Industrial Specialization

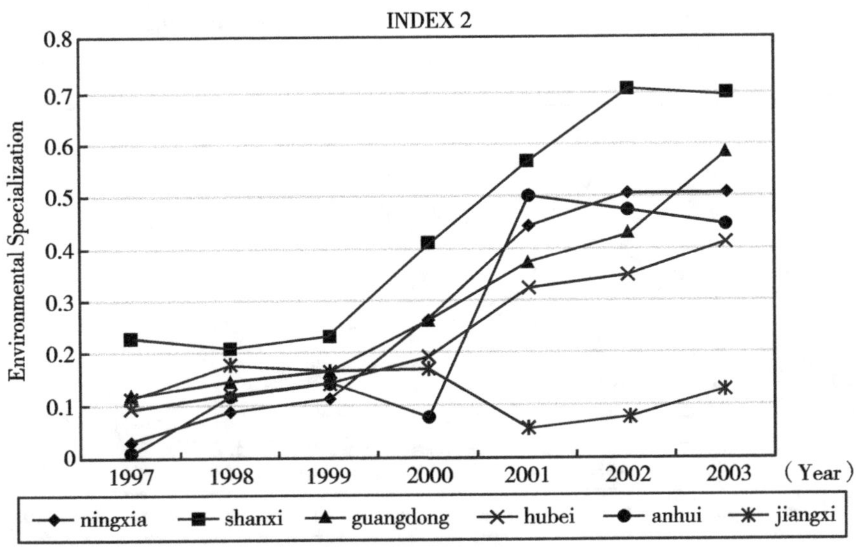

Figure 4.14 Environmental Specialization (Index 2) for Regions with the Highest and Lowest Industrial Specialization

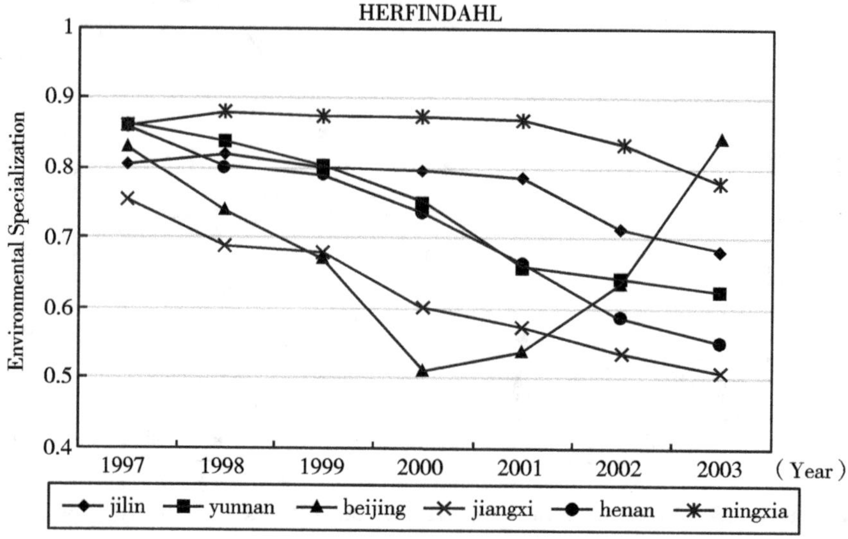

Figure 4.15 Environmental Specialization (Herfindahl) for Regions with the Highest and Lowest Industrial Specialization

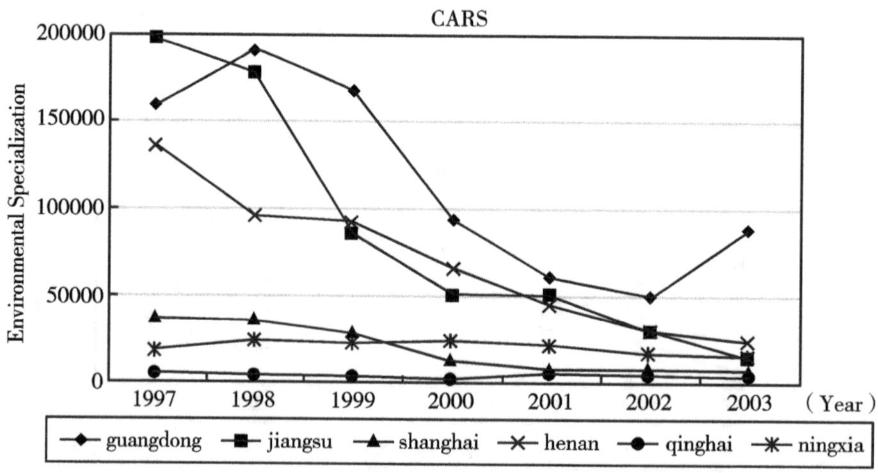

Figure 4.16 Environmental Specialization (CARS) for Regions with the Highest and Lowest Industrial Specialization

To conclude, contrary to the US results in Millimet and Slottje (2003), I find no clear relationship between environmental specialization and industrial specialization in China. However, whether industrial specialization could determine environmental specialization still require more empirical analysis. Although nothing is found generally, analysis on certain regions provides some hints. For instance, Ningxia is found as one of the top three provinces in terms of index 2 and one of the bottom three provinces in terms of the Herfindahl and CARS. The share of output of a few manufacturing sectors may be substantially above the average in Ningxia, but the distance between output shares of Ningxia and shares of other provinces is not yet quickly widened, therefore, its absolute measures are not high whilst its relative measures are high. In the following empirical analysis, the distinction between the relative measures and absolute measures have to be cautiously taken into account when explaining the results.

4.4.2.2 Industrial Specialization in the 10 East coast Provinces

Using a sub – sample of 10 East coast provinces, Figure 4.17 – 4.20 plot the mean value of each index averaged on the 10 provinces. Figure 4.17 plots index 1 from 1997 to 2003 and the estimate remains fairly stable over time except for an outlier in 2001. ① Figure 4.18 plots index 2 and the estimate remains stable over time as well. Two relative measures both demonstrate that there is no significant change of industrial specialization in 10 East coast provinces, where it is dif-

① There is a missing value in the province Hainan in 2001 for index 1, causing an over – estimated value of index 1.

ferent from the trend of specialization in the whole country. Industrial specialization increases over time in the whole country in terms of two relative measures. Figure 4. 19 plots the Herfindahl index that has increased by 20. 1% from 1997 to 2003. Figure 4. 20 plots CARS that has increased by 202% from 1997 to 2003. Both absolute measures clearly display an increasing industrial specialization in the East coast region, which is consistent with the time trend in the whole country. The relative measures have not seen a rising level of industrial specialization in the 10 East coast region because provinces in this region are developing at fairly similar stage, share of each sector's output in total output is very similar across the 10 provinces, therefore, there is no wide gap of growth between provinces, and the distance of output shares between provinces is small as well.

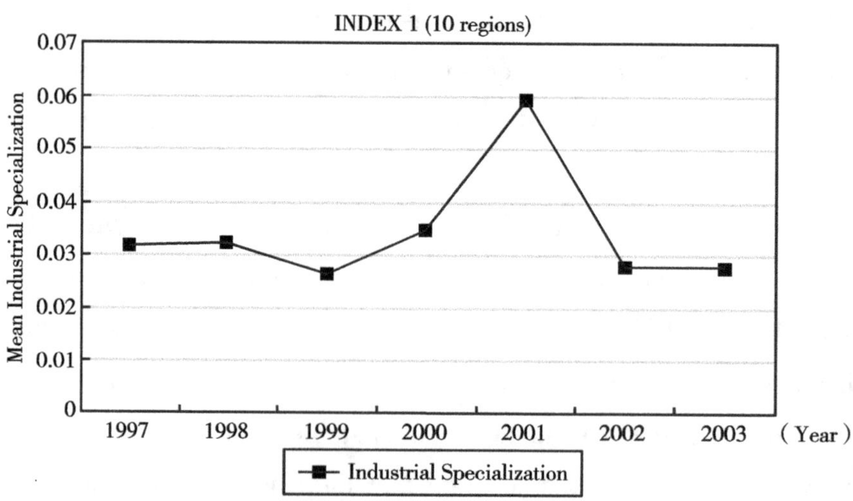

Figure 4. 17 Industrial Specialization (Index 1) 1997 – 2003

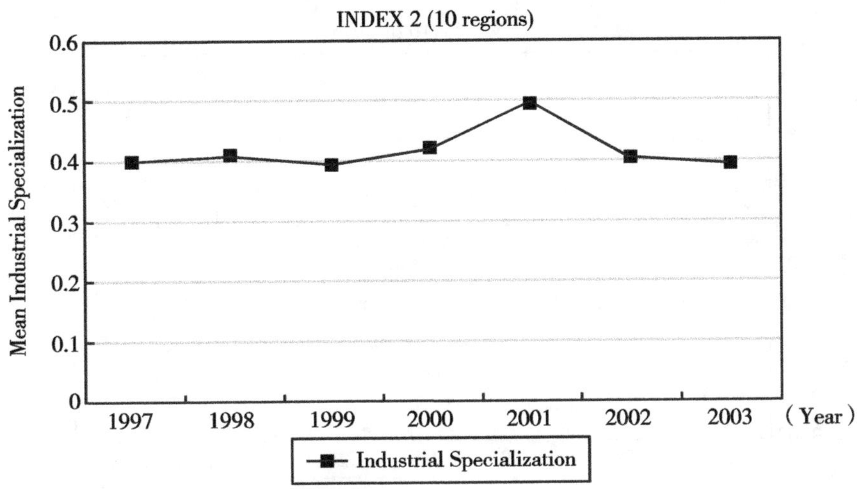

Figure 4. 18 Industrial Specialization (Index 2) 1997 – 2003

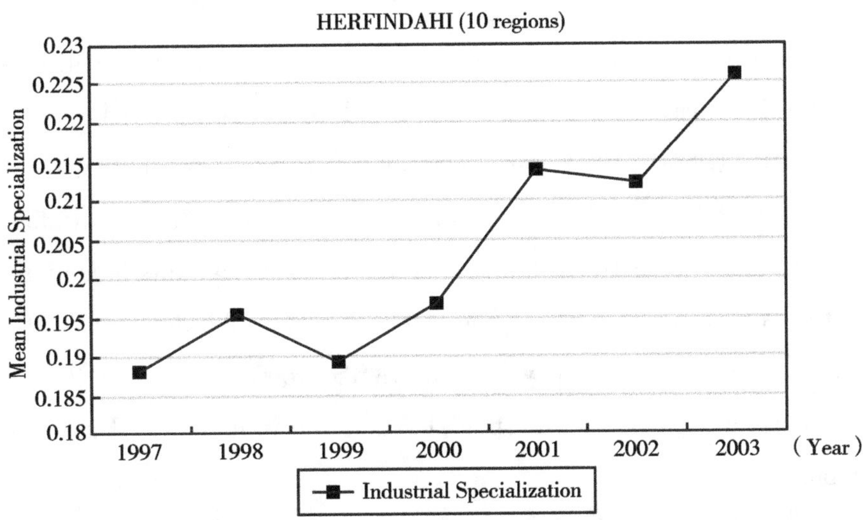

Figure 4. 19 Industrial Specialization (Herfindahl) 1997 – 2003

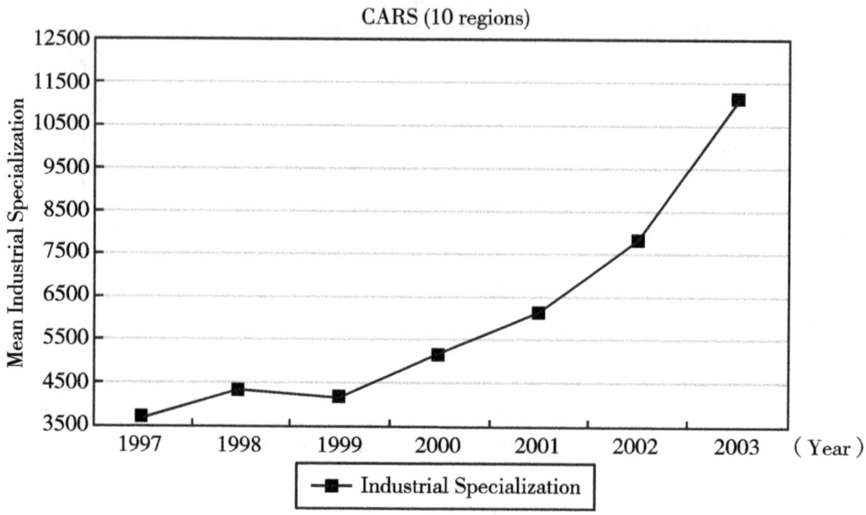

Figure 4.20 Industrial Specialization (CARS) 1997 – 2003

As previously did, a simple regression that regresses each index in natural logarithm on a linear time trend and regional fixed effects is estimated. Table 4.7 reports estimates. It is consistent with the graphs that the insignificant estimates of time dummies for index 1 and 2 indicate a fairly unchanging trend of industrial specialization in the East coast region. Meantime, the Herfindahl index grows at an average rate of 1.8% per year and CARS grows at a rate of 2.3%, demonstrating a deepening specialization on industry in East coast region.

The relationship between environmental specialization and industrial specialization in the 10 East coast provinces needs further investigations. Based on estimates of industrial specialization, three provinces with the largest specialization and three provinces with the lowest specialization are selected out. Figure 4.21 – 4.24 plot the environmental specialization of six selected provinces, and for each index the selection of six provinces is not the same.

Table 4.7 The Time Trend of Industrial Specialization Indices (10 provinces)

year	Index 1	Index 2	Herfindahl	CARS
T2	-0.00045 (-0.00)	0.0179 (0.28)	0.0383 (0.82)	0.145 (1.61)
T3	-0.163 (-1.05)	-0.0240 (-0.44)	0.0202 (0.45)	0.212 (2.62) **
T4	-0.0222 (-0.13)	0.0199 (0.34)	0.0495 (1.04)	0.410 (4.73) ***
T5	0.215 (1.09)	0.138 (1.68) *	0.125 (2.25) **	0.543 (5.87) ***
T6	-0.0617 (-0.41)	0.0041 (0.07)	0.126 (2.81) ***	0.809 (9.91) ***
T7	-0.0440 (-0.24)	-0.00861 (-0.11)	0.183 (3.97) ***	1.134 (13.24) ***
Constant	-3.725 (-27.52) ***	-0.964 (-19.01) ***	-1.702 (-43.52) ***	7.691 (102.11) ***
Observation	70	70	70	70

Figure 4.21 plots the environmental specialization in terms of index 1. Top three East coast provinces are Hainan, Beijing and Tianjin, and the last three provinces are Shandong, Jiangsu and Fujian. It shows no clear relationship between the environmental specialization and industrial specialization for the six selected provinces, however, since 2000 the relationship turns out to be clear where the time trend of top three provinces all stays above the time trend of the last three

provinces. It suggests that greater regional specialization on industry could lead to higher specialization on environment, but the causality may hold only after 2000. Figure 4.22 plots the environmental specialization in terms of index 2. Top three East coast provinces are Hainan, Beijing and Tianjin, and the last three provinces are Shandong, Jiangsu and Guangdong. The plots of six selected provinces are mixed and no clear relationship between environmental specialization and industrial specialization stand out.

Compared to the relative measures of specialization, absolute measures have shown a much clearer relationship. Figure 4.23 plots the environmental specialization in terms of the Herfindahl index. Top three provinces are Hainan, Tianjin and Beijing, and the last three provinces are Shandong, Jiangsu and Guangdong. Two of the last three provinces (Jiangsu and Guangdong) have a greater level of environmental specialization than the top three provinces. It appears that regional industrial specialization and environmental specialization are negatively related in terms of the Herfindahl index. Figure 4.24 plots the environmental specialization in terms of CARS. The top three provinces are Shanghai, Tianjin and Beijing, and the last three provinces are Fujian, Shandong and Hainan. The relationship between environmental specialization and industrial specialization is even more clear. Shandong and Fujian with the least industrial specialization have experienced the highest environmental specialization. Tianjin and Beijing with the greatest industrial specialization have experienced the least environmental specialization, suggesting that regional environmental specialization is negatively related to industrial specialization.

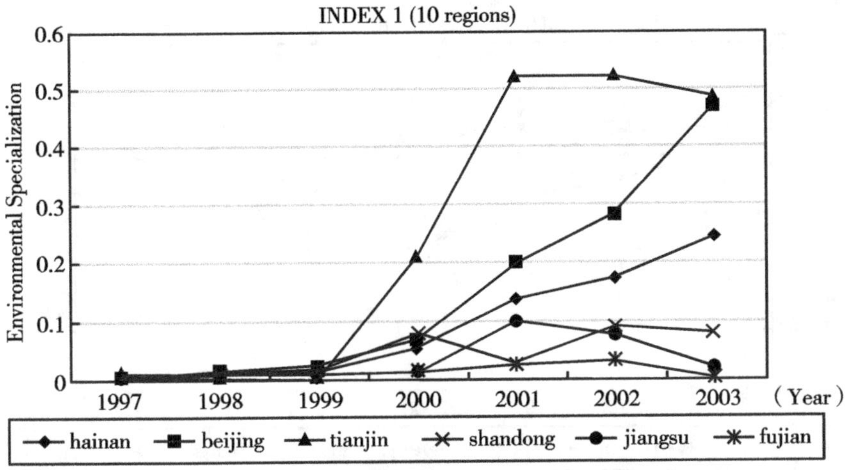

Figure 4.21 Environmental Specialization (index 1) for Regions with the Highest and Lowest Industrial Specialization

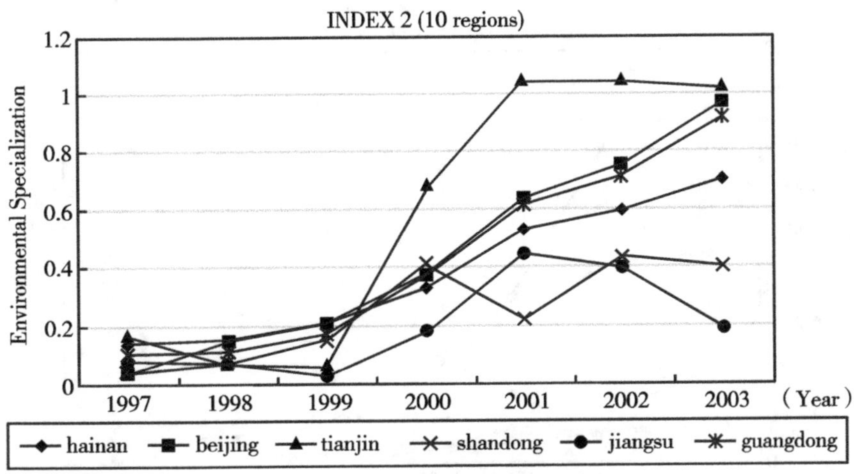

Figure 4.22 Environmental Specialization (index 2) for Regions with the Highest and Lowest Industrial Specialization

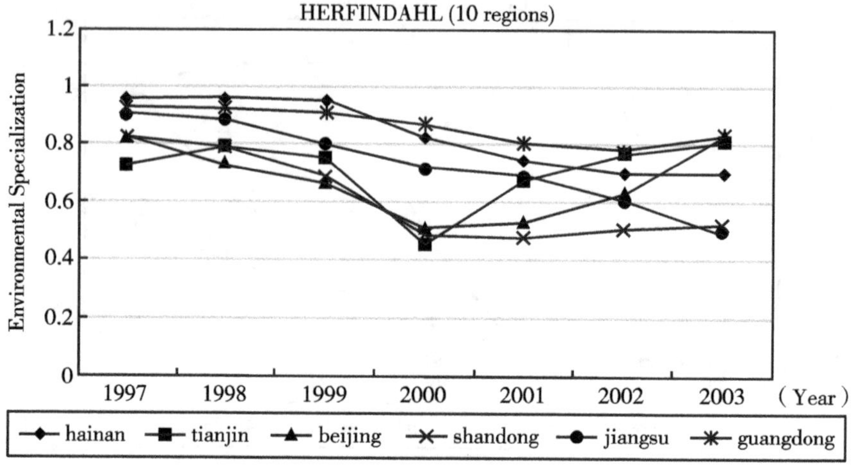

Figure 4.23 Environmental Specialization (Herfindahl) for Regions with the Highest and Lowest Industrial Specialization

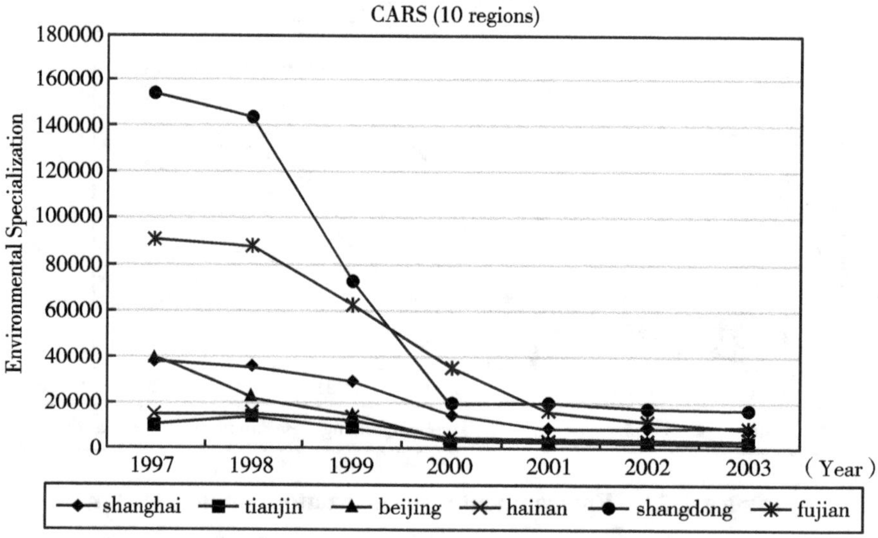

Figure 4.24 Environmental Specialization (CARS) for Regions with the Highest and Lowest Industrial Specialization

4.5 Econometric Specification and Data Considerations

Millimet and Slottje (2003) construct a regression model that examines industrial specialization as a determinant of environmental specialization. The econometric model of this research is based upon Millimet and Slottje's (2003) and the estimation model is given by:

$$\ln(P-spec_{it}) = \alpha_i + \lambda_t + \delta\ln(I-spec_{it}) + \beta_1\ln(Percapitaincome_{it}) + \beta_2[\ln(Percapitaincome_{it})]^2 + \beta_3\ln(Population_{it}) + \beta_4[\ln(Population_{it})]^2 + \beta_5\ln(Industrialoutput_{it}) + \varepsilon_{it} \quad (4-9)$$

where the dependent variable, $P-spec_{it}$, is environmental specialization and there are four measures. Term α_i denotes location fixed effects whilst term λ_t denotes time fixed effects. $I-spec_{it}$, denotes industrial specialization, and δ is the parameter of interest that estimates elasticity of environmental specialization with respect to industrial specialization.

The model in equation (4-9) includes time-varying and location-specific characteristics. *Per capita income*, defined as a region's total gross product scaled by its total population, controls for the mechanism proposed by the Environmental Kuznets Curve. In particular, if pollution specialization is related to larger health risks, wealthier regions are more likely to have lower levels of specialization. *Population* measured by a region's total population and *Industrial output* measured by a region's gross industrial output, both may determine regional environmental specialization due to the scale effect. All else being equal, an increase in the scale of output in the pollution intensive industries could be more detrimental to the environment, and the region with large population and industrial output are more likely to attract pollution intensive industries. Environmental specialization defined by shares of pollution could be probably influenced by the scale effect. The model also includes the quadratic term of *Per capita income* and *Population*. All related monetary variables are deflated to 1990 prices using a GDP deflator.

Equation (4 –9) is estimated using three samples of panel data from 1997 to 2003: the whole country with 28 provinces, 10 East coast provinces and the remaining 18 provinces. Both fixed and random effects specifications are employed and year dummies are included in all specifications. Location fixed effects (α_i) captures factors specific to individual province but do not change over time, and time fixed effects (λ_t) capture factors common to all provinces but change over time.

4.6 Estimation Results

4.6.1 Main Results

Table 4.8 presents fixed and random effects estimates using the sample of 28 provinces.① The Hausman test cannot reject the null hy-

① Econometric software STATA 9.0 is applied to run all the regressions and the major syntaxes include *xtreg* with *fe* and *re robust*.

pothesis for all random effects specifications and the estimate of the random effects specification consistently and efficiently estimate the true parameter. Therefore, both fixed and random effects estimates will be discussed.[①] The Spearman correlation test demonstrates a positive correlation between industrial specialization and pollution specialization in terms of index 1, index 2 and CARS, but the correlation is statistically significant for index 1 only (p - value = 0.096). The correlation is -0.07 (p - value = 0.33) for the Herfindahl index and it indicates a very weakly and insignificantly negative relationship between industrial specialization and pollution specialization.

The parameter of interest in this research is the estimate of industrial specialization that can inform whether industrial specialization has contributed to environmental specialization. It is positive but statistically insignificant in most models, suggesting that no causal relationship between industrial specialization and environmental specialization is available for China. Although Millimet and Slottje (2003) find empirical evidence of a positive relationship for US, it is not the same case in China. Such a difference may present due to the industrial patterns of two countries. China specializes in labour intensive, relatively low value - added industries, whilst US specializes in capital intensive, high - tech industries, and the pollution content of industrial production is thus different in two countries.

① Models fitted on data of *index* 2 fail to meet the asymptotic assumptions of the Hausman test, and therefore no Hausman test result is provided in Table 4.8 for the dependent variable *index* 2.

Table 4.8 **Determinants of Provincial Level Environmental Specialization (Fixed and Random Effects) 1997 – 2003**

ln(Environmental specialization)	FIXED EFFECTS				RANDOM EFFECTS			
	(1)	(2)	(3)	(4)	(5)	(6)	(7)	(8)
	Index1	Index2	Herfindahl	Cars	Index1	Index2	Herfindahl	Cars
ln(Industrial specialization)	0.833 (1.52)	0.144 (0.24)	-0.0418 (-0.53)	-0.080 (-1.08)	0.185 (0.77)	-0.0359 (-0.14)	0.0416 (0.73)	-0.006 (-0.12)
ln(Per capita income)	-21.449 (-1.37)	-9.322 (-1.28)	1.250 (1.33)	0.807 (1.16)	4.816 (0.47)	2.463 (0.52)	0.478 (0.73)	0.303 (0.66)
[*ln(Per capital income)*]^2	1.350 (1.46)	0.583 (1.37)	-0.0519 (-0.92)	-0.035 (-0.84)	-0.166 (-0.27)	-0.101 (-0.35)	-0.0177 (-0.43)	-0.011 (-0.37)
ln(Population)	21.116 (0.64)	14.735 (0.86)	6.868 (2.70) ***	5.030 (2.80) ***	-4.837 (-1.06)	-1.935 (-0.91)	-0.355 (-0.63)	-0.207 (-0.52)
[*ln(Population)*]^2	-0.682 (-0.35)	-0.635 (-0.63)	-0.414 (-2.60) **	-0.303 (-2.71) ***	0.402 (1.27)	0.152 (1.04)	0.0313 (0.88)	0.019 (0.73)
ln(Industrial output)	-3.542 (-1.62)	-1.310 (-1.43)	-0.100 (-0.74)	-0.059 (-0.61)	-1.467 (-1.53)	-0.542 (-1.15)	-0.133 (-1.51)	-0.088 (-1.38)
R^2	0.46	0.46	0.65	0.78	0.33	0.34	0.40	0.71

Continued

ln(Environmental specialization)	FIXED EFFECTS				RANDOM EFFECTS			
	(1)	(2)	(3)	(4)	(5)	(6)	(7)	(8)
	Index1	Index2	Herfindahl	Cars	Index1	Index2	Herfindahl	Cars
Hausman(FE. V RE.)					3.93 (0.985)		14.41 (0.275)	5.23 (0.950)
Spearman Correlation† (*Environmental specialization & Industrial specialization*)	0.120 (0.096)*	0.106 (0.140)	-0.069 (0.334)	0.084 (0.240)				
Observations	196	196	196	196	196	196	196	196

NOTES: environmental specialization and industrial specialization use the same measurement of specialization in each model.

t-statistics in parentheses for fixed effects and z-statistics in parentheses for random effects. Time dummies are included.

* significant at 10% level; ** significant at 5% level; *** significant at 1% level; † P-value in parentheses for Spearman correlation.

Therefore, it is possible that an increase of industrial specialization may have impacts on environmental specialization in US but not in China.

The estimate of per capita income and its squared term has mixed sign and it is insignificant all the time. Regional population is positively significant in model (3) and (4). As suggested by Krugman (1991), transportation cost determines the location of manufacturing industries, where industries with high transportation cost are likely to locate in densely populated areas and industrial specialization may vary with population density thereafter. The squared term of population is negative and significant in model (3) or (4) as well. The finding literally provides evidence for the presence of a non – linear relationship between population and environmental specialization in China. The estimate of industrial output that controls for the scale effect is insignificant throughout all models. The impact of industrial output on environmental specialization seems trivial.

4.6.2 Results for the 10 East Coast Provinces

Table 4.9 presents both fixed and random effects estimates using the sample of 10 East coast provinces. ① The Hausman test has rejected the null hypothesis that the estimator of random effects specification is a consistent and efficient estimator of the true parameters in terms of CARS, the analysis should thus focus on the estimate of fixed effects specification for CARS. The Hausman test cannot reject the

① Econometric software STATA 9.0 is applied to run all the regressions and the major syntaxes include *xtreg* with *fe* and *re robust*.

Table 4.9 Determinants of Provincial Level Environmental Specialization: 10 East Coast Provinces. (Fixed and Random Effects) 1997 – 2003

ln(Environmental specialization)	FIXED EFFECTS				RANDOM EFFECTS			
	(9)	(10)	(11)	(12)	(13)	(14)	(15)	(16)
	Index1	Index2	Herfindahl	Cars	Index1	Index2	Herfindahl	Cars
ln(Industrial specialization)	-0.0204 (-0.05)	-0.299 (-0.52)	-0.435 (-2.06)**	-0.660 (-3.20)***	0.245 (0.73)	0.283 (0.72)	-0.114 (-0.82)	-0.213 (-1.45)
ln(Per capita income)	11.344 (0.31)	7.659 (0.41)	0.0781 (0.03)	-0.329 (-0.16)	3.326 (0.17)	0.226 (0.02)	-1.087 (-0.60)	-0.795 (-0.62)
$[ln(Per\ capital\ income)]^2$	-0.275 (-0.16)	-0.218 (-0.24)	0.0536 (0.38)	0.051 (0.53)	-0.172 (-0.18)	-0.0111 (-0.02)	0.0867 (0.94)	0.064 (0.97)
ln(Population)	35.891 (0.71)	19.733 (0.80)	1.704 (0.47)	2.168 (0.77)	-16.566 (-1.54)	-8.082 (-1.60)	-1.681 (-1.22)	-1.310 (-1.27)
$[ln(Population)]^2$	-1.438 (-0.51)	-0.849 (-0.62)	-0.0283 (-0.12)	-0.085 (-0.47)	1.035 (1.39)	0.500 (1.42)	0.128 (1.38)	0.097 (1.40)
ln(Industrial output)	1.583 (0.45)	0.807 (0.48)	-0.564 (-2.24)**	-0.298 (-1.69)*	-0.0145 (-0.01)	0.0618 (0.08)	-0.276 (-1.36)	-0.186 (-1.22)
R^2	0.59	0.61	0.72	0.91	0.51	0.52	0.38	0.92

Continued

ln(Environmental specialization)	FIXED EFFECTS				RANDOM EFFECTS			
	(9)	(10)	(11)	(12)	(13)	(14)	(15)	(16)
	Index1	Index2	Herfindahl	Cars	Index1	Index2	Herfindahl	Cars
Hausman(FE. V RE.)					12.15 (0.433)	11.90 (0.45)	10.02 (0.614)	64.41 (0.000)
Spearman Correlation† (*Environmental specialization & Industrial specialization*)	0.192 (0.112)	0.177 (0.142)	0.042 (0.728)	0.158 (0.191)				
Observations	70	70	70	70	70	70	70	70

NOTES: environmental specialization and industrial specialization use the same measurement of specialization in each model.

t - statistics in parentheses for fixed effects and z - statistics in parentheses for random effects. Time dummies are included.

* significant at 10% level; ** significant at 5% level; *** significant at 1% level; † P - value in parentheses for Spearman correlation.

null hypothesis for the other three indices, thus, estimates of both specifications should be taken into account. The Spearman rank correlation test cannot find statistically significant correlations between environmental specialization and industrial specialization in the East coast region, however, after the regression controls for other relevant factors, they seem to be related somehow.

The estimate of industrial specialization is negative and statistically significant in model (11) and (12), suggesting that industrial specialization is a negative determinant of environmental specialization in the East coast region of China. ① One possible reason for this negative relationship is that the East coast region is the most developed and affluent region in China, the industrial specialization of this region is found to be increasing in terms of the two absolute specialization measures. The specialization mainly presents in high-tech, high value-added sectors in this region, therefore, total pollution as well as pollution of each type all experience a decreasing level, which results in a fall in the environmental specialization.

Secondly, the estimate of per capita income still remains insignificant in the East coast region, maybe at the current economic stage income not yet plays a critical role in managing the environment in China. The estimates of population and its squared term is insignificant throughout all models. Industrial output that controls for the scale effects is negative and significant in model (11) and (12), respec-

---

① The positive and significant coefficient of industrial specialization for CARS in the random effects specification is out of consideration because it fails the Hausman test.

tively. It is consistent with the finding in US. Industries in the East coast China are more likely to be high – tech, efficient and high value – added. Due to the economy of scale, pollution abatement cost may decline and level of pollution of each type drops thereafter. Consequently, the environmental specialization will fall along with an increase in the industrial output.

4.6.3 Results for the other 18 provinces

Table 4.10 reports both fixed and random effects estimates using the sub – sample of the other 18 provinces. It also reports the results of the Spearman correlation test and the Hausman test.① The Hausman test has rejected the random effects estimate as a consistent and efficient estimator of the true parameters for CARS. The Spearman correlation test shows a positive and significant correlation between environmental specialization and industrial specialization in terms of CARS and the value of the Spearman correlation is 0.28 ($p = 0.001$). There is no significant correlation between environmental pollution and industrial specialization in terms of other three specialization measures. However, after controlling for other variables, the estimate of the regression presents a significant causality of industrial specialization on environmental specialization.

According to the estimate in Table 4.10, industrial specialization is now a positive and significant determinant of environmental specialization in terms of the index 1 (model 17). Previous analysis has

① Econometric software STATA 9.0 is applied to run all the regressions and the major syntaxes include *xtreg* with *fe* and *re robust*.

Table 4.10 Determinants of Provincial Level Environmental Specialization: 18 Provinces. (Fixed and Random Effects) 1997 – 2003

ln(Environmental specialization)	FIXED EFFECTS				RANDOM EFFECTS			
	(17)	(18)	(19)	(20)	(21)	(22)	(23)	(24)
	Index1	Index2	Herfindahl	Cars	Index1	Index2	Herfindahl	Cars
ln(Industrial specialization)	0.683 (1.67) *	0.0896 (0.24)	0.0440 (0.68)	-0.00562 (-0.04)	0.0955 (0.38)	-0.318 (-1.28)	0.0625 (0.96)	-0.0360 (-0.26)
ln(Per capita income)	-59.000 (-2.10) **	-31.291 (-2.36) **	00510 (0.03)	6.963 (1.11)	-22.135 (-1.29)	-10.686 (-1.32)	-0.114 (-0.06)	4.769 (0.75)
[*ln(Per capital income)*]^2	3.391 (1.98) *	1.782 (2.20) **	-0.00115 (-0.01)	-0.406 (-1.08)	1.600 (1.48)	0.760 (1.48)	0.0140 (0.13)	-0.281 (-0.71)
ln(Population)	12.075 (0.24)	9.237 (0.39)	13.149 (5.75) ***	60.628 (5.78) ***	1.674 (0.26)	1.597 (0.55)	0.269 (0.29)	5.306 (1.42)
[*ln(Population)*]^2	-0.495 (-0.16)	-0.425 (-0.28)	-0.847 (-5.81) ***	-3.834 (-5.77) ***	0.0211 (0.05)	-0.0706 (-0.37)	-0.0244 (-0.43)	-0.329 (-1.43)
ln(Industrial output)	-2.849 (-0.78)	-1.051 (-0.61)	0.168 (1.48)	0.822 (1.47)	-2.511 (-1.33)	-0.916 (-1.06)	0.119 (1.09)	0.683 (1.34)

Continued

ln(Environmental specialization)	FIXED EFFECTS				RANDOM EFFECTS			
	(17)	(18)	(19)	(20)	(21)	(22)	(23)	(24)
	Index1	Index2	Herfindahl	Cars	Index1	Index2	Herfindahl	Cars
R^2	0.47	0.47	0.80	0.82	0.24	0.31	0.22	0.53
Hausman(FE. V RE.)					11.76 (0.465)	3.97 (0.984)	14.47 (0.272)	23.56 (0.023)
Spearman Correlation† (*Environmental specialization & Industrial specialization*)	0.055 (0.54)	0.027 (0.76)	−0.13 (0.14)	0.28 (0.0012)				
Observations	126	126	126	126	126	126	126	126

NOTES: environmental specialization and industrial specialization use the same measurement of specialization in each model.

t - statistics in parentheses for fixed effects and z - statistics in parentheses for random effects. Time dummies are included.

* significant at 10% level; ** significant at 5% level; *** significant at 1% level; † P - value in parentheses for Spearman correlation.

shown an increasing level of industrial specialization in the inland 18 provinces, however, these industries with great specialization are more likely to depend on natural resources and raw materials, therefore, they are relatively low value – added, low – tech industries and some of them could be quite pollution intensive. Meantime, because the level of development across 18 provinces does not stay on similar economic stages, the share of pollution in total pollution may vary from one province to another, resulting in a widening distance of pollution shares between provinces, environmental specialization in terms of relative measures thus increases.

Per capita income and its squared term both significantly determine the environmental specialization in model (17) and (18), so that environmental specialization turns out to be a quadratic function of per capita income, and a U – shaped curve for per capita income and environmental specialization in terms of index 1 and 2 could be found in Figure 4. 25. There is a turning point of per capita income at RMB6000 for index 1 and RMB6501. 2 for index 2, and per capita income of 18 provinces all remains on the left of the curve, it thus demonstrates a negative relationship between regional environmental specialization and level of per capita income. It finds no such a relationship in the East coast China. The environmental specialization is also a quadratic function of regional population size for the Herfindahl index and CARS. Industrial output that controls for the scale effects is insignificant throughout all models.

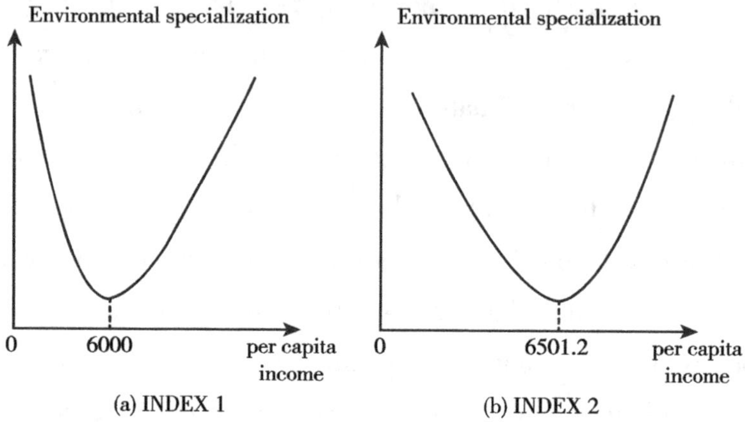

Figure 4. 25 U – curve in the other 18 provinces (index 1 and index 2)

4. 7 Sensitivity Checks

The literature suggests that efficiency improvement, technological progress, economy of scale, growing free trade and deepening international division of labour, would have impacts on the existing pattern of regional specialization on industrial production (Liang and Xu, 2004). Kalemi – Ozcan *et al.* (2003) also argues that population density may affect localization since transportation costs determine where manufacturing industries locate and industries with high transportation cost are likely to locate in densely populated areas, and such patterns of localization may cause industrial specialization to vary with population density as well (Krugman, 1991). They are therefore expected possible correlations between explanatory variables in the regression and more robustness checks are necessary.

Using three sample of 28 provinces, 10 East coast provinces and 18 inland provinces, I reestimate equation (4 – 9) by dropping one explanatory variable once at a time, staring with dropping the variable of industrial output. Table 4. 11 presents estimates of robustness checks using the fixed effects specifications and the sample of 28 provinces.

The estimates of robustness checks are similar for both relative specialization measures. The estimate of industrial specialization remains roughly stable and insignificant in model (25) to (30). Per capita income is negative and significant in model (28) and insignificant throughout other models. If not including the squared term of population (model 27), the estimate of population turns positive and significant. Model (31) to (36) that employ index 2 report very similar estimates. For the two absolute specialization measures, the estimate of industrial specialization remains roughly stable in model (37) to (42), per capita income and its squared term do not change as well. Without including the squared term of population (model 39), the estimate of population turns insignificant. Model (43) to (48) that employ CARS report very similar estimates.

Overall, the sensitivity checks for the sample of 28 provinces find no significant changes to estimatons of all variables. The possible correlation between variables is not a critical issue and estimates of the main results remain reliable.

Table 4. 12 reports estimates of robustness checks using the sub – sample of 10 East coast provinces. For the two relative measures, all variables except for per capita income do not significantly change. After dropping several control variables, the estimate of per capita in-

Table 4.11 **Sensitivity Analysis (Fixed Effects)**

FIXED EFFECTS ln(Environmental specialization)	INDEX 1						INDEX 2					
	(25)	(26)	(27)	(28)	(29)	(30)	(31)	(32)	(33)	(34)	(35)	(36)
ln(Industrial specialization)	0.833 (1.52)	0.606 (0.89)	0.651 (0.96)	0.639 (0.95)	0.543 (0.82)	0.566 (0.83)	0.144 (0.24)	−0.131 (−0.17)	−0.111 (−0.15)	−0.145 (−0.20)	−0.289 (−0.40)	−0.233 (−0.33)
ln(per capita income)	−21.449 (−1.37)	−20.018 (−1.32)	−20.885 (−1.36)	−26.286 (−1.69)*	1.542 (0.38)		−9.322 (−1.28)	−8.639 (−1.21)	−9.082 (−1.26)	−11.528 (−1.58)	1.095 (0.55)	
[*ln(per capita income)*]^2	1.350 (1.46)	1.027 (1.18)	1.096 (1.23)	1.441 (1.59)			0.583 (1.37)	0.459 (1.12)	0.495 (1.18)	0.652 (1.53)		
ln(population)	21.116 (0.64)	36.972 (1.15)	9.541 (1.98)**				14.735 (0.86)	19.960 (1.22)	4.375 (1.79)*			
[*ln(population)*]^2	−0.682 (−0.35)	−1.733 (−0.92)					−0.635 (−0.63)	−0.985 (−1.03)				
ln(Industrial output)	−3.542 (−1.62)						−1.310 (−1.43)					
R^2	0.46	0.45	0.45	0.44	0.42	0.42	0.46	0.45	0.45	0.44	0.43	0.42
Observations	196	196	196	196	196	196	196	196	196	196	196	196

Continued

FIXED EFFECTS ln(Environmental specialization)	HERFINDAHL						CARS					
	(37)	(38)	(39)	(40)	(41)	(42)	(43)	(44)	(45)	(45)	(47)	(48)
ln(Industrial specialization)	-0.042 (-0.53)	-0.048 (-0.61)	0.002 (0.03)	-0.002 (-0.02)	-0.017 (-0.25)	-0.016 (-0.24)	0.068 (0.38)	0.050 (0.30)	0.053 (0.32)	0.049 (0.30)	-0.143 (-0.76)	-0.153 (-0.83)
ln(per capita income)	1.250 (1.33)	1.254 (1.33)	1.176 (1.19)	0.989 (1.03)	0.270 (1.24)		14.050 (4.72) ***	13.984 (4.67) ***	13.595 (4.34) ***	13.222 (4.32) ***	-0.287 (-0.34)	
[*ln(per capita income)*]^2	-0.052 (-0.92)	-0.059 (-1.11)	-0.049 (-0.87)	-0.037 (-0.68)			-0.766 (-4.71) ***	-0.769 (-4.80) ***	-0.735 (-4.43) ***	-0.712 (-4.44) ***		
ln(population)	6.868 (2.70) ***	7.276 (2.79) ***	0.315 (0.83)				15.646 (1.47)	16.033 (1.55)	0.620 (0.54)			
[*ln(population)*]^2	-0.414 (-2.60) **	-0.441 (-2.71) ***					-0.948 (-1.45)	-0.974 (-1.53)				
ln(Industrial output)	-0.100 (-0.74)						-0.103 (-0.18)					
R^2	0.65	0.64	0.62	0.62	0.62	0.62	0.78	0.78	0.77	0.77	0.74	0.73
Observations	196	196	196	196	196	196	196	196	196	196	196	196

NOTES: environmental specialization and industrial specialization use the same measurement of specialization in each model.

t-statistics in parentheses for fixed effects. Time dummies are included.

* significant at 10% level; ** significant at 5% level; *** significant at 1% level.

Table 4.12 Sensitivity Analysis (10 East Coast Provinces, Fixed Effects)

FIXED EFFECTS ln(Environmental specialization)	INDEX 1						INDEX 2					
	(49)	(50)	(51)	(52)	(53)	(54)	(55)	(56)	(57)	(58)	(59)	(60)
ln(Industrial specialization)	-0.020 (-0.05)	-0.020 (-0.04)	0.032 (0.08)	-0.094 (-0.21)	-0.146 (-0.32)	0.148 (0.32)	-0.299 (-0.52)	-0.257 (-0.45)	-0.177 (-0.33)	-0.268 (-0.49)	-0.442 (-0.83)	0.063 (0.14)
ln(per capita income)	11.344 (0.31)	12.444 (0.35)	7.739 (0.25)	-17.837 (-0.68)	8.592 (1.84)*		7.659 (0.41)	7.899 (0.43)	4.627 (0.30)	-7.251 (-0.54)	4.674 (1.92)*	
[*ln(per capita income)*]^2	-0.275 (-0.16)	-0.271 (-0.16)	-0.037 (-0.03)	1.275 (0.98)			-0.218 (-0.24)	-0.204 (-0.23)	-0.043 (-0.06)	0.565 (0.87)		
ln(population)	35.891 (0.71)	27.081 (0.61)	12.500 (1.38)				19.733 (0.80)	14.927 (0.69)	5.879 (1.33)			
[*ln(population)*]^2	-1.438 (-0.51)	-0.887 (-0.36)					-0.849 (-0.62)	-0.548 (-0.46)				
ln(Industrial output)	1.583 (0.45)						0.807 (0.48)					
R^2	0.59	0.59	0.59	0.57	0.56	0.54	0.61	0.61	0.60	0.59	0.58	0.56
Observations	70	70	70	70	70	70	70	70	70	70	70	70

Continued

FIXED EFFECTS ln(Environmental specialization)	HERFINDAHL						CARS					
	(61)	(62)	(63)	(64)	(65)	(66)	(67)	(68)	(69)	(70)	(71)	(72)
ln(Industrial specialization)	-0.435 (-2.06) **	-0.461 (-1.86) *	-0.417 (-1.85) *	-0.481 (-2.11) **	-0.347 (-1.84) *	-0.320 (-1.92) *	-0.538 (-1.70) *	-0.625 (-2.27) **	-0.551 (-1.50)	-0.545 (-1.53)	-0.478 (-1.39)	-0.432 (-1.22)
ln(per capita income)	0.078 (0.03)	-0.444 (-0.15)	-1.359 (-0.43)	-4.047 (-1.48)	0.913 (1.70) *		-20.715 (-3.06) ***	-21.494 (-3.41) ***	-9.891 (-1.81) *	-9.422 (-2.24) **	0.948 (0.81)	
[*ln(per capita income)*]^2	0.054 (0.38)	0.059 (0.40)	0.106 (0.68)	0.242 (1.80) *			1.102 (3.57) ***	1.131 (3.87) ***	0.530 (2.06) **	0.506 (2.68) **		
ln(population)	1.704 (0.47)	4.944 (1.42)	1.136 (1.46)				-37.728 (-3.71) ***	-36.176 (-3.98) ***	-0.215 (-0.11)			
[*ln(population)*]^2	-0.028 (-0.12)	-0.232 (-1.10)					2.266 (3.50) ***	2.160 (3.84) ***				
ln(Industrial output)	-0.564 (-2.24) **						-0.346 (-0.46)					
R^2	0.72	0.69	0.69	0.68	0.65	0.63	0.91	0.91	0.89	0.89	0.88	0.88
Observations	70	70	70	70	70	70	70	70	70	70	70	70

NOTES: environmental specialization and industrial specialization use the same measurement of specialization in each model.

t-statistics in parentheses for fixed effects. Time dummies are included.

* significant at 10% level; ** significant at 5% level; *** significant at 1% level.

come turns significant in model (53) and (59). It implies that the effect of per capita income on environmental specialization may be captured by other variables. For both absolute measures, the estimate of industrial specialization is robust in model (61) to (66). After dropping several control variables, per capita income and its squared term both turn to significant (model 64 and 65) so that the effect of per capita income on environmental specialization has been captured by other variables. Model (69) to (72) report no significant change to estimates. The same procedure of robustness checks is applied to the 18 inland provinces, and results are presented in Table A4. 2 in the appendix.

4. 8 Conclusions

Environmental specialization is a critical issue raised after an improvement on levels of total pollution. According to several studies in US, industrial specialization could be a significant determinant of environmental specialization, and the research in this chapter thus investigates whether industrial specialization is also a major contributor to environmental specialization in a developing economy such as China.

Based on samples of 28 provinces that represent the whole country, 10 East coast provinces and 18 inland provinces, respectively, and on the observed time period from 1997 to 2003, the research finds an increasing industrial specialization in the whole country as well as in the East coast region. The East coast China is likely to specialize in high - tech, productive industries, whilst inland China is likely to specialize in industries with great consumption of natural resources and raw materials.

Environmental specialization is rising in terms of the relative specialization measures and is falling in terms of the absolute measures. A rising environmental specialization may cause serious health risks. Such an increase presents due to regional imbalanced development and shares of pollution between regions may have widened thereafter, however, this does not mean that share of pollution in a given region has increased. Actually, shares of pollution within regions have been decreasing, resulting in a falling environmental specialization in terms of absolute measures. I believe absolute measures more important for advising on health outcomes because they are based on absolute levels of exposure to pollution.

A clear relationship between industrial specialization and environmental specialization is not found in the whole country. The graphical analysis demonstrates that both industrial specialization and environmental specialization have been rising in China, but the econometric estimations found no causality between the two specializations. However, while defined in terms of absolute measures, industrial specialization is a negative and statistically significant determinant of environmental specialization in the East coast China, and while defined in terms of relative measures, it is a positive and statistically significant determinant of environmental specialization in the inland China. Therefore, it suggests industrial specialization may not have impact on the whole country's environmental specialization, but it has impact on regional environmental specialization, and such impact crucially depends on the specialization measures utilized.

Other regional variables somehow have determined environmental specialization as well. Regional per capita income is a significant determinant in the inland China. Regional population size has a significantly non – linear relationship with environmental specialization irrespective of which sample is used, population is thus an important determinant of regional environmental specialization. Industrial output that controls for the scale effect is not a significant determinant either.

Appendix

Table A4. 1 Data definitions and sources

Variable	Definition/Source
Environmental specialization	Calculated from emissions of five pollutants: waster water, solid waste, SO_2, SOOT and DUST. Source: China Statistical Yearbook.
Industrial specialization	Calculated from gross output of 15 manufacturing sectors. Source: China Statistical Yearbook.
Per capita income	Per capita gross regional product (RMB yuan/person). Source: China Statistical Yearbook.
Population	Regional total population year – end (10 000 persons). Source: China Statistical Yearbook.
Industrial output	Regional gross industrial output value (100 million RMB yuan). Source: China Statistical Yearbook.

Notes for Pollutants:

1. Waste water = (Waste water discharged by industry) – (In-

dustrial waste water meeting discharge standards)

Waste water discharged by industry refers to the volume of waste water discharged by industrial enterprises through all their outlets, including waste water from production process, directly cooled water, groundwater from mining wells that does not meet discharge standards and sewage from households mixed with waste water produced by industrial activities.

Industrial waste water meeting discharge standards refers to volume of industrial waste water discharge which, with or without treatment reaches national or local standards.

2. Solid waste = Industrial solid waste produced

Industrial solid waste produced refers to total volume of solid, semi – solid and high concentration liquid residues produced by industrial enterprises from production process in a given period of time including hazardous wastes, slag, coal ash, gangue, tailings, radioactive residues and other wastes.

3. *Industrial SO_2 emission* refers to volume of sulphur dioxide emission from fuel burning and production process in premises of enterprises for a given period of time.

4. *Industrial SOOT emission* refers to volume of SOOT in smoke emitted in process of fuel burning in premises of enterprises.

5. *Industrial DUST emission* refers to volume of DUST emitted by production process of enterprises and suspended in the air for a given period of time, including DUST form refractory material of iron and steel works, DUST from coke – screening systems and sintering machines of coke plants, DUST from lime kilns and DUST from cement production in building material enterprises.

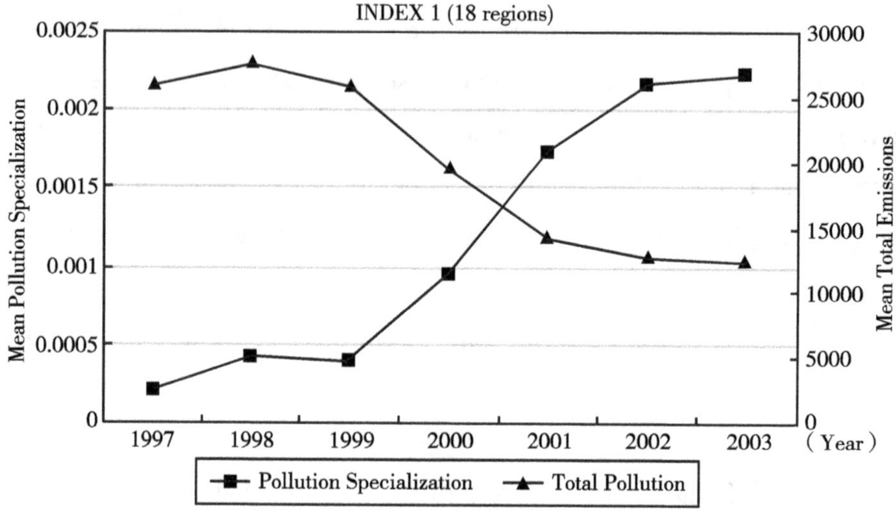

Figure A4.1 Pollution Specialization (Index 1) and Total Pollution, 1997 – 2003

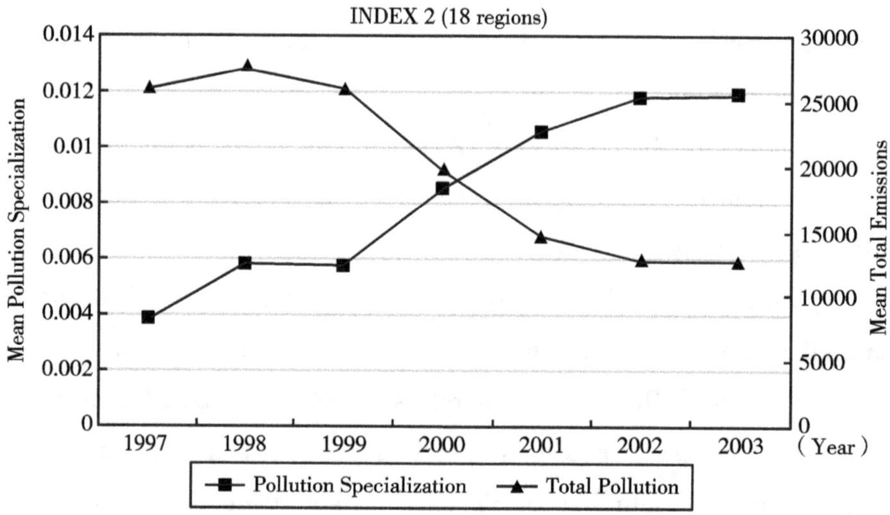

Figure A4.2 Pollution Specialization (Index 2) and Total Pollution, 1997 – 2003

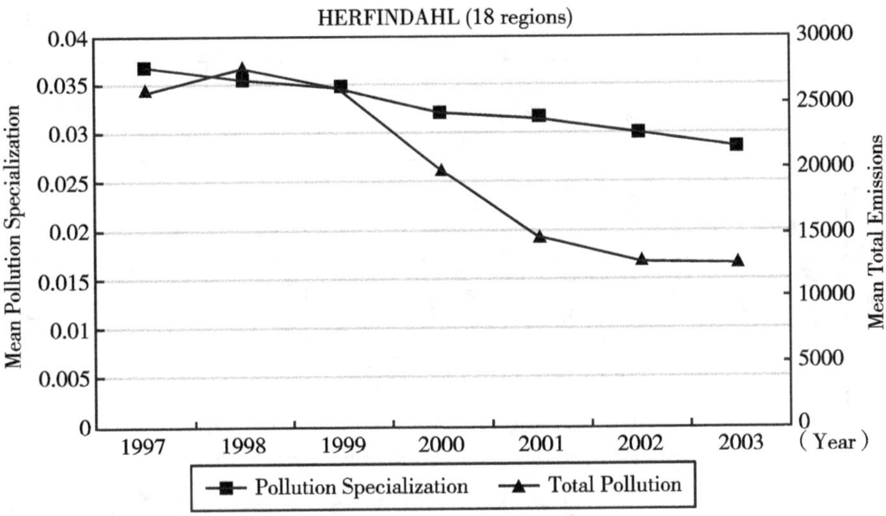

Figure A4.3 Pollution Specialization (Herfindahl) and Total Pollution, 1997 – 2003

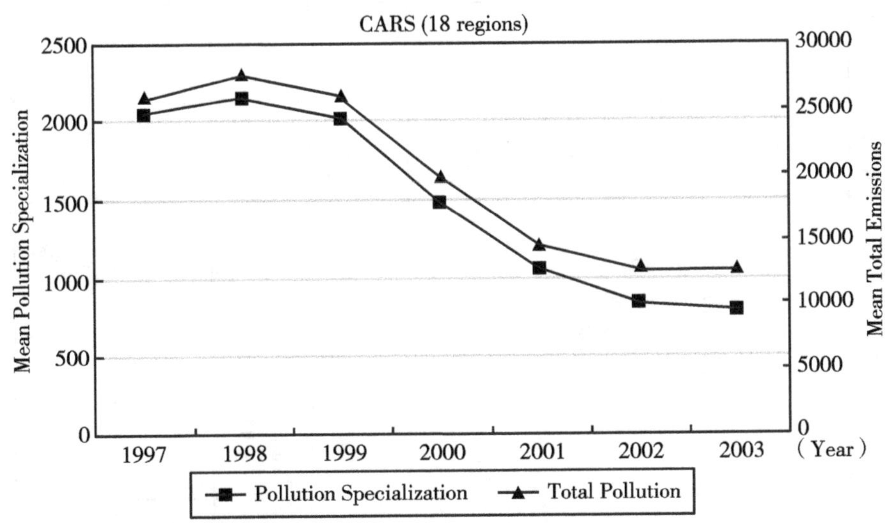

Figure A4.4 Pollution Specialization (CARS) and Total Pollution, 1997 – 2003

Table A4. 2 Sensitivity Analysis (18 Provinces, Fixed Effects)

FIXED EFFECTS ln(Environmental specialization)	INDEX 1						INDEX 2					
	(73)	(74)	(75)	(76)	(77)	(78)	(79)	(80)	(81)	(82)	(83)	(84)
ln(Industrial specialization)	0.683 (1.67) *	0.555 (1.35)	0.563 (1.39)	0.588 (1.44)	0.673 (1.62)	0.688 (1.65)	0.090 (0.24)	-0.005 (-0.01)	0.002 (0.00)	0.036 (0.08)	0.021 (0.05)	-0.004 (-0.01)
ln(per capita income)	-59.000 (-2.10) **	-67.796 (-2.62) **	-67.901 (-2.65) ***	-66.092 (-2.49) **	-6.997 (-1.53)		-31.291 (-2.36) **	-34.256 (-2.80) ***	-34.371 (-2.83) ***	-33.221 (-2.65) ***	-3.358 (-1.52)	
[ln(per capita income)]^2	3.391 (1.98) *	3.725 (2.28) **	3.743 (2.32) **	3.639 (2.17) **			1.782 (2.20) **	1.890 (2.44) **	1.906 (2.49) **	1.839 (2.31) **		
ln(population)	12.075 (0.24)	12.225 (0.26)	3.339 (0.58)				9.237 (0.39)	8.869 (0.39)	2.299 (0.85)			
[ln(population)]^2	-0.495 (-0.16)	-0.584 (-0.20)					-0.425 (-0.28)	-0.433 (-0.31)				
ln(Industrial output)	-2.849 (-0.78)						-1.051 (-0.61)					
R^2	0.47	0.46	0.46	0.46	0.42	0.39	0.47	0.46	0.46	0.46	0.42	0.39
Observations	126	126	126	126	126	126	126	126	126	126	126	126

Continued

FIXED EFFECTS ln(Environmental specialization)	HERFINDAHL					CARS						
	(85)	(86)	(87)	(88)	(89)	(90)	(91)	(92)	(93)	(94)	(95)	(96)
ln(Industrial specialization)	0.044 (0.68)	0.069 (1.00)	0.096 (1.40)	0.100 (1.52)	0.095 (1.63)	0.094 (1.54)	-0.006 (-0.04)	0.127 (0.88)	0.132 (0.80)	0.157 (0.97)	0.094 (0.64)	0.134 (0.87)
ln(per capita income)	0.051 (0.03)	0.687 (0.41)	0.638 (0.35)	0.847 (0.46)	0.521 (2.63) **		6.963 (1.11)	10.960 (1.87) *	9.996 (1.53)	11.634 (1.73) *	2.631 (3.04) ***	
[*ln(per capita income)*]^2	-0.001 (-0.01)	-0.028 (-0.27)	-0.008 (-0.07)	-0.020 (-0.18)			-0.406 (-1.08)	-0.597 (-1.66)	-0.460 (-1.15)	-0.557 (-1.35)		
ln(population)	13.149 (5.75) ***	13.160 (6.15) ***	0.352 (0.98)				60.628 (5.78) ***	60.873 (6.29) ***	2.668 (1.56)			
[*ln(population)*]^2	-0.847 (-5.81) ***	-0.843 (-6.18) ***					-3.834 (-5.77) ***	-3.836 (-6.26) ***				
ln(Industrial output)	0.168 (1.48)						0.822 (1.47)					
R^2	0.80	0.80	0.74	0.74	0.74	0.72	0.82	0.81	0.75	0.75	0.74	0.72
Observations	126	126	126	126	126	126	126	126	126	126	126	126

NOTES: environmental specialization and industrial specialization use the same measurement of specialization in each model.

t-statistics in parentheses for fixed effects. Time dummies are included.

* significant at 10% level; ** significant at 5% level; *** significant at 1% level.

Chapter 5

An Account of Geographic Concentration: An Analysis of Spatial Distribution of Pollution in China

5.1 Introduction

Researchers start to apply tools developed in the study of income inequality to analyze pollution inequality (Millimet and Slottje 2001, 2002; Heil and Wodon 1997, 2000; List 1999). Most studies still stick to the inequality measure of the Gini coefficient to examine regional distribution of pollution, and most studies have been taken in US. This research explores regional distribution of pollution using the Gini coefficient and many other inequality measures in order to provide a comprehensive account of spatial concentration of pollution. Brülhart and Traeger (2005) discuss a family of entropy indices that are commonly used to estimate inequality. Out of several entropy indices the research has selected the Theil index and its extensions (index of relative concentration and index of topographic concentration) to estimate regional distribution of pollution in China.

Regional distribution of pollution is an important subject in the environmental dimension because pollution is supposed to distribute equally across regions for several reasons as suggested by Millimet and Slottje (2002) and Heil and Wodon (1997). First, the literature on income inequality suggests that equity is important. Although income is a 'good' and pollution is a 'bad', *ceteris paribus*, society may wish to distribute cost of pollution evenly just as it may wish to distribute benefit of income equally. Secondly, there are health costs associated with pollution due to the threshold effects and nonlinear dose response functions. Equality of exposure to emissions can potentially minimize health costs. Thirdly, distribution of pollution is related to the distribution of quality of life at regional level. Inequality of emissions may result in the inequality of welfare, therefore, to accomplish an equal distribution of pollution may contribute to the equality of welfare.

This chapter examines regional distribution of pollution across the Chinese cities. It must distinguish from the subject in Chapter four. Chapter 4 examines environmental specialization using relative and absolute specialization measures. The specialization measures define if a region specializes in pollution of similar type or similar industries, whilst inequality measures define if pollution of similar type is evenly distributed over geographic area of the region. Therefore, a region may specialize in emissions of a given pollutant and have a large estimate of specialization measures, but the type of pollution may be evenly distributed in this region that would have a small estimate of inequality measure. Although the regional specialization on pollution is high, as long as the pollution is equally distributed within this region, the environmental hazards caused by pollution specialization may not be as serious as we previously expected.

The research uses city – level emission data and three sample sizes. The level of pollution could be reported in terms of concentrations or in terms of emissions, but it must be clear that information of concentrations and information of emissions refer to different contents. Concentration data provide more information about health impact of pollution, whilst emission data provide information on a wide range of environmental issues such as climate change or acid deposition, which are less likely related to pollution concentration. When the government policy targets on reducing detrimental health risks from air pollution, authorities could set a standard for height of factory chimneys or require firms to relocate outside the city, such policies aim at reducing pollution concentration rather than reducing pollution emissions. The goal of this research is based on a concern that detrimental health outcomes may be caused by unequal regional distribution of pollution, therefore, data of pollution concentration should be more appropriate for this study, but unfortunately, concentration data is not yet available at city level, and it has to be replaced with emission data.

I design three samples according to the regional level of economic development. The first one includes 112 cities from 30 provinces that spread all over the whole country. The second one includes 47 cities from 10 East coast provinces that cover the most developed areas in China, and the third one includes 65 cities from 20 inland provinces generally less developed. Since level of income may have impact on regional distribution of pollution (Benjamin *et al.* 2005; Kanbur and Zhang 2005; Wan and Zhang 2004; Wang 2006) and the gap of income is wide between the East coast China and the inland China, the regional distribution of pollution is thus expected to be quite different between the two regions.

The key methodology of this research is the bootstrap method, which has certain advantages that are specific to the inequality measures. The results show that toxic air pollution SO_2 and TSP are more uniformly distributed than wastewater and solid waste. Emissions of wastewater concentrate in the East coast China and they also take a large percentage of total emissions, driving an unequal regional distribution. The estimates of topographic concentration demonstrate results very similar to those found by estimates of the Gini coefficient or the general Theil index, but estimates of relative concentration show different outcomes. TSP and solid waste are most concentrated in the whole country. TSP concentrates in inland China that drives a higher relative concentration in the whole country. There is no significant change of time trend for pollution inequality in terms of the Gini coefficient, the general Theil index and the topographic concentration measure, but the time trend of relative concentration has significantly increased for emissions of wastewater, and decreased for solid waste.

The remainder of the chapter is organized as follows: Section 2 reviews the literature; Section 3 carefully explains the measurement of inequality; Section 4 describes the data; Section 5 presents the econometric methodology specific to the inequality measures; Section 6 reports the results and Section 7 concludes.

5.2 Literature Review

There has been an increasing number of literatures that use inequality measures to estimate the spatial distribution of pollution and other environmental hazards. Millimet and Slottje (2002) use the Gini coefficient to estimate impact of environmental regulations on the spatial distribution of pollution in their study. They suggest three reasons for the importance of studies on the pollution inequality, motivating the research of this chapter.

First, borrowing from the literature of income inequality, equity is important. Although income is a 'good' and pollution is a 'bad', society may wish to distribute cost of pollution evenly just as it may wish to distribute benefits of income equally.

Secondly, equality of emission exposure potentially minimizes the health cost associated with pollution due to the threshold effect and nonlinear dose response functions. Threshold effects refer to a minimum level of toxin to which one can be exposed before suffering any side effects. Such effects have shown important while human responses to various environmental hazards. Nonlinear dose response functions refer to the relationship between harmful outcomes and exposure levels. Such functions are typically assumed to be S – shaped. However, nonlinear dose response functions so far have been applied only to the developed countries such as US, and there is no scientific evidence that confirms if the functions also apply to developing countries such as China. This chapter is thus more likely to focus on the threshold effects as the scientific motivation to investigate the pollution distribution in China.

Thirdly, an unequal distribution of pollution implies inequality in the distribution of the quality of life. Differences of quality of life have impact on the internal migration in US, particularly for educated workers, and it may be the same case in China. Therefore, an unequal distribution of pollution may have more far – reaching impacts than simply affect the distribution of toxic exposure. It is worth investigating the distribution of pollution not only in developed countries, but also in developing countries.

The Gini coefficient is the best known and most frequently used measure of inequality, usually to estimate the distribution of income. Some studies extend the Gini coefficient and define a new environmental Gini coefficient (Heil and Wodon 1997, 2000). Millimet and Slottje (2002) use the environmental Gini coefficient to examine pollution inequality in US. They estimate the environmental Gini coefficient at both national and state level using data of total emissions per capita and emissions by type, and find national estimate of environmental Gini coefficient much larger than the state – level estimate, moreover, air pollution is more evenly distributed whilst water, land and underground releases are unevenly distributed across US.

Millimet and Slottje (2001) convert the environmental Gini coefficient to the environmental Paglin – Gini coefficient. The 45 – degree line in the studies of income inequality is a reference line that stands for the perfect equality, meaning each individual or household has identical income. However, Paglin (1975) questions the 45 – degree line and argue that the age – earning profile has an inverted U – shape, the society should not strive to identical income across all households at a point of time, rather only identical income across households at the same stage of life cycles. The idea of Paglin's should also be applied to the Gini coefficient in estimating pollution inequality. If individuals have preferences for the level of per capita income (a good) and pollution (a bad), individuals should be compensated for higher exposure to emissions with greater income, so that individuals in 'dirty' locations are no worse off than individuals in 'clean' locations.

Heil and Wodon (1997) investigate the inequality of CO_2 emissions in the poor and rich countries based on the environmental Gini coefficient. They also explain why the Gini coefficient should be applied to estimate inequality of emissions. The Gini coefficient is associated with the relative deprivation theory where levels of welfare depend not only on absolute income but also on individual's income relative to income of other individuals of society. Similarly, government policies target not only on their own levels of emissions, but also on the levels of emissions in other countries. In this sense, the Gini coefficient is supposed to be a reasonable measure because it contains information on emissions per capita as well as the rank of countries in the distribution of emissions.

Following Yitzhaki and Lerman (1991) who propose the decomposition of the Gini index into within – group and between – group components, Heil and Wodon (1997) define countries as groups of poor and rich countries, and they examine within – group and between – group inequality. Using data of per capita emissions of 111 countries from 1960 to 1990, they find a falling Gini over time, and it is due to a rising per capita emissions in the poor nations that have reduced disparity globally. The between – groups Gini takes account of half of total inequality and decreases over time, whilst for the within – group Gini, rich countries firstly contribute to the within – group inequality and then poor and rich both contribute equally to the within – group inequality.

Heil and Wodon (2000) forecast future inequality of carbon emissions in terms of decomposed Gini coefficient. They also forecast scenarios of country – level carbon emissions per capita to 2100. The forecast is based on a simple carbon emission model where emissions are modeled as a quadratic function of GDP and per capita GDP. It shows a long – term convergence in per capita GDP and a diminishing marginal propensity to emit (MPE) between per capita emissions and per capita GDP, both implies that per capita emissions grow rapidly when income remains at low levels, the growth of per capita emissions is back to be stable at middle income levels, and then drop quick when income reaches high levels. Their estimates of decomposed Gini demonstrate that a decreasing Gini coefficient is due to a fall of between – groups Gini.

List (1999) runs a unit root test and examines whether income convergence is accompanied by a convergence of air pollution, and this paper provides another motivation for studying the inequality of pollution. It argues, although evidence indicates that the disparity of per capita income between regions has lessened across US, only one measure of well – being has been applied to estimate such a disparity, that is a measure of wealth in terms of income or production. Since poor regions may specialize in pollution – intensive industries and growth of per capita income could be higher, whilst rich regions may specialize in clean industries and experience a relatively lower growth of per capita income, therefore, it is possible that regions converge in terms of monetary wealth but diverge in terms of "green incomes" or levels of income adjusted by environmental quality. It is thus essential to employ some other measures of well – being, such as a measure of environmental quality. List uses the β – convergence technique for cross – sectional convergence, ADF unit root test for stochastic convergence and the trend break model for a structural break in the time path of emissions. It finds that per capita emissions of nitrogen oxides and sulphur dioxide have converged conditionally across ten EPA (Environmental Protection Agency) Regions, which implies a decreasing inequality of emissions in US.

There are few studies that work on pollution inequality in developing countries like China. However, since Heil and Wodon (2000) and List (1999) both find links between income inequality and inequality of pollution, my research reviews several literatures related to the income inequality in China, from which a scenario of pollution inequality in China could be potentially detected.

Wan and Zhou (2005) examine the fundamental determinants of income inequality in rural China using household data. They find per capita income of rural household higher in the East coast China, around national average in the central China and much lower in the West China. Such a circumstance stays unchanged in long term and it implies that there is no convergence of income across regions despite rapid economic growth in China. They also find that not only a wide income disparity exists between provinces, but income inequality also significantly presents between villages within a province and present between households within a village. The inter – village income differences take about 40 percent of total inequality and the gap is even larger at household level.

Wang (2006) also examines the potential determinants of income inequality in China using province – level data. It finds out an inverted U – shaped curve between income inequality and economic development. They define a model of the Gini coefficient as a quadratic function of per capita GDP and the model is set up in level and in natural logarithm respectively. The estimates show a turning point of per capita GDP at RMB 30000 in urban China and at RMB 20000 in rural China. The model in terms of the natural logarithm indicates that urban inequality does not diminish in the extremely long term until GDP per capita has reached a level of RMB 2 million, which is practically indifferent to a non – decreasing function. Wang finally concludes that income inequality does not automatically decline as the economy grows and it is risky to predict a drop of income inequality in the near future.

There are other literatures that study income inequality in China from a historical perspective. Benjamin *et al.* (2005) takes an overview on the evolution of income inequality during China's economic transition period from 1987 to 2002. There has been a clear increase of income inequality since 1987 that presents in both urban and rural China where the increase is more rapid in urban China. They also find a significant disparity of inequality dynamics between inland and coast provinces where inland provinces experience more serious inequality. Kanbur and Zhang (2005) also find an increase of inequality between inland and coast China, and they argue that it is caused by some policies that favor coastal regions, such as the establishment of special economic zones and favourable tax breaks.

These studies discussed above literally provide indirect information about regional distribution of pollution in China. Given the possible link between income inequality and pollution inequality, a proven increase of income inequality in China may lead to a rising trend in pollution inequality and consequently cause more environmental hazards in China.

Another key point of this chapter is about how to measure environmental inequality. The Gini coefficient is the best known and widely applied measure of inequality, Yitzhaki and Lerman (1984, 1991) develop this measure for the first time. They create a simple approach that estimates the Gini coefficient using individual data and a regression program, which has thoroughly improved the complicated calculation introduced in previous literature. Heil and Wodon (1997) thereafter apply the Gini coefficient to measure distribution of emissions across countries and thus have developed the environmental Gini coefficient, and then Millimet and Slottje (2001) use the environmental Gini coefficient to estimate distribution of emissions in US.

Aside from the Gini coefficient, another group of inequality measure is also commonly applied and known as the entropy index. Brülhart and Traeger (2005) suggest that under some circumstances, entropy indices are better suited than the Gini index. One advantage of geographic concentration measures is their decomposability into within - country and between - country components. The Gini index is decomposable only if the range of values taken by the variable of interest does not overlap across subgroups of individual observations, however, it is not the case for almost all studies. Instead, they use entropy indices to estimate distribution of eight major sectors as well as some manufacturing sectors at a more disaggregated level in the Western European regions from 1975 to 2000. Since entropy measures are decomposable, they have examined several types of decomposition, including within - subgroups and between - subgroups general entropy, and entropy index of topographic concentration and of relative concentration.

5.3 Measurement of Inequality

In this chapter I employ two classes of inequality measures, the Gini coefficient and the family of entropy indices. They are both well - known and widely applied in the studies of income inequality. This research applies the measures in the field of environmental studies and develops measures of pollution inequality.

5.3.1 The Gini Coefficient

Yitzhaki and Lerman (1991) develop a simple approach that estimates the Gini coefficient using individual data and a regression program. They prove that the Gini of a variable is equal to the covariance between the variable and the rank of the variable, multiplied by two, and then divided by the product of the sample size and the mean value of the variable. Let y_i be the incomes in a sample of n observations, and rank individuals so that to set y_i in a non-decreasing order ($j < k$ implies $y_j < y_k$). The Gini coefficient of y is given by:

$$G = 2\text{cov}[y, F(y)]/\bar{y} \qquad (5-1)$$

where F(y) is the cumulative distribution and $\bar{y}$ is the mean of y. The estimate of F(y) in a random sample is the rank of the variable divided by n, the number of observations.

Heil and Wodon (1997) extend this method to develop an environmental Gini coefficient. Assume a sample of per capita emissions at regional level, denote p as per capita emissions, and F as each region's rank in the cumulative distribution of per capita emissions (F is 0 for the least polluting region and 1 for the most polluting region). If the covariance between x and y across regions is denoted by *cov* (x, y), the environmental Gini index G is thus given by:

$$G = 2\text{cov}(p, F)/\mu \qquad (5-2)$$

where μ is defined as the mean value of per capita emissions averaged on all regions. The Gini coefficient takes values between 0 (perfect equality) and 1 (maximum inequality). A larger value of environmental Gini indicates a greater inequality of pollution across regions.

5.3.2 Family of Entropy Indices

Brülhart and Traeger (2005) is one of the studies that use entropy indices to describe sectoral location patterns across Western European regions. Following their methodology, this research applies entropy indices to describe location patterns of pollution across the

Chinese cities.

5.3.2.1 General Entropy Index

Given a population of spatial basic units $i \in \{1, 2, \ldots, N\}$, each basic unit is associated with a unique value of variable y_{si} that represents an economic activity (measured in terms of employment or value added) of a particular sector $s \in \{1, 2, \ldots, S\}$. A basic unit is defined as a square kilometre of geographic area. In this research, I define a spatial basic unit as a city and an economic activity as level of pollution of a particular pollutant.

Members of the generalized entropy (GE) class of inequality indices are defined as follows:

$$GE(\alpha)_s = \frac{1}{\alpha^2 - \alpha}\left[\frac{1}{N}\sum_{i=1}^{N}\left(\frac{y_{si}}{\bar{y}_s}\right)^{\alpha} - 1\right] \tag{5-3}$$

where

$$\bar{y}_s = \frac{1}{N}\sum_{i=1}^{N} y_{si} = \frac{Y_s}{N} \tag{5-4}$$

Y_s denotes an activity in sector s summed across all N basic units. Alpha is a sensitivity parameter and it identifies the weight put on distances among values of y_{si} across the distribution over i. In principle it can be set to any real number. Following standard practice, α can be set to 1 or 2. Equation (5-3) is defined as the *Theil index* of inequality when $\alpha = 1$, and defined as *half the squared coefficient of variation*, CV, when $\alpha = 2$. The research focuses on the application of *Theil index*, and the general function of the *Theil index* is given by:

$$GE(1)_s = \frac{1}{N}\sum_{i=1}^{N}\frac{y_{si}}{\bar{y}_s}\log\frac{y_{si}}{\bar{y}_s}, \tag{5-5}$$

where GE (1) denotes the *Theil index*, s denotes the type of pollutant, N denotes total number of cities in the sample, y_{si} denotes emissions of pollutant s within city i, and $\bar{y}_s$ denotes mean value of emissions of pollutant s averaged on N cities. A larger value of GE (1) indicates a greater inequality of pollution across regions.

5.3.2.2 Topographic Concentration and Relative Concentration

The *Theil index* has two extensions, one is the *topographic concentration* index, and the other is the *relative concentration* index.① These two concentration indices are proposed due to limitations in the inequality studies. Previous studies argue that the sub – national regions such as a city is not supposed to be defined as a basic unit because cities differ significantly in terms of geographic and economic size. It is well known that spatial inequality measures are quite sensitive to the definition of regions, and the issue commonly refers to the "modifiable areal unit problem" (MAUP). Due to such a problem, the statistical analysis of a spatial zone could result in very different estimates by just changing boundaries of zones. Then how to put a weight on an economic activity of a basic unit has shown a great concern, and the choice of weight thereafter has raised a discussion on two types of geographic concentration: topographic concentration and relative concentration.

When measuring an economic activity per square kilometre without weighting, the non – concentration benchmark is that an activity spreads perfectly and evenly over physical space. Conversely, any

① The relative versus topographic definition is equivalent to the distinction in spatial statistics between heterogeneous and homogeneous space.

departure from such an evenly spatial spread registers as geographic concentration, irrespective of the spatial distribution of endowments or of other economic factors. This conception of geographic concentration refers to as the *topographic concentration.*

Alternatively, the sectoral activity per square kilometre can be weighted by the amount of aggregate economic activity on that square kilometre. In other words, the physical space is conditioned on the distribution of aggregate activity. If, for example, this research works on pollution as an economic activity, the non – concentration benchmark indicates that the proportions of types of pollutant in a given square kilometre are exactly equal to the proportions of types of pollutant in all observed regions. To make it clear, if the level of total pollution is high in the East coast region while it is low in the inland region, then discharge of wastewater, for instance, should be high in the East coast region and be low in the inland region, in this case, discharge of wastewater is defined to have non – relative concentration. This conception of geographic concentration refers to the *relative concentration.*

Overall, given the uneven geographic distribution of pollution, a given type of pollutant that happens to perfectly evenly spread in physical space would have zero topographic concentration but positive relative concentration. Conversely, in a region given types of pollutant spread exactly according to proportions of those types of pollutant across all observed regions, this region would then have zero relative concentration but positive topographic concentration.

Now consider a region $r \in \{1, 2, \ldots, R\}$ is set to be a basic unit i. The size of each region is defined in terms of the number of basic units it contains and thus $\sum_r n_r = N$. Regional economic activity is denoted by $\tilde{Y}_{sr}$ and indicates emissions of pollutant at regional level. Based on the type of geographic concentration, $\tilde{Y}_{sr} = \sum_i y_{sir}$ without weights indicates the *topographic concentration*, and $\tilde{Y}_{sr} = \sum_i \frac{y_{sir}}{\sum_s y_{sir}}$ with weights indicates the *relative concentration*.

In this setting, the Theil index is given by:

$$GE(1)_s = \sum_{r=1}^{R} \frac{n_r}{N} \frac{\bar{y}_{sr}}{\bar{y}_s} \log \frac{\bar{y}_{sr}}{\bar{y}_s}, \quad (5-6)$$

where

$$\bar{y}_{sr} = \frac{\tilde{Y}_{sr}}{n_r}, \text{ and } \bar{y}_s = \frac{\tilde{Y}_s}{N}, \quad (5-7)$$

and where $\tilde{Y}_s = \sum_r \sum_i y_{sir}$ for topographic concentration and $\tilde{Y}_s = \sum_r \sum_i \frac{y_{sir}}{\sum_s y_{sir}}$ for relative concentration. r denotes region in the sample that consists of a set of basic units. Other subscripts are previously defined. As described above, a large value of the indices implies a high level of concentration of a given type of pollutant, in other words, the geographic distribution of a given pollution is unequal when there is a large value of measure for either topographic concentration or relative concentration.

5.4 Data Description

The data of this research is set up at city level. Observations are collected in 112 cities from 2001 to 2005, where the number of cities ranges from 1 to 10 across regions (see appendix). ① The time period of 2001 to 2005 in China is on a stage of substantial development and has demonstrated many significant features of China that are essential to this research. There are four pollutants in the sample including wastewater, sulphur dioxide (SO_2), total suspended particle (TSP), and solid waste (see appendix for definition), each pollutant is measured by the same unit of tonne. City – level per capita GDP is also collected to estimate income inequality for comparison.

The pollution data in this research does not take account of pollution from sources other than industry (i. e. transportation) due to the lack of data at city – level. In order to acquire a sample size as large as possible, data of industrial pollution is therefore employed. For the four pollutants, emission data of TSP is newly constructed through taking a sum of industrial emissions of soot and dust. Since soot and dust differ only in terms of sources, they can be aggregated as suspended particles. Moreover, soot and dust are produced at different stages of production but in the same production process of a plant,

① Regions that have only one city include four municipalities, Beijing, Tianjin, Shanghai, Chongqing, and one province, Qinghai. Region with 10 cities is Shandong province.

therefore, the distribution of soot and dust both depends on the location of plants. Because of such a high correlation between soot and dust, it would be better treating them as one pollutant.

The basic unit that estimates the Theil index is defined as a city in this research, and a region that contains a set of basic units refers to a Chinese province. There are 112 cities and 30 provinces in the sample of this research. ①

Table 5. 1 reports the summary of statistics for each pollutant as well as total pollution. Statistics of city – level GDP per capita is also reported. It has seen a substantially decline of wastewater releases, but an increase of SO_2 emissions and solid waste produced. Emissions of TSP remain fairly stable over time. Both wastewater and solid waste take a large percentage of total pollution, in contrast, the air pollution of SO_2 and TSP takes only a small share of total pollution. Therefore, a significant reduction in total pollution is primarily due to the decline in wastewater releases, whilst other pollutants have made no substantial contribution to the decline of total pollution. Per capita emissions demonstrate very similar trends to the level of emissions for each pollutant. A decline of per capita wastewater releases is the main reason that total emissions per capita have decreased. Per capita emissions of other pollutants either rise or remain stable. GDP per capita has substantially increased over time and it has been driven by the rapid growth of the Chinese economy since 1980s.

① Tibet is not included due to lack of data.

Table 5.1 Summary Statistics, Mean Value at City Level

Variable	2001	2002	2003	2004	2005
Waste water releases	1214.94 (1752.33)	948.69 (1280.83)	885.19 (1350.98)	725.63 (983.59)	615.34 (838.72)
SO_2 emissions	7.74 (7.42)	7.74 (7.36)	8.53 (7.74)	9.32 (8.08)	10.16 (8.59)
TSP emissions	7.24 (6.12)	6.78 (5.96)	7.17 (6.17)	7.47 (6.79)	7.50 (6.78)
Solid waste produced	427.64 (564.59)	444.06 (558.09)	476.68 (590.27)	598.88 (1159.70)	628.18 (877.29)
Total emissions	1653.74 (1931.59)	1407.26 (1482.25)	1377.57 (1585.86)	1335.96 (1617.10)	1261.11 (1298.10)
Per capita waste water releases	3.29 (4.88)	2.61 (3.98)	2.09 (2.86)	1.73 (2.54)	1.50 (1.91)
Per capita SO_2 emissions	0.022 (0.032)	0.022 (0.030)	0.023 (0.032)	0.025 (0.033)	0.027 (0.032)
Per capita TSP emissions	0.020 (0.024)	0.019 (0.023)	0.020 (0.028)	0.020 (0.021)	0.019 (0.020)
Per capita solid waste produced	1.27 (2.14)	1.33 (2.22)	1.38 (2.29)	1.65 (2.87)	1.79 (2.99)
Total emissions per capita	4.59 (5.74)	3.98 (4.98)	3.52 (4.20)	3.41 (4.37)	3.34 (3.94)
GDP per capita	7987.84 (8839.08)	8117.61 (5748.48)	8962.68 (6308.83)	10119.34 (6939.34)	10991.93 (7169.75)

Note: per capita values are weighed by population at city level. Standard deviations in parentheses.

Table 5.2 reports the Spearman correlations between per capita GDP and level of emissions as well as per capita emissions. The null hypothesis of Spearman correlation test is that two variables observed are independent of each other and the rejection of the null indicates that these two variables are correlated to some extent. It has shown that level of emissions is significantly correlated to per capita GDP for all pollutants. Wastewater releases and emissions of TSP are both negatively related to per capita GDP, whilst SO_2 emissions and solid waste produced are both positively related to per capita GDP. However, the estimate of correlation coefficient is relatively small for all pollutants, which implies that the correlation between pollution and income may not be that strong in China. It is the same result for pollutant in terms of per capita emissions except for per capita releases of wastewater. Different from the level of wastewater releases, per capita wastewater is not correlated to per capita GDP. Total pollution is not related to per capita GDP either. These findings suggest a possible but relatively weak link between income and pollution, it needs more investigation on whether the distribution of income may have impact on the distribution of pollution in China.

Table 5.2 Spearman Correlations between Emissions and Per Capita GDP, City Level

Variable	Per capita GDP
Waste water releases	-0.10 (0.02)**
SO_2 emissions	0.20 (0.00)***
TSP emissions	-0.10 (0.02)**

Continued

Variable	Per capita GDP
Solid waste produced	0.10 (0.02) **
Total emissions	-0.04 (0.40)
Per capita waste water releases	-0.06 (0.16)
Per capita SO_2 emissions	0.32 (0.00) ***
Per capita TSP emissions	-0.11 (0.01) **
Per capita solid waste produced	0.13 (0.00) ***
Total emissions per capita	0.01 (0.88)

Note: P-value in parentheses. * significant at 10% level; ** significant at 5% level; *** significant at 1% level.

5.5 Non-Parametric Estimation Methodology

I conduct a non-parametric estimation methodology called the bootstrap method. Mills and Zandvakili (1997) highlight the bootstrap techniques that can estimate the standard errors of inequality measures. They argue that a major shortcoming of the studies that use inequality measure is the absence of statistical inference. Most studies have not made any attempt to determine the statistical significance of the observed difference in the computed values of a particular measure, despite studies using the asymptotic methods. It is necessary to set up a statistical inference within small samples, however, it is difficult to construct statistical inference for any inequality measures because these measures are non – linear functions of random variables. Furthermore, the decomposable measures of inequality are bounded, for example, the Gini coefficient lies in the interval of [0, 1], the application of standard asymptotic estimates may result in an estimated interval that extend beyond the theoretical bound of a particular measure. Therefore, bootstrap method as an alternative to construct statistical inference is introduced thereafter.

Brülhart and Traeger (2005) also demonstrate reasons for taking the bootstrap method in inequality studies. They point out that any concentration index describes the dispersion of a distribution through a scalar, and it therefore has its own sampling distribution. Traditionally, inference on entropy measures is based on the asymptotic results obtained through the delta method that tests the equality of two distributions on the same units at different times, however, this method requires very complex covariance calculations to take account of the intertemporal dependencies in the data. One solution is to ignore data dependencies and assume instead that the spatial distributions compared are independent. Some literature therefore favours the application of the bootstrap inference (Biewen 2001, Mills and Zandvakili 1997). In this approach, the sampling distribution of an inequality index is estimated by multiple random re – sampling with replacement from the data set at hand. Through the bootstrap one can account for dependencies in the data without having to estimate covariance matrices explicitly.

All in all, this research prefers the bootstrap method for reasons discussed above. The concentration indices of this research are non-linear functions of a random variable. The estimates of the measures are bounded within the [0, 1] interval. This research has a relatively small sample size. The goal of this research is also to test changes of measures statistically. Therefore, the bootstrap method can sort out all these issues and is indeed superior to other method.

As Heij *et al.* (2004) suggests, there is an attractive property of the bootstrap method that does not require knowledge of the shape of the probability distribution for either the data or the estimator. It is, therefore, said to be distribution free. The bootstrap method uses the sample distribution to construct an interval. Taking a random sample as an example, assuming that all observations have different values, i. e. $y_i \neq y_j$ for $i \neq j$, $(i, j = 1, \ldots, n)$, then the bootstrap probability distribution of the random variable y is the discrete distribution with outcome set $V = \{y_1, \ldots, y_n\}$ and with probabilities

$$P[y = y_i] = \frac{1}{n} \tag{5-8}$$

the distribution of a statistic $t\ (y_1, \ldots, y_n)$ is simulated as follows. In one simulation run, n observations are randomly drawn (with replacement) from the distribution (5-8) and the corresponding value of t is calculated. Repeating it in a large number of runs (always with the same distribution based on the original data) provides an accurate approximation of the distribution of t if equation (5-8) would be the data generating process. Generally, the bootstrap is a simple method that creates an idea of possible random variations when there is little information about the probability distribution of the data.

STATA version 8 explains the bootstrap method in such a way that bootstrapping provides a way of estimating standard errors and other measures of statistical precision. It provides a way to obtain such measures when no formula is otherwise available, or when available formulas make assumptions that are not tenable.

Mechanically, the procedure works like this: one has a dataset containing N observations and an estimator that, when applied to the data, produces certain statistics. One draws, with replacement, N observations from the N observation dataset. In this random drawing, some of the original observations will appear once, some more than once, and some not at all. Using that dataset, one reapplies the estimator. One does this repeatedly, each time drawing a new random sample and re – estimating. Last, one builds a dataset of estimated statistics. From these data, one can calculate the standard deviation using the standard formula: $\{\sum(\theta_i^* - \bar{\theta}^*)^2/(k-1)\}^{\frac{1}{2}}$, where θ_i^* is the statistic calculated using the i th bootstrap sample, $\bar{\theta}^*$ is the average of θ_i^*, and k is the number of replications. This formula gives an estimate of the standard error of the statistic.

The STATA command 'INEQERR' is to estimate the bootstrap standard errors for indices of inequality, including three indices of inequality: the Gini coefficient, the Theil index and Variance of Logs. The research uses the first two measures, the Gini coefficient and the Theil index.

5.6 Results

The estimates of inequality measures are reported in the following tables. I use three data samples, including the whole country that contains 112 cities in 30 provinces, the most developed region in China that contains 47 cities in the 10 East coast provinces, and the inland region that contains 65 cities in 20 provinces.

5.6.1 The Gini Coefficient

According to the definition of Gini coefficient, I use per capita emissions at city level to estimate the Gini coefficient. Table 5.3, 5.4 and 5.5 present estimates for three samples, respectively.

Table 5.3 presents the estimate of environmental Gini coefficient for the whole country. The estimate is reported for each pollutant as well as total pollution. The Gini of income inequality is also reported. The estimate of the Gini coefficient ranges from 0.552 to 0.618 for wastewater, demonstrating the largest inequality out of four pollutants. The estimate of the Gini coefficient ranges from 0.382 to 0.433 for SO_2 emissions, indicating the least inequality out of four pollutants. The inequality of the TSP emissions is the second lowest and the inequality of solid waste produced is the second highest. The estimate of the Gini ranges from 0.458 to 0.517 for total pollution, which also demonstrates a high degree of inequality. If compare the Gini estimates across pollutants, the distribution of wastewater and solid waste is more unequal relative to the distribution of total pollution, and the distribution of air pollution is less unequal relative to the distribution of total pollution. Because the discharge of wastewater takes over half of total pollution (Table 5.1), it is reasonable that the distribution of total pollution is primarily driven by an unequal distribution of wastewater.

Table 5.3 Gini Coefficient of Emissions and Income (sample size of 112 cities in 30 provinces)

The Gini Coefficient						
Year	Water	SO_2	TSP	Solid Waste	Total Pollution	Per capita GDP
2001	0.552 (0.041)	0.433 (0.035)	0.436 (0.026)	0.546 (0.040)	0.491 (0.039)	0.403 (0.041)
2002	0.584 (0.031)	0.432 (0.032)	0.447 (0.028)	0.544 (0.034)	0.499 (0.029)	0.351 (0.019)
2003	0.618 (0.027)	0.409 (0.030)	0.440 (0.028)	0.532 (0.035)	0.517 (0.027)	0.355 (0.019)
2004	0.580 (0.027)	0.396 (0.033)	0.443 (0.030)	0.569 (0.060)	0.496 (0.043)	0.350 (0.019)
2005	0.578 (0.035)	0.382 (0.036)	0.434 (0.030)	0.547 (0.039)	0.458 (0.032)	0.333 (0.022)

Note: Emissions are weighted by population. The index is calculated using Equation (5-2) from the text. Bootstrap standard errors in parentheses are generated from 100 bootstrap replications.

The estimate of the Gini ranges from 0.333 to 0.403 for per capita GDP, which is much lower compared to the inequality of pollution. Previous correlation analysis finds no clear relationship between pollution and income. It still remains a question that if inequality of pollution is related to the inequality of income.

Table 5.4 presents estimates of the environmental Gini for the East coast region. The estimate of the Gini ranges from 0.500 to

0.676 for wastewater, it again indicates the highest inequality out of four pollutants. The estimate of the Gini ranges from 0.343 to 0.399 for SO_2 emissions, indicating the least inequality out of four pollutants. The estimates of the Gini for TSP and solid waste stay in the middle of the four pollutants. The estimate of the Gini ranges from 0.468 to 0.552 for total pollution. Distribution of wastewater and solid waste spread more unequally relative to the distribution of total pollution, but distribution of SO_2 and TSP spread more evenly relative to the distribution of total pollution.

Table 5.4 Gini Coefficient of Emissions and Income (sample size of 47 cities in 10 East coast provinces)

	The Gini Coefficient					
Year	Water	SO_2	TSP	Solid waste	Total Pollution	Per capita GDP
2001	0.500 (0.061)	0.397 (0.033)	0.440 (0.038)	0.531 (0.039)	0.475 (0.055)	0.370 (0.060)
2002	0.620 (0.043)	0.399 (0.038)	0.443 (0.039)	0.529 (0.037)	0.522 (0.047)	0.292 (0.025)
2003	0.676 (0.045)	0.383 (0.032)	0.439 (0.039)	0.519 (0.039)	0.552 (0.045)	0.303 (0.021)
2004	0.605 (0.049)	0.363 (0.035)	0.419 (0.043)	0.499 (0.037)	0.499 (0.037)	0.296 (0.021)
2005	0.630 (0.047)	0.343 (0.039)	0.404 (0.037)	0.526 (0.030)	0.468 (0.042)	0.275 (0.023)

Note: Emissions are weighted by population. The index is calculated using Equation (5-2) from the text. Bootstrap standard errors in parentheses are generated from 100 bootstrap replications.

Similar patterns of distribution exist in the East coast region and in the whole country. There is a larger estimate of the Gini in the East coast region than in the whole country for wastewater, suggesting that discharge of wastewater heavily concentrates in the East coast China and it primarily drives the unequal distribution of wastewater in the whole country. The concentration of wastewater in the East coast region may be caused by the concentration of several manufacturing industries in this region, such as Textile and wearing apparel, Paper and products, Chemicals, and Non – metallic mineral products. These sectors are major sources of industrial wastewater, every year total wastewater of the 10 provinces takes over half of the country' total releases of wastewater so that it is possible that the concentration of water – polluting industries in the East coast region is the main reason for the inequality of wastewater across the whole country.

The estimate of the Gini ranges from 0.275 to 0.370 for per capita GDP in the East coast region. The distribution of income in the most developed region of China is more equal relative to the distribution of income in the whole country. However, relatively equal distribution of income does not bring in the same equality of pollution in the most developed region. Again, the findings suggest no clear relationship between inequality of income and inequality of pollution.

Table 5.5 presents estimates of the environmental Gini for the inland China. It has also seen a pattern of pollution distribution similar to that in the whole country. The estimate of the Gini ranges from 0.538 to 0.578 for wastewater that shows the largest inequality of four pollutants. The estimate of the Gini stays within the interval [0.40, 0.46] for SO_2 and TSP. Solid waste also has a greater Gini coefficient that demonstrates the second highest level of inequality in the four pollutants. The estimate of the Gini ranges from 0.447 to 0.489 for total pollution that is higher than the Gini of SO_2 and TSP and lower than the Gini of wastewater and solid waste. Also note that the distribution of SO_2 emissions in the inland region is more unequal than that in the East coast region. The explanation is that industrial SO_2 emissions is primarily produced by burning coal and coal is still the major energy source of industrial production in China. Natural resources such as coal are relatively abundant in the inland region and several inland provinces such as Shanxi are big consumers of coal that leads to a relatively high inequality of SO_2 in the inland region.

Table 5.5 Gini Coefficient of Emissions and Income (sample size of 65 cities in 20 inland provinces)

The Gini Coefficient						
Year	Water	SO_2	TSP	Solid waste	Total Pollution	Per capita GDP
2001	0.562 (0.050)	0.454 (0.053)	0.418 (0.031)	0.555 (0.048)	0.486 (0.048)	0.313 (0.049)
2002	0.553 (0.038)	0.453 (0.050)	0.430 (0.033)	0.552 (0.042)	0.473 (0.039)	0.299 (0.048)
2003	0.578 (0.045)	0.426 (0.042)	0.414 (0.034)	0.538 (0.051)	0.483 (0.041)	0.286 (0.034)
2004	0.560 (0.041)	0.417 (0.049)	0.426 (0.036)	0.605 (0.082)	0.489 (0.058)	0.291 (0.037)
2005	0.538 (0.042)	0.406 (0.043)	0.416 (0.035)	0.557 (0.064)	0.447 (0.043)	0.300 (0.043)

Note: Emissions are weighted by population. The index is calculated using Equation (5-2) from the text. Bootstrap standard errors in parentheses are generated from 100 bootstrap replications.

The estimate of the Gini for per capita GDP is slightly larger in the inland region than in the East coast region, suggesting that income is more evenly distributed either within the East coast regions or within the inland region, but there is a greater inequality of income in the whole country. Therefore, such an inequality of income in the country could be driven by the difference between the East coast and inland regions. Due to a variety of governmental policies that is favourable towards the East coast region, it has developed more rapidly than the inland region, and the gap of income in the two regions consequently causes an inequality of income in the whole country.

Figure 5.1, 5.2 and 5.3 plot the Gini coefficient from 2001 to 2005, allowing us to examine the time trend of pollution inequality as well as income inequality. Figure 5.1 displays the Gini coefficient estimated on 112 cities in the whole country. The Gini coefficient of wastewater increases at the beginning and then declines after 2003, whilst the Gini of solid waste slightly declines at the beginning and then increases after 2003. The Gini of SO_2 and TSP remains fairly stable over time with a slightly decrease for SO_2. Compared to the time trend of total pollution, the time trend of wastewater and solid waste are both higher and the time trend of SO_2 and TSP are both lower, suggesting that wastewater and solid waste are more unequally distributed than the distribution of total pollution, whilst air pollution are more evenly distributed relative to the distribution of total pollution. There is a significant finding in Figure 5.1 that distribution of wastewater literally dominates the distribution of total pollution. In 2003 – 2004, it has apparently seen a decline in the inequality of wastewater, at the same time, the inequality of total pollution declines as well even though the inequality of other pollutants increases or remains fairly stable. The Gini of per capita GDP increases at first, and then drops and remains stable afterwards. Income is distributed more equally relative to the pollution.

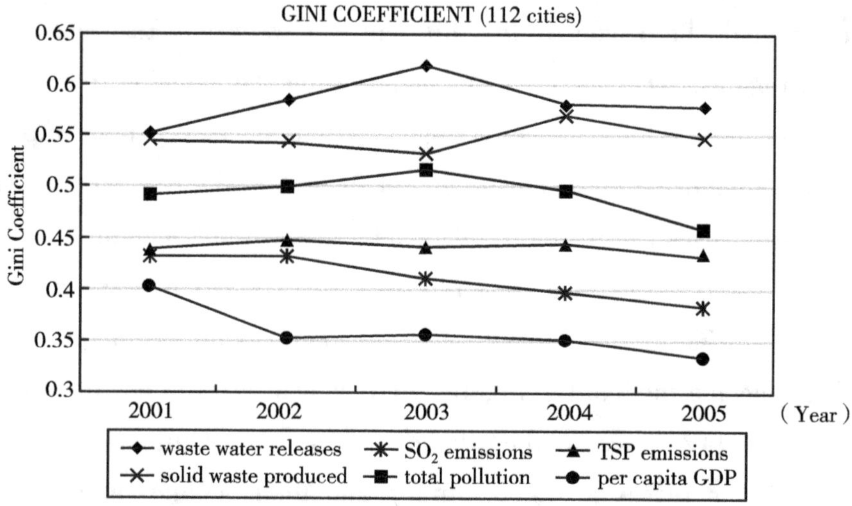

Figure 5. 1 The Environmental Gini and Income Gini (112 cities in 30 provinces)

Figure 5. 2 displays the Gini estimated on 47 cities in the East coast China. The time trend on the top demonstrates the largest inequality of wastewater. It increases at first and then decreases after 2003. Other pollutants have seen a falling Gini over time. Therefore, the shift of time trend for the inequality of total pollution could be primarily due to the shift of inequality of wastewater. The inequality of per capita GDP remains at low level in the East coast China. Figure 5. 3 displays the Gini estimated on 65 cities in the inland China. Wastewater and solid waste again demonstrate the largest inequality in the four pollutants. The inequality of per capita GDP remains stable relative to the income inequality in the East coast region.

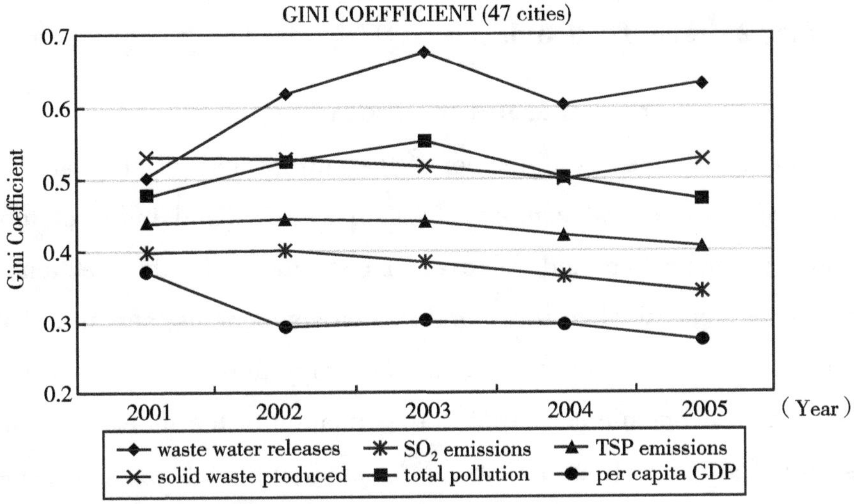

Figure 5.2 The Environmental Gini and Income Gini
(47 cities in 10 East coast provinces)

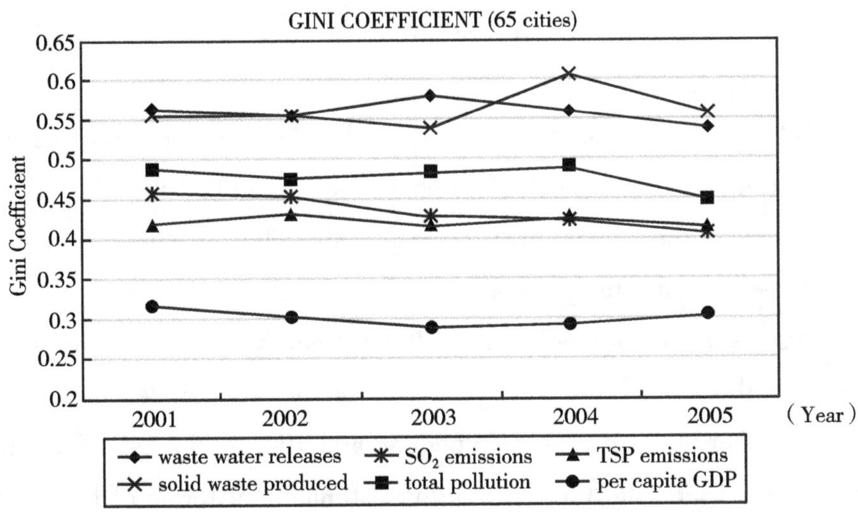

Figure 5.3 The Environmental Gini and Income Gini
(65 cities in 20 inland provinces)

5.6.2 The Theil Index

5.6.2.1 The General Theil Index

The Theil index is a member of the entropy index family and can be extended to several components such as the Theil index of topographic concentration and relative concentration. In this section, I explore the general Theil index and its two components thereafter. According to the definition of the general entropy index, there is a basic unit with an economic activity in the estimation of the index, and this research defines such an activity as the environmental pollution generated by industrial production. Table 5.6 – 5.8 report the general Theil index of total pollution as well as four types of pollutant, namely wastewater releases, SO_2 emissions, TSP emissions and solid waste produced, for the whole country and East coast and inland regions, respectively.

Table 5.6 presents the general Theil index estimated on 112 cities in the whole country. The estimate ranges from 0.568 to 0.702 for wastewater, indicating a high level of inequality in the four pollutants. The estimate ranges from 0.265 to 0.333 for SO_2 and it is the least inequality in four pollutants. It has seen very similar results as shown by the Gini. However, in terms of the Theil index, distribution of wastewater turns more unequal and distribution of SO_2 turns more equal relative to the distribution estimated in terms of the Gini. The Theil index ranges from 0.376 to 0.472 for total pollution and ranges from 0.180 to 0.328 for per capita GDP, both of which demonstrate more equal distribution relative to the distribution estimated in terms of the Gini. It has also seen a lower inequality of income relative to the inequality of pollution, implying that the distribution of pollution could be determined by factors other than the income.

Table 5.6 Theil Index of Emissions and Income (sample size of 112 cities in 30 provinces)

The Theil Index						
Year	Water	SO_2	TSP	Solid waste	Total Pollution	Per capita GDP
2001	0.568 (0.108)	0.333 (0.066)	0.322 (0.038)	0.546 (0.098)	0.445 (0.084)	0.328 (0.089)
2002	0.604 (0.079)	0.332 (0.055)	0.339 (0.044)	0.530 (0.077)	0.429 (0.054)	0.205 (0.023)
2003	0.702 (0.072)	0.300 (0.054)	0.327 (0.041)	0.509 (0.084)	0.472 (0.053)	0.207 (0.021)
2004	0.599 (0.064)	0.280 (0.057)	0.341 (0.048)	0.702 (0.221)	0.459 (0.095)	0.199 (0.022)
2005	0.604 (0.083)	0.265 (0.058)	0.331 (0.044)	0.559 (0.114)	0.376 (0.060)	0.180 (0.025)

Note: Emissions are measured by the aggregate level of emissions. The index is calculated using Equation (5 – 5) from the text. Bootstrap standard errors in parentheses are generated from 100 bootstrap replications.

Table 5.7 presents the estimated Theil index on 47 cities in the East coast China. Wastewater has shown the largest inequality in four pollutants with the estimate of the Theil from 0.466 to 0.870, and SO_2 has shown the least inequality with the estimate of the Theil from 0.208 to 0.274. The Theil index ranges from 0.372 to 0.551 for total pollution, that is more equal than the distribution estimated in terms of the Gini. Wastewater is highly concentrated whilst SO_2 and solid wastes are less concentrated in the East coast region, thus, in the whole country the inequality of wastewater is due to the concentration in the East coast region and the inequality of SO_2 and solid wastes is due to the concentration in inland region. The Theil index gives very similar estimates for TSP emissions in the East coast region and in the country, showing similar patterns of distribution in the East coast region and in the country. The Theil index ranges from 0.118 to 0.286 for per capita GDP in the East coast region, namely low levels of income inequality.

Table 5.7 Theil Index of Emissions and Income

(sample size of 47 cities in 10 East coast provinces)

	The Theil Index					
Year	Water	SO_2	TSP	Solid waste	Total Pollution	Per capita GDP
2001	0.466 (0.120)	0.268 (0.046)	0.333 (0.056)	0.483 (0.077)	0.406 (0.092)	0.286 (0.107)
2002	0.689 (0.106)	0.274 (0.054)	0.334 (0.057)	0.483 (0.074)	0.472 (0.089)	0.133 (0.022)
2003	0.870 (0.137)	0.253 (0.043)	0.324 (0.055)	0.463 (0.073)	0.551 (0.102)	0.143 (0.019)
2004	0.660 (0.121)	0.228 (0.047)	0.297 (0.062)	0.423 (0.069)	0.423 (0.067)	0.137 (0.019)
2005	0.723 (0.122)	0.208 (0.049)	0.280 (0.051)	0.469 (0.059)	0.372 (0.069)	0.118 (0.019)

Note: Emissions are measured by the aggregate level of emissions. The index is calculated using Equation (5-5) from the text. Bootstrap standard errors in parentheses are generated from 100 bootstrap replications.

Table 5.8 presents the Theil index estimated on 65 cities in the inland China. The Theil index ranges from 0.535 to 0.839 for solid waste, representing highest level of inequality in four pollutants. The Theil index ranges from 0.284 to 0.307 for TSP, providing the least inequality in four pollutants. The Theil index ranges from 0.371 to 0.473 for total pollution. Again, very similar to that found by the Gini, SO_2 and solid wastes are both concentrated in the inland region. Income inequality is larger in the inland region than that in the East coast region because provinces in the inland region are more likely to show various stages of economic development while provinces in the East coast region are more likely to remain on the same stage of economic development.

Table 5.8 The Theil Index of Emissions and Income (sample size of 65 cities in 20 inland provinces)

The Theil Index						
Year	Water	SO_2	TSP	Solid waste	Total Pollution	Per capita GDP
2001	0.586 (0.132)	0.382 (0.104)	0.291 (0.042)	0.589 (0.127)	0.439 (0.104)	0.209 (0.073)
2002	0.539 (0.086)	0.375 (0.102)	0.306 (0.047)	0.562 (0.109)	0.385 (0.070)	0.185 (0.066)
2003	0.607 (0.114)	0.335 (0.079)	0.284 (0.047)	0.535 (0.128)	0.415 (0.077)	0.153 (0.040)
2004	0.560 (0.095)	0.317 (0.088)	0.307 (0.051)	0.839 (0.290)	0.473 (0.125)	0.156 (0.047)
2005	0.530 (0.091)	0.307 (0.078)	0.295 (0.047)	0.609 (0.176)	0.371 (0.080)	0.171 (0.055)

Note: Emissions are measured by the aggregate level of emissions. The index is calculated using Equation (5-5) from the text. Bootstrap standard errors in parentheses are generated from 100 bootstrap replications.

Figure 5.4, 5.5 and 5.6 plot the general Theil index from 2001 to 2005. Figure 5.4 exhibits the Theil index estimated on 112 cities across the whole country. The inequality of wastewater rises at first but then falls. The inequality of solid waste instead falls at first but then increases with a jump from 2003 to 2004. The inequality of SO_2, TSP and total pollution all remains stable over time. The top two time trends of inequality stand for wastewater and solid wastes, and the two time trends below the trend of total pollution stand for SO_2 and TSP. The figure suggests that wastewater and solid wastes are more concentrated, whilst air pollution is distributed more equally. The Theil index of per capita income remains at very low level over time.

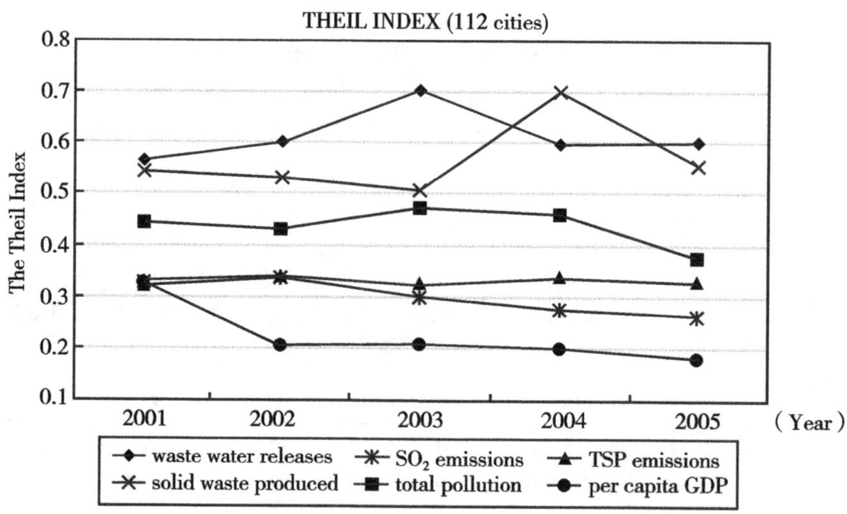

Figure 5.4 The Theil Index for Emissions and Income (112 cities in 30 provinces)

Figure 5.5 exhibits the general Theil index estimated on 47 cities in the East coast China. Wastewater shows the largest as well as the most volatile trend of inequality, it is thus believed that the inequality of wastewater in the whole country is driven by the more unequal distribution of wastewater in the East coast region. The Theil index of other pollutants and total pollution are stable over time. Income inequality in terms of the Theil index of per capita GDP still remains at very low level all the time.

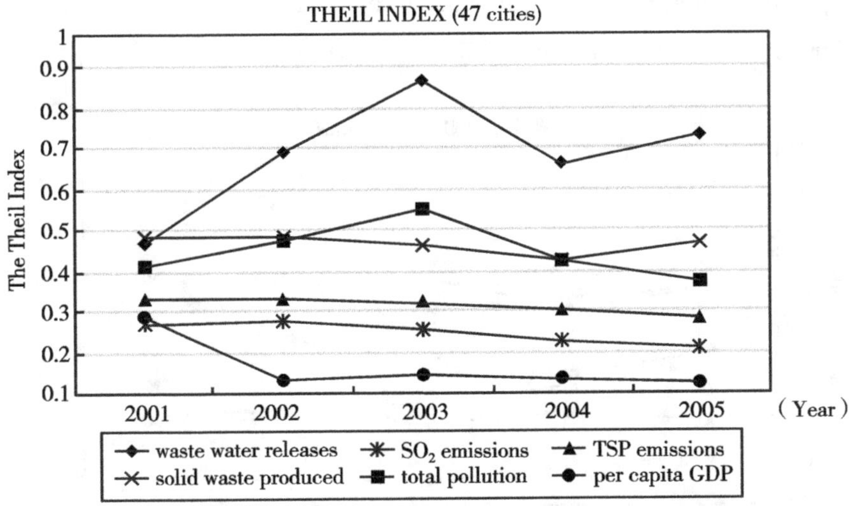

Figure 5.5 The Theil Index for Emissions and Income
(47 cities in 10 East coast provinces)

Figure 5.6 exhibits the general Theil index estimated on 65 cities in the inland China. The Theil index of wastewater no longer shows the largest inequality, instead, it shows a fairly stable time trend. The Theil index of SO_2, TSP as well as total pollution remains stable over time. Now the Theil index of solid waste deserves our attention. The inequality shows a jump between 2003 and 2004 for solid waste and it is due to a significant increase of the solid waste produced. The solid waste produced in Tangshan city of Hebei province increased from 4605 (measured in 10000 tons) in 2003 to 11609 (10000 tons) in 2004, and in Huhhot of Inner Mongolia it increased from 92 (10000 tons) in 2003 to 203 (10000 tons) in 2004. Other cities also show either an increase or a decrease for solid waste produced, but the change is not as significant as those in Tangshan and Huhhot. The income inequality remains at low level in the inland region, but it is larger than the inequality of income in the East coast region.

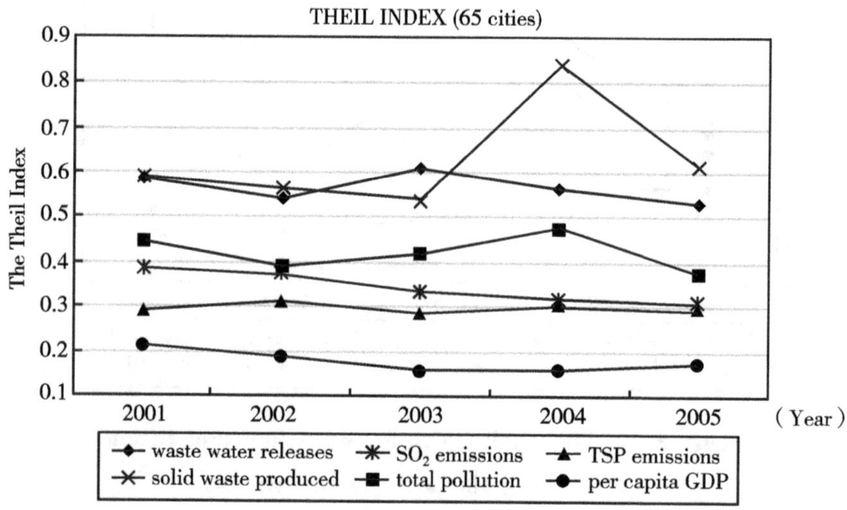

Figure 5.6 The Theil Index for Emissions and Income (65 cities in 20 inland provinces)

5.6.2.2 The Theil Index of Relative Concentration

As previously introduced, the non-concentration benchmark of relative concentration indicates pollutants in a given region are distributed exactly the same to the distribution of pollutants in all regions observed. A large value of the relative concentration indicates a more unequal distribution of pollution at regional level relative to the distribution of pollution in the whole country. Topographic and relative concentration measures are no longer estimated for per capita GDP since they are only applicable to sectoral distribution.

Table 5.9, 5.10 and 5.11 report the Theil index of relative concentration for four pollutants, respectively. Table 5.9 presents the relative concentration estimated on 112 cities in the whole country. The relative concentration ranges from 0.145 to 0.172 for TSP and from 0.101 to 0.176 for solid waste, both show the highest relative concentration in four pollutants though the values of estimate are very small. The relative concentration ranges from 0.052 to 0.124 for waste water, the least relative concentration in four pollutants. Note that wastewater has shown the largest inequality in terms of the general Theil index but the least inequality in terms of the relative concentration. Therefore, although wastewater is found to be highly concentrated in the East coast region, the pattern of distribution at regional level must be quite similar to the pattern of distribution in the whole country.

Table 5.9 also presents changes of relative concentration from year to year. Wastewater is the only pollutant that has seen a statistically significant decrease of relative concentration, and such a fall was more pronounced in early period from 2001 to 2003. Solid waste has seen a statistically significant increase from 2001 to 2002 and there is no significant change thereafter. No statistically significant changes of relative concentration are found for air pollution of SO_2 and TSP.

Table 5.9 The Theil Index of Relative Concentration for Emissions (sample size of 112 cities in 30 provinces)

Relative Concentration				
Year	Water	SO_2	TSP	Solid Waste
2001	0.052 (0.012)	0.144 (0.034)	0.162 (0.039)	0.176 (0.040)
2002	0.082 (0.026)	0.150 (0.036)	0.148 (0.034)	0.150 (0.032)
2003	0.110 (0.035)	0.119 (0.026)	0.154 (0.036)	0.158 (0.035)
2004	0.109 (0.027)	0.097 (0.022)	0.172 (0.054)	0.130 (0.033)
2005	0.124 (0.039)	0.081 (0.017)	0.145 (0.040)	0.101 (0.024)
Change in relative concentration over time				
Δ02 – 01	–0.114*	0.002	0.000	0.113*
Δ03 – 02	–0.147*	0.000	–0.001	0.148
Δ04 – 03	0.046	0.000	0.000	–0.045
Δ05 – 04	–0.062	0.000	–0.001	0.063

Note: Emissions are measured by the aggregate level of emissions. The index is calculated using Equation (5 – 6) from the text. Bootstrap standard errors in parentheses are generated from 100 bootstrap replications. * denotes rejection of H0 that year difference equals 0, based on bootstrap 90% confidence intervals (100 replications).

Table 5. 10 presents the Theil index of relative concentration estimated on 47 cities in the East coast China. The relative concentration ranges from 0. 094 to 0. 143 for TSP and from 0. 083 to 0. 162 for solid waste, indicating very large relative concentration in four pollutants. However, the relative concentration of TSP is smaller in the East coast region than in the whole country implying that relative concentration of TSP is driven by the relative concentration in the inland region. The relative concentration ranges from 0.071 to 0.106 for of SO_2, the least relative concentration in four pollutants. Wastewater found highly concentrated in the East coast region no longer has the largest relative concentration, its relative concentration ranges from 0.052 to 0.171, though it is slightly greater than the relative concentration in the whole country.

Table 5.10 The Theil index of Relative Concentration for Emissions (sample size of 47 cities in 10 East coast provinces)

	Relative Concentration			
Year	Water	SO_2	TSP	Solid Waste
2001	0.052 (0.016)	0.093 (0.063)	0.119 (0.061)	0.114 (0.048)
2002	0.096 (0.041)	0.073 (0.055)	0.094 (0.046)	0.083 (0.030)
2003	0.171 (0.061)	0.106 (0.051)	0.133 (0.057)	0.162 (0.070)
2004	0.136 (0.052)	0.082 (0.039)	0.143 (0.077)	0.150 (0.059)
2005	0.164 (0.085)	0.071 (0.036)	0.097 (0.052)	0.101 (0.041)

Note: Emissions are measured by the aggregate level of emissions. The index is calculated using Equation (5-6) from the text. Bootstrap standard errors in parentheses are generated from 100 bootstrap replications.

Table 5.11 presents the Theil index of relative concentration estimated on 65 cities in the inland China. The relative concentration ranges from 0.120 to 0.167 for TSP and from 0.098 to 0.221 for solid waste, which are large relative concentration in four pollutants. The relative concentration of TSP is larger in the inland region than in the East coast region, which suggests that the relative concentration of TSP in the inland region primarily drives the concentration of the whole country. The relative concentration ranging from 0.049 to 0.096 for wastewater shows the least relative concentration in four pollutants. The wastewater is more equally distributed in terms of the relative concentration in the inland region, which therefore provides evidence that the relative concentration of wastewater in the East coast region drives the relative concentration in the whole country.

Table 5.11 The Theil Index of Relative Concentration for Emissions (sample size of 65 cities in 20 inland provinces)

	Relative Concentration			
Year	Water	SO_2	TSP	Solid Waste
2001	0.049 (0.013)	0.099 (0.032)	0.167 (0.043)	0.221 (0.059)
2002	0.062 (0.018)	0.110 (0.026)	0.161 (0.038)	0.189 (0.048)
2003	0.067 (0.018)	0.079 (0.026)	0.140 (0.035)	0.142 (0.046)
2004	0.089 (0.029)	0.095 (0.026)	0.141 (0.036)	0.114 (0.040)
2005	0.096 (0.027)	0.064 (0.025)	0.120 (0.040)	0.098 (0.033)

Note: Emissions are measured by the aggregate level of emissions. The index is calculated using Equation (5-6) from the text. Bootstrap standard errors in parentheses are generated from 100 bootstrap replications.

In Figures 5.7 – 5.9 we plot the Theil index of relative concentration from 2001 to 2005. Figure 5.7 plots the relative concentration estimated on 112 cities in 30 provinces. Wastewater is the only pollutant that has seen a monotonic and significant increase in relative concentration, however, the relative concentration of wastewater remains at low level compared to other pollutants. The relative concentration of SO_2 and solid waste falls over time, and the relative concentration of TSP stays in the range of (0.14, 0.16). Very small estimates of relative concentration for all four pollutants imply that the distribution of pollution at regional level is similar to the that in the country as a whole.

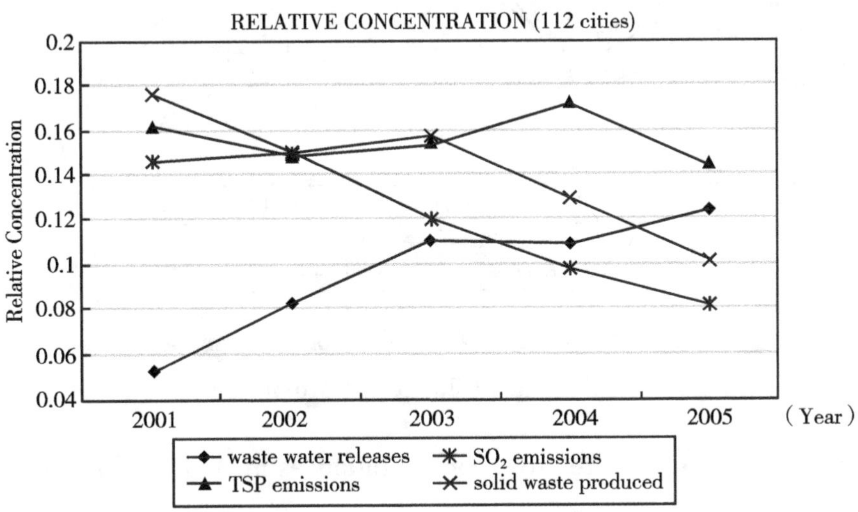

Figure 5.7 Relative Concentration for Emissions (112 cities in 30 provinces)

Figure 5.8 plots the relative concentration estimated on 47 cities in the East coast China. The time trend of relative concentration is more volatile compared to the trends in the whole country. It indicates significant changes of relative concentration in the East coast region. Wastewater is again the only pollutant that shows an increase of relative concentration that stays at higher level than other pollutants after 2002. The relative concentration of SO_2 remains the least in four pollutants after 2002, which shows very similar pattern between regional distribution and national distribution.

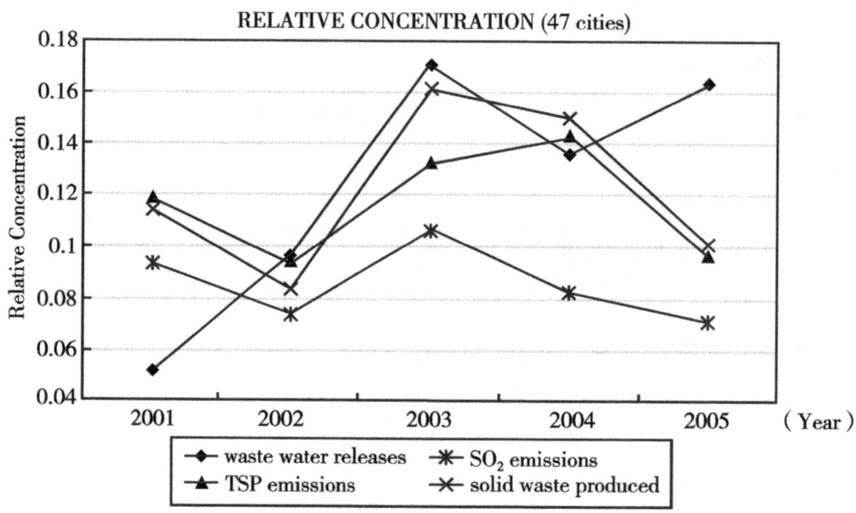

Figure 5.8 Relative Concentration for Emissions (47 cities in 10 East coast provinces)

Figure 5.9 plots relative concentration estimated on 65 cities in the inland China. The relative concentration of pollution remains fairly stable. Wastewater is the only pollutant that has seen an increase of relative concentration. Solid waste is the only pollutant that has seen a significant decrease of relative concentration. It implies that the pattern of regional distribution is moving away from that of national distribution for wastewater and converging to the pattern of national distribution for solid waste. The relative concentration of TSP and SO_2 slightly falls, also indicating the convergence of regional distribution and national distribution for air pollution.

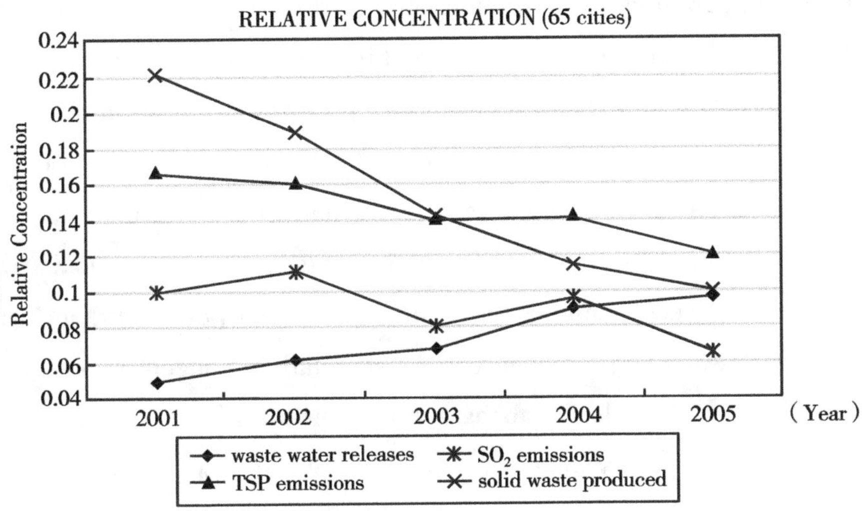

Figure 5.9 Relative Concentration for Emissions (65 cities in 20 inland provinces)

5.6.2.3 The Theil Index of Topographic Concentration

As previously introduced, the non – concentration benchmark of the topographic concentration obtains where an activity spreads perfectly and evenly over physical space. The non – topographic concentration for pollution means that pollution of each type spread perfectly even over the physical space of a given region and any departure from such an even spatial spread registers as geographic concentration. The index of topographic concentration is estimated using city – level pollution scaled by population of individual city. It is slightly different from the index of topographic concentration inBrülhart and Traeger (2005) where they scale pollution by the geographic area of individual city.

Table 5. 12, 5. 13 and 5. 14 report the Theil index of topographic concentration for four pollutants from 2001 to 2005. Table 5. 12 presents the topographic concentration estimated on 112 cities in 30 provinces. Solid waste has the topographic concentration ranging from 0. 763 to 0. 810 and demonstrates the highest concentration over the physical space. The difference between topographic concentration and relative concentration is significantly evidenced by wastewater. The topographic concentration of wastewater ranges from 0. 565 to 0. 672 that shows the second highest concentration in four pollutants, in contrast, wastewater has shown the least relative concentration (see Table 5. 9). The large topographic concentration indicates that wastewater is unevenly distributed over the physical space in the country and it is due to that wastewater is highly concentrated in the East coast region. However, the patterns of regional distribution and national distribution are very similar for wastewater, therefore, the relative concentration of wastewater is small. The difference is also evidenced by TSP emissions. The topographic concentration of TSP ranges from 0. 403 to 0. 519 that shows the least concentration in four pollutants, but TSP has the largest relative concentration at the same time (see Table 5. 9). TSP emissions spread equally over the physical space of the country, but it shows quite different regional distribution relative to its national distribution. Air pollution could be produced everywhere, whilst discharge of wastewater is restricted in regions where water is available. Therefore, the characteristics of pollution determines patterns of distribution. Changes of topographic concentration from year to year are reported in Table 5. 12 as well. There is no statistically significant change over time.

Table 5. 12 The Theil Index of Topographic Concentration for Emissions (sample size of 112 cities in 30 provinces)

Topographic Concentration				
Year	Water	SO_2	TSP	Solid Waste
2001	0. 612 (0. 034)	0. 491 (0. 157)	0. 455 (0. 036)	0. 780 (0. 099)
2002	0. 672 (0. 099)	0. 462 (0. 132)	0. 462 (0. 086)	0. 771 (0. 084)
2003	0. 612 (0. 070)	0. 456 (0. 112)	0. 519 (0. 124)	0. 763 (0. 084)
2004	0. 595 (0. 106)	0. 439 (0. 105)	0. 429 (0. 050)	0. 810 (0. 092)
2005	0. 565 (0. 068)	0. 396 (0. 097)	0. 403 (0. 048)	0. 781 (0. 087)
Change in topographic concentration over time				
Δ02 - 01	-0. 255	-0. 001	-0. 003	-0. 087
Δ03 - 02	-0. 186	-0. 001	-0. 002	0. 094
Δ04 - 03	0. 070	0. 001	0. 000	0. 088
Δ05 - 04	-0. 089	-0. 002	-0. 001	-0. 072

Note: Emissions are measured in terms of per capita emissions. The index is calculated using Equation (5 - 6) from the text. Bootstrap standard errors in parentheses are generated from 100 bootstrap replications.

Table 5. 13 presents the Theil index of topographic concentration estimated on 47 cities in the East coast China. Wastewater and solid waste both show high concentration over the physical space. TSP emissions show high relative concentration but low topographic concentration. Air pollution of SO_2 and TSP also shows lower topographic concentration than wastewater and solid waste, again supporting the previous argument that air pollution is more evenly distributed over the physical space whilst pollution such as wastewater or solid waste is more likely to concentrate in certain regions due to location limitations.

Table 5.13 The Theil Index of Topographic Concentration for Emissions (sample size of 47 cities in 10 East coast provinces)

	Topographic Concentration			
Year	Water	SO_2	TSP	Solid Waste
2001	0.459 (0.071)	0.176 (0.039)	0.377 (0.051)	0.712 (0.169)
2002	0.558 (0.083)	0.178 (0.038)	0.388 (0.062)	0.689 (0.181)
2003	0.694 (0.097)	0.185 (0.035)	0.377 (0.064)	0.697 (0.198)
2004	0.641 (0.144)	0.160 (0.036)	0.370 (0.060)	0.639 (0.201)
2005	0.685 (0.133)	0.190 (0.045)	0.436 (0.105)	0.723 (0.201)

Note: Emissions are measured in terms of per capita emissions. The index is calculated using Equation (5 – 6) from the text. Bootstrap standard errors in parentheses are generated from 100 bootstrap replications.

Table 5.14 presents the Theil index of topographic concentration estimated on 65 cities in the inland China. The topographic concentration of solid waste ranges from 0.757 to 0.836 that shows the highest concentration in four pollutants. The topographic concentration of wastewater ranges from 0.486 to 0.611, which shows the second highest concentration in four pollutants, but at the same time it gives the least relative concentration (Table 5.11). The difference between topographic concentration and relative concentration is once again evidenced by the distribution of wastewater. TSP emissions, on the other hand, show the least topographic concentration but the highest relative concentration, which further proves that air pollution is more equally distributed because industrial sectors spread out all over the whole country and air pollution could be produced everywhere.

Table 5.14 The Theil Index of Topographic Concentration for Emissions (sample size of 65 cities in 20 inland provinces)

	Topographic Concentration			
Year	Water	SO_2	TSP	Solid Waste
2001	0.611 (0.051)	0.636 (0.191)	0.410 (0.100)	0.788 (0.106)
2002	0.625 (0.091)	0.447 (0.096)	0.416 (0.106)	0.786 (0.101)
2003	0.553 (0.075)	0.564 (0.156)	0.473 (0.133)	0.757 (0.091)
2004	0.564 (0.112)	0.544 (0.142)	0.358 (0.051)	0.836 (0.101)
2005	0.486 (0.072)	0.482 (0.118)	0.313 (0.043)	0.771 (0.099)

Note: Emissions are measured in terms of per capita emissions. The index is calculated using Equation (5-6) from the text. Bootstrap standard errors in parentheses are generated from 100 bootstrap replications.

It is also noticeable that regardless of any sample utilized, the inequality in terms of the topographic concentration turns out to be much larger than the inequality in terms of the relative concentration. Specifically the topographic concentration literally dominates the distribution of pollution in China, therefore, at present policy makers should focus on solutions to tackle topographic concentration rather than relative concentration.

Figure 5. 10 – 5. 12 plot the topographic concentration of pollution from 2001 to 2005. Figure 5. 10 plots the topographic concentration estimated on 112 cities in the whole country. The time trend on the top stands for solid waste, although it shows high concentration, the concentration does not change much over time. Wastewater also has high concentration, but its time trend does not change much either. The time trend of air pollution SO_2 and TSP remains low and fairly stable too. Figure 5. 11 plots the topographic concentration estimated on 47 cities in the East coast China. The time trend of solid waste, TSP and SO_2 all stays fairly stable. The concentration of wastewater quickly grows at first and remains stable at a high level thereafter. Figure 5. 12 plots the topographic concentration estimated on 65 cities in the inland China. It has seen no significant change of concentration for solid waste, TSP emissions and wastewater. The concentration of SO_2 falls at first but gets back to high levels later on. To conclude, the topographic concentration of pollution is larger in the inland region because pollution spreads unequally over the physical space of the region. At the same time, pollution spreads more evenly over the physical space in the East coast region where the topographic concentration is low relative to that in the inland region.

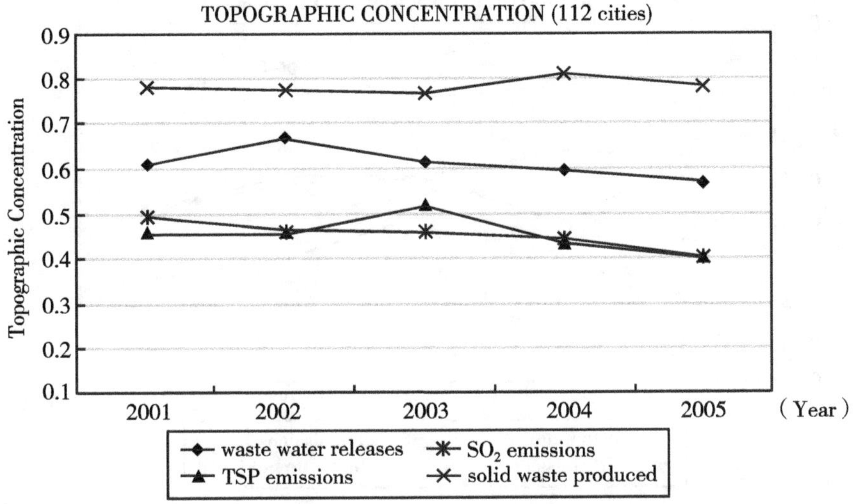

Figure 5. 10 Topographic Concentration for Emissions (112 cities in 30 provinces)

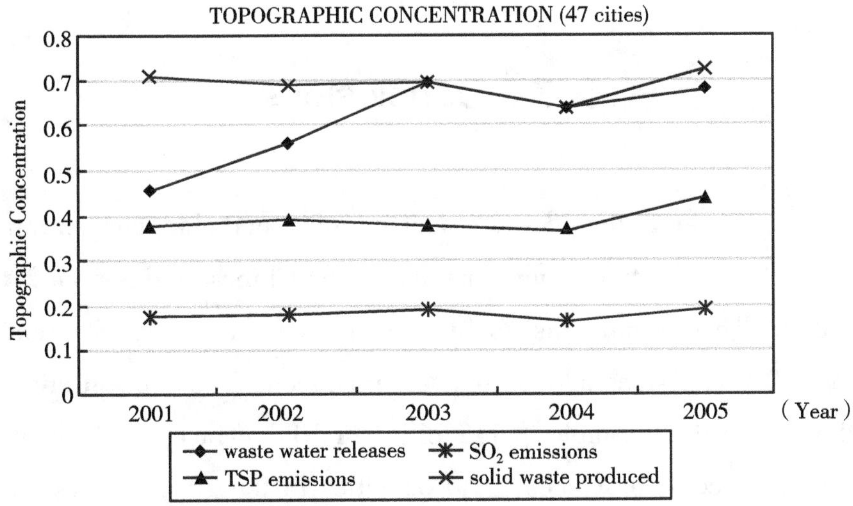

Figure 5. 11 Topographic Concentration for Emissions (47 cities in 10 East coast provinces)

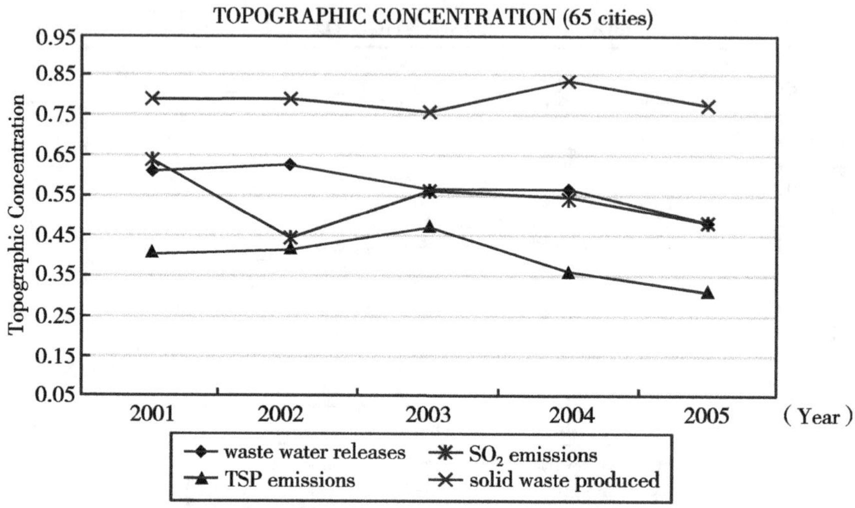

Figure 5.12 Topographic Concentration for Emissions (65 cities in 20 inland provinces)

5.7 Conclusions

This research provides an account of geographic concentration patterns for a variety of pollutants across the Chinese cities from 2001 to 2005. These pollutants include wastewater releases, SO_2 emissions, TSP emissions and solid waste produced. The concentration is estimated on three samples: 112 cities in 30 provinces, 47 cities in the 10 East coast provinces, and 65 cities in the 20 provinces. The estimates of geographic concentration are defined as the Gini coefficient and the entropy indices. This research is novel in terms of applying the Gini coefficient to estimate the environmental inequality in a developing country. Members of entropy indices family are also employed as a novel attempt to estimate concentration of pollution in China. The research uses the general Theil index as well as its two components, topographic concentration and relative concentration, where relative concentration estimates the pattern of regional distribution relative to the pattern of national distribution, and topographic concentration estimates the distribution over the physical space of a given region.

This research uses a non – parametric estimation methodology, the bootstrap method to estimate all concentration measures. The bootstrap method provides standard errors of inequality measures as well as probability intervals. The method can take account of dependencies of the data without having to estimate covariance matrices through very complex calculation. All these features of the bootstrap make it advantaged in the estimation of inequality measures.

According to the estimate of the Gini coefficient, air pollution such as SO_2 and TSP is more uniformly distributed than wastewater and solid waste, and the result is consistent in the whole country as well as in the East coast and inland regions. The inequality of total pollution is primarily driven by the unequal distribution of wastewater in the country. Moreover, the inequality of wastewater and solid waste changes much volatile compared to the inequality of SO_2 and TSP over time.

Estimates of the general Theil index show very similar results to those found by the Gini coefficient. Wastewater has the highest inequality and SO_2 has the least inequality in all regions. The inequality of wastewater in the country is primarily driven by the high concentration of wastewater in the East coast region, whilst the inequality of SO_2 and solid waste in the country is primarily driven by the concentration in the inland region. The inequality of TSP remains similar in all regions. The time trend of the Theil index does not demonstrate significant changes of inequality for pollution over time.

According to the Theil index of relative concentration, TSP and solid waste show the highest concentration in the country, SO_2 emissions show the least concentration in the East coast region and wastewater shows the least concentration in the inland region. The concentration of wastewater in the East coast region primarily drives the relative concentration of wastewater in the country, and the concentration of TSP in the inland region primarily drives the relative concentration of TSP in the country. The research also examines the time trend of relative concentration. The relative concentration of wastewater increases in the East coast region as well as in the country, whilst the relative concentration of solid waste decreases in the inland region as well as in the country. On the other hand, the estimates of the topographic concentration are very similar to the estimates of the general Theil index but quite different from the estimates of the relative concentration. Specifically, such a difference between concentration measures are strongly evidenced by estimates for wastewater and TSP emissions. The topographic concentration also remains stable over time except for a few outliers in given years.

Based on findings discussed above, I can conclude that, compared to the level of pollution, the distribution of pollution is not yet a critical issue in China. The study finds less unequal distribution of pollution at city - level in China, and the distribution of pollution also remains stable over time. However, significantly uneven distribution is still found for particular pollutants in particular regions. For example, wastewater is highly concentrated in the East coast region where health risk could be high in this region. Therefore, the abatement policies are not supposed to maintain uniform across regions in the country, instead, the policy should be tailored for particular pollutant in particular region. The research needs longer time series for future work, and more decomposed concentration measures could be employed to estimate pollution inequality in China.

Appendix

Data Set:

■ Variable: emissions by type, per capita GDP.

■ Pollutants: waste water releases, SO_2 emissions, TSP emissions, solid waste produced.

■ Source: China Environment Yearbook (2002 – 2006) for pollution data, China City Statistical Yearbook (2002 – 2006) for per capita GDP.

■ Time period: annual data 2001 – 2005.

■ Regional breakdown: 112 cities, see Table A5. 1.

Table A5. 1 Regional Breakdown of Data Set

Province/Region	Number of cities from which data are available	Classification
Beijing	1	East coast
Tianjin	1	East coast
Hebei	5	Interior
Shanxi	5	Interior
Inner Mongolia	3	Interior

Continued

Province/Region	Number of cities from which data are available	Classification
Liaoning	6	East coast
Jilin	2	Interior
Heilongjiang	4	Interior
Shanghai	1	East coast
Jiangsu	8	East coast
Zhejiang	7	East coast
Anhui	3	Interior
Fujian	3	East coast
Jiangxi	2	Interior
Shandong	10	East coast
Henan	6	Interior
Hubei	3	Interior
Hunan	6	Interior
Guangdong	8	East coast
Guangxi	4	Interior
Hainan	2	East coast
Chongqing	1	Interior
Sichuan	5	Interior
Guizhou	2	Interior
Yunnan	2	Interior
Shannxi	5	Interior
Gansu	2	Interior
Qinghai	1	Interior
Ningxia	2	Interior
Xinjiang	2	Interior
Total East coast Interior	112 47 65	

Notes for Pollutants

1. Waste water = (Waste water discharged by industry) − (Industrial waste water meeting discharge standards)

Waste water discharged by industry refers to the volume of waste water discharged by industrial enterprises through all their outlets, including waste water from production process, directly cooled water, groundwater from mining wells that does not meet discharge standards and sewage from households mixed with waste water produced by industrial activities.

Industrial waste water meeting discharge standards refers to volume of industrial waste water discharge which, with or without treatment reaches national or local standards.

2. Solid waste = Industrial solid waste produced

Industrial solid waste produced refers to total volume of solid, semi – solid and high concentration liquid residues produced by industrial enterprises from production process in a given period of time including hazardous wastes, slag, coal ash, gangue, tailings, radioactive residues and other wastes.

3. *Industrial* SO_2 *emission* refers to volume of 197 ulphur dioxide emission from fuel burning and production process in premises of enterprises for a given period of time.

4. TSP (total suspended particle) is defined as the sum of industrial soot and dust emissions:

■ *Industrial Soot emission* refers to volume of soot in smoke emitted in process of fuel burning in premises of enterprises.

■ *Industrial Dust emission* refers to volume of dust emitted by production process of enterprises and suspended in the air for a given period of time, including dust form refractory material of iron and steel works, dust from coke – screening systems and sintering machines of coke plants, dust from lime kilns and dust from cement production in building material enterprises.

Chapter 6

Conclusions

6. 1 Summary of Results

This book carefully explores four topics within the broad area of trade, industrial activity and the environment in China. The first topic is to examine the effect of trade liberalization on industrial specialization given that factor intensities and environmental regulations are both defined as determinants of industrial specialization. The second topic is to examine industrial characteristics and formal and informal regulations as determinants of industrial pollution. The third topic examines the environmental specialization using several specialization measures and the last topic is to study the spatial distribution of pollution using several inequality measures. Chapter 2 to chapter 5 cover one topic, respectively. This chapter concludes and outlines possible future research.

Chapter 2 employs two specialization indices to measure industry – level specialization. The chapter examines the competing impact of factor intensities and environmental regulations on industrial pollution. Factor intensities could be determinants as expected by the traditional endowment's theory, and the stringency of environmental regulations could be a determinant as hypothesized by the pollution haven hypothesis. Using the Chinese industrial data at 3 – digit ISIC level, the empirical results show that physical capital intensity (PCI), a negative determinant is the most significant determinant of industrial specialization in China. Pollution abatement cost that represents the stringency of environmental regulations has no significant impact on industrial specialization. However, while the environmental stringency is measured in terms of pollution removed, it shows a negative relationship with industrial specialization. Human capital intensity is not a significant determinant of industrial specialization either. The results therefore could explain why specialization of 'dirty' industries is neither high nor increasing more rapidly in China. Pollution intensive industries also intensively use physical capital compared to clean industries, and physical capital intensity negatively determines industrial specialization while other characteristics are controlled for. Therefore, when determining specialization of pollution intensive industries, the effect of less stringent regulations may be offset by the effect of physical capital intensity in China so that pollution intensive industries do not experience high or growing specialization in China.

Chapter 3 carefully examines several possible factors that may have a direct impact on industrial pollution intensity in China from an empirical perspective. This chapter emphasizes on air pollution and discusses the issue for three air pollutants, SO_2, SOOT, and DUST. Using both industrial and regional data from 1997 to 2003, the empirical results find energy use, human capital intensity, productivity and investment in innovation as the most significant determinants of industrial pollution intensity. Pollution intensity is found to be positively determined by energy use and human capital intensity, and negatively determined by productivity and expenditure on innovation. On the other hand, since there is no direct measure of formal and informal regulations, the models use regional characteristics to capture the effect of regulations. The proxies for regulations do not perform well in the estimations and many regional characteristics do not have impact on industrial pollution intensity. Therefore, it suggests that the most efficient measures that reduce industry pollution should be to reduce energy use, to improve productivity and to raise expenditure on research and development.

Chapter 4 examines regional environmental specialization in China. As suggested by scientific literature, exposure to pollution of similar type or category may cause more health risks than exposure to pollution of several types or categories. Environmental specialization refers to a similar type of pollutant in the composition of pollution. The chapter focuses on the possible relationship between environmental specialization and industrial specialization. Two groups of specialization measures, relative specialization indices and absolute specialization indices, are employed to estimate both environmental and industrial specialization. Environmental specialization increases in terms of the relative specialization measures and falls in terms of the absolute specialization measures. Industrial specialization is insignificant in determining environmental specialization of the country, but it is a significant determinant of environmental specialization in the East coast China or in the inland China. An increase of industrial specialization has resulted in a decrease of environmental specialization in the East coast region and an increase of environmental specialization in the inland region. Such a difference may be due to different patterns of regional industrial specialization.

Chapter 5 examines the spatial distribution of pollution in terms of the Gini coefficient and a family of entropy indices, and these inequality measures are estimated through bootstrapping. There are four pollutants in this research, including wastewater, SO_2 emissions, TSP emissions and solid waste. Estimates of inequality measures show that air pollution, such as SO_2 and TSP, is more uniformly distributed across regions than other pollutions, such as wastewater and solid waste. Wastewater is highly concentrated in the East coast China and SO_2 and solid waste are more concentrated in the inland China. There is no significant change of pollution inequality over time. It eventually suggests that, compared to developed economies, the distribution of pollution is not yet a critical issue in China. However, high concentration of particular pollutants in particular regions still need us to pay much attention.

6.2 Future Research

The research in this book would have benefited from a richer dataset with a longer time series, greater industry coverage and smaller regional units. In future, while such a data set is forthcoming, more sophisticated analyses could be performed and more reliable evidence with greater benefit to the Chinese policymakers could be found.

The relationship between trade and the environment in China still requires further investigation. There is no evidence that trade liberalization would lead to a higher or deepening specialization of pollution – intensive industries in China, however, the existing literature suggests that many other factors that may cause missing evidence of the pollution haven hypothesis, and these factors should be taken into account in future research. Except for the determinants of industrial pollution taken in this research, there would be many other industrial activities as well as regional characteristics that may have impact on industrial pollution, future research should include relevant determinants as many as possible to enrich the existing empirical model. Furthermore, while testing the relationship between environmental specialization and industrial specialization, more relevant factors should be controlled for in the estimation though only a few studies ever discuss determinants of environmental specialization. Lastly, while examining the distribution of pollution, econometric regressions should be employed to test the causality of regional characteristics on regional pollution distribution.

参考文献 References

[1] Antweiler W, Copeland B R, Taylor M S, et al. Is Free Trade Good for the Environment [J]. The American Economic Review, 2001, 91 (4): 877 - 908.

[2] Arora S, Cason T N. An Experiment in Voluntary Environmental Regulation: Participation in EPA's 33/50 Program [J]. Journal of Environmental Economics and Management, 1995, 28 (3): 271 - 286.

[3] Arora S, Cason T N. Do Community Characteristics Influence Environmental Outcomes? Evidence from the Toxic Release Inventory [J]. Journal of Applied Economics, 1998, 1 (2): 413 - 453.

[4] Bartik T J. The Effects of Environmental Regulation on Business Location in the United States [J]. Growth and Change, 1988, 19 (3): 22 - 44.

[5] Balassa B. Trade Liberalization and Revealed Comparative Advantage [J]. The Manchester School of Economic and Social Studies, 33: 99 -124.

[6] Balassa B. The Changing Pattern of Comparative Advantage in Manufacturing Goods [J], Review of Economics and Statistics, 1979, 61 (2): 259 -266.

[7] Balassa B. Comparative Advantage in Manufactured Goods: A reappraisal [J], Review of Economics and Statistics, 1986, 68 (2): 315 -319.

[8] Bartik T J. The Effects of Environmental Regulation on Business Location in the United States [J]. Growth and Change, 1988, 19 (3): 22 -44.

[9] Baumol W J, Oates W E. The Theory of Environmental Policy [M]. Cambridge University Press, 1998.

[10] Benjamin D, Brandt L, Giles J, Wang S. Income Inequality during China's Economic Transition. Working Papers No. tecipa -238, 2005. Department of Economics, University of Toronto.

[11] Biewen M. Bootstrap inference for inequality, mobility and poverty measurement [J]. Journal of Econometrics, 2002, 108 (2): 317 -342.

[12] Bowen H P. On the Theoretical Interpretation of Indices of Trade Intensity and Revealed Comparative advantage [J]. Weltwirtschaftliches Archiv, 1983, 119: 464 -472.

[13] Bowen H P. On Measuring Comparative Advantage: A Rely and Extensions [J]. Weltwirtschaftliches Archiv, 1985, 121: 351 -354.

[14] Bowen H P. On Measuring Comparative Advantage: Fur-

ther Comments [J]. Weltwirtschaftliches Archiv, 1986, 122: 379 - 381.

[15] Brooks N, Sethi R. The Distribution of Pollution: Community Characteristics and Exposure to Air Toxics [J]. Journal of Environmental Economics and Management, 1997, 32 (2): 233 - 250.

[16] Brulhart M, Traeger R. An Account of Geographic Concentration Patterns in Europe [J]. Regional Science and Urban Economics, 2005, 35 (6): 597 - 624.

[17] Chai J C. Trade and environment: evidence from China's manufacturing sector [J]. Sustainable Development, 2002, 10 (1): 25 - 35.

[18] Chay K Y, Greenstone M. The Impact of Air Pollution on Infant Mortality: Evidence from Geographic Variation in Pollution Shocks Induced by a Recession [J]. Quarterly Journal of Economics, 2003, 118 (3): 1121 - 1167.

[19] Chestnut G M, Schwartz J, Savitz D A, et al. Pulmonary function and ambient particulate matter: Epidemiological evidence from NHANES I [J]. Archives of Environmental Health, 1991, 46 (3): 135 - 144.

[20] Chichilnisky G. North - South Trade and the Global Environment [J]. The American Economic Review, 1994, 84 (4): 851 - 874.

[21] Cole M A, Elliott R J. Determining the Trade - Environment Composition Effect: The Role of Capital, Labour and Environmental Regulations [J]. Journal of Environmental Economics and Management, 2003a, 46 (3): 363 - 383.

[22] Cole M A, Elliott R J. Do Environmental Regulations Influence Trade Patterns? Testing Old and New Trade Theories [J]. The World Economy, 2003b, 26 (8): 1163 – 1186.

[23] Cole M A, Elliott R J, Shimamoto K. Why the grass is not always greener: the competing effects of environmental regulations and factor intensities on US specialization [J]. Ecological Economics, 2005, 54 (1): 95 – 109.

[24] Cole M A, Elliott R J, Shimamoto K. Industrial Characteristics, Environmental Regulation and Air Pollution: An Analysis of the UK Manufacturing Sector [J]. Journal of Environmental Economics and Management, 2005, 50 (1): 121 – 143.

[25] Dasgupta S, Wang H, Wheeler D. Surviving Success: Policy Reform and the Future of Industrial Pollution in China. World Bank Policy Research Paper No. 1856. 1997.

[26] Doull J. Specificity and Dosimetry of Toxicologic Responses [J]. Regulatory Toxicology and Pharmacology, 1996, 24 (1).

[27] Ederington J, Minier J. Is Environmental Policy a Secondary Trade Barrier? An Empirical Analysis [J]. Canadian Journal of Economics, 2003, 36 (1): 137 – 154.

[28] Gianessi L P, Peskin H M, Wolff E N, et al. The Distributional Effects of Uniform Air Pollution Policy in the United States [J]. Quarterly Journal of Economics, 1979, 93 (2): 281 – 301.

[29] Gollop F M, Roberts M J. Environmental Regulations and Productivity Growth: The Case of Fossil – fueled Electric Power Generation [J]. Journal of Political Economy, 1983, 91 (4): 654 – 674.

[30] Gray W B, Shadbegian R J. Pollution Abatement Cost,

Regulation and Plant Level Productivity. National Bureau of Economic Research, working paper 4994. 1995.

[31] Gray W B, Shadbegian R J. When do Firms Shift Production Across States to Avoid Environmental Regulations? National Bureau of Economic Research, working paper 8705. 2002.

[32] Gray W B, Shadbegian R J. Plant Vintage, Technology, and Environmental Regulation [J]. Journal of Environmental Economics and Management, 2003, 46 (3): 384 –402.

[33] Gray W B, Shadbegian R J. Optimal Pollution Abatement – Whose Benefits Matter, and How Much? [J]. Journal of Environmental Economics and Management, 2004, 47 (3): 510 –534.

[34] Hamilton J T. Politics and Social Costs: Estimating the Impact of Collective Action on Hazardous Waste Facilities [J]. The RAND Journal of Economics, 1993, 24 (1): 101 –125.

[35] Heij C, Boer P de, Franses P H, Kloek T and Herman K. van D. Econometric Methods with Applications in Business and Economics [M], 1st ed. Oxford University Press, 2004.

[36] Heil M T, Wodon Q. Inequality in CO2 Emissions Between Poor and Rich Countries [J]. The Journal of Environment & Development, 1997, 6 (4): 426 –452.

[37] Heil M T, Wodon Q. Future Inequality in CO2 Emissions and the Impact of Abatement Proposals [J]. Environmental and Resource Economics, 2000, 17 (2): 163 –181.

[38] Helland E, Whitford A B. Pollution Incidence and Political Jurisdiction: Evidence from the TRI [J]. Journal of Environmental Economics and Management, 2003, 46 (3): 403 –424.

[39] Henderson J V. Effects of Air Quality Regulation [J].

The American Economic Review, 1995, 86 (4): 789 – 813.

[40] Hewings G J. The Empirical Identification of Key Sectors in an Economy: a Regional Perspective [J]. Developing Economies, 1982, 20 (2): 173 – 195.

[41] Jackson R W. An evaluation of alternative measures of regional industrial diversification [J]. Regional Studies, 1984, 18 (2): 103 – 112.

[42] Jaffe A B. Environmental Regulation and the Competitiveness of U. S. Manufacturing: What Does the Evidence Tell Us? [J]. Journal of Economic Literature, 1995, 33 (1): 132 – 163.

[43] Kahn M E. The Silver Lining of Rust Best Manufacturing Decline [J]. Journal of Urban Economics, 1999, 46 (3): 360 – 376.

[44] Kahn M. The Geography of US Pollution Intensive Trade: Evidence from 1958 – 94 [J]. Regional Science and Urban Economics, 2003, 33 (4): 483 – 500.

[45] Kalemliozcan S, Sorensen B E, Yosha O, et al. Risk Sharing and Industrial Specialization: Regional and International Evidence [J]. The American Economic Review, 2003, 93 (3): 903 – 918.

[46] Kanbur R, Zhang X. Fifty Years of Regional Inequality in China: A Journey through Central Planning, Reform, and Openness [J]. Review of Development Economics, 2005, 9 (1): 87 – 106.

[47] Laursen K. Revealed comparative advantage and the alternatives as measures of international specialization [J]. Eurasian Business Review, 2015, 5 (1): 99 – 115.

[48] Lerman R I, Yitzhaki S. A note on the calculation and in-

terpretation of the Gini index [J]. Economics Letters, 1984: 363 - 368.

[49] Lerman R I, Yitzhaki S. Income Inequality Effects by Income Source: A New Approach and Application to the United States [J]. Review of Economics and Statistics, 1985, 67 (1): 151 - 156.

[50] Lerman R I, Yitzhaki S. Improving the accuracy of estimates of Gini coefficients [J]. Journal of Econometrics, 1989, 42 (1): 43 - 47.

[51] Levinson A. Environmental Regulations and Manufacturing Location Choices: Evidence from the Census of Manufactures [J]. Journal of Public Economics, 1996, 62 (1): 5 - 30.

[52] Levinson A, Taylor M S. Unmasking the Pollution Haven Effect [J]. International Economic Review, 2008, 49 (1): 223 - 254.

[53] Levinsohn, J. and Petrin, A. (2003), Estimating Production Functions Using Inputs to Control for Unobservables, Review of Economic Studies, Vol. 70, pp. 317 - 341.

[54] Levinsohn J A, Petrin A. Estimating Production Functions Using Inputs to Control for Unobservables [J]. The Review of Economic Studies, 2003, 70 (2): 317 - 341.

[55] Liang Z, Xu L. Regional Specialization and Dynamic Pattern of Comparative Advantage: Evidence from China's Industries 1988 - 2001 [J]. Review of Urban and Regional Development Studies, 2004, 16 (3): 231 - 44.

[56] List J A. Have Air Pollutant Emissions Converged Among U. S. Regions? Evidence from Unit Root Tests [J]. Southern Eco-

nomic Journal, 1999, 66 (1): 144 –155.

[57] Lu J, Tao Z. Industrial Agglomeration and Regional Specialization in China, Presentation Summary at the China – Russia Conference in Beijing in December 2005.

[58] Lu J, Tao Z. Determinants of Industrial Agglomeration: Recent Evidence from China, Centre for China in the World Economy, Working Paper 2006/08.

[59] Mills J A, Zandvakili S. Statistical Inference via Bootstrapping for Measures of Inequality [J]. Journal of Applied Econometrics, 1997, 12 (2): 133 –150.

[60] Millimet D L, Slottje D J. Environmental Compliance Costs and the Distribution of Emissions in the U. S. [J]. Journal of Regional Science, 2002, 42 (1): 87 –105.

[61] Millimet D L, Slottje D J. An environmental Paglin – Gini [J]. Applied Economics Letters, 2002, 9 (4): 271 –274.

[62] Millimet D L, Slottje D J. Industrial and environmental specialization [J]. Applied Economics Letters, 2003, 10 (3): 123 –128.

[63] Naughton B. How Much Can Regional Integration Do to Unify China's Market (August 2000). Centre for Research on Economic Development, Working Paper No. 58. Stanford University.

[64] Neumayer E. Greening Trade and Investment: Environmental Protection without Protectionism [M]. 1st ed. Routledge, 2001. London.

[65] Paglin M. The Measurement and Trend of Inequality: A Basic Revision [J]. The American Economic Review, 1975, 65 (4): 598 –609.

[66] Paglin M. On the Measurement and Trend of Inequality: A Reply [J]. The American Economic Review, 1989, 79 (1): 265 -266.

[67] Pargal S, Wheeler D. Informal Regulation of Industrial Pollution in Developing Countries: Evidence from Indonesia [J]. Journal of Political Economy, 1996, 104 (6): 1314 -27.

[68] Porter M E, Der Linde C V. Toward a New Conception of the Environment - Competitiveness Relationship [J]. Journal of Economic Perspectives, 1995, 9 (4): 97 -118.

[69] Tobey J A. The Effects of Domestic Environmental Policies on Patterns of World Trade: An Empirical Test [J]. Kyklos, 1990, 43 (2): 191 -209.

[70] Thirlwall A P. Regional Unemployment as a Cyclical Phenomenon [J], Scottish Journal of Political Economy, 1966, 13 (2): 205 -19.

[71] Wan G, Zhou Z. Income Inequality in Rural China: Regression - based Decomposition Using Household Data [J]. Review of Development Economics, 2005, 9 (1): 107 -120.

[72] Wang X. Income inequality in China and its influencing factors, WIDER Research Paper, No. 2006/126, ISBN 9291909106, The United Nations University World Institute for Development Economics Research (UNU - WIDER), Helsinki, 2006.

[73] Wheeler D, Wang H, Dasgupta S. Can China Grow and Safeguard its Environment? The Case of Industrial Pollution. Centre for Research on Economic Development and Policy Reform, Working Paper No. 68. Stanford University, 2000.

[74] WHO Air quality guidelines for particulate matter, ozone,

nitrogen dioxide and sulfur dioxide, Global update 2005 summary of risk assessment, World Health Organization.

[75] Wren C, Taylor J. Industrial Restructuring and Regional Policy [J]. Oxford Economic Papers, 1999, 51 (3): 487 -516.

This book is the result of a co-publication agreement between China Financial and Economic Publishing House (China) and Paths International Ltd (UK).

Title: Trade, Industrial Activity and the Environment in China
Author: Wu Shanshan
ISBN: 978-1-84464-744-6
Ebook ISBN: 978-1-84464-745-3

Paths International Ltd

Published in the United Kingdom
www.pathsinternational.com

www.ingramcontent.com/pod-product-compliance
Lightning Source LLC
LaVergne TN
LVHW081208240426
836338LV00004B/49